The Children of Athena

The Children of Athena

Greek Intellectuals in the Age of Rome:
150 BC-400 AD

CHARLES FREEMAN

PEGASUS BOOKS

NEW YORK LONDON

THE CHILDREN OF ATHENA

Pegasus Books, Ltd.
148 West 37th Street, 13th Floor
New York, NY 10018

Copyright © 2023 by Charles Freeman

First Pegasus Books cloth edition December 2023

ISBN: 978-1-63936-515-9

10 9 8 7 6 5 4 3 2 1

Printed in the United States of America
Distributed by Simon & Schuster
www.pegasusbooks.com

For my son Barney

Contents

Prologue

The Banquet

It is the middle of the second century AD, in the Greek world of Asia Minor. We are at a banquet that is being held to celebrate a wedding. The host is Aristainetos and we assume that he is a Stoic since his daughter, Cleanthis, the bride, appears to share a name with Cleanthes, one of the most famous early Stoic philosophers. His son, too, has a Stoic name, Zeno, after the founder of Stoicism, Zeno of Citium. The bridegroom, the son of a wealthy banker, is a good catch. The other guests represent the diverse schools of philosophy that flourish in the second century. So an important local Stoic, Zenothemis, is present at the banquet, along with Zeno's teacher, Diphilos. Those who follow the philosopher Plato are represented by Ion, the teacher of the bridegroom; he is a serious man who considers his judgement superior to that of his rival philosophers. He is treated with reserve by the other guests. The followers of the philosopher Aristotle, known as the Peripatetics, the 'walkers around', from their custom of walking while talking in Aristotle's school, the Lyceum, are represented by Kleodemos. He has the reputation of making angry interventions that ridicule others, which habit has earned him the nickname of 'the Cleaver'. The presence of Platonists and Aristotelians at Aristainetos' party is evidence that the two great philosophies of the fourth century BC, one concentrating on the truths of the immaterial world and the other on empirical experience, are still powerful five hundred years later. Also present is a follower of Epicurus (341–270 BC), by the name of Hermon. The Epicureans taught that one should withdraw from the world to focus on the pleasures of the mind. In this they are in firm opposition to the Stoics, who believe it is the duty of all to participate actively in society. Zenothemis and Hermon turn away from each other in disgust, a sure sign of trouble ahead. Two guests of more lowly status are the grammarian Histiaios and a rhetor (a teacher of rhetoric), Dionysodoros. They will be placed at the bottom of the table.

There is intense embarrassment over the allocation of the best seat, next to the bridal group. Hermon is of noble birth and a priest of one of the city's temples and so might have been granted it, but Zenothemis claims precedence on account of his age. The Stoics claim to set little store by material desires but Zenothemis greedily grabs the first plates of food, spilling gravy over himself, and then makes sure the leftovers are passed on to the retinue of slaves that he has brought with him. Now a gatecrasher appears – Alkidamas, a Cynic. The Cynics show contempt for any form of worldly pleasure. They pride themselves on defying convention, living in the streets and insulting passers-by. Alkidamas is offered the lowest seat of all but he refuses to sit down and wanders about, helping himself to the delicacies being served while criticising the gold and silver plates they are offered on. The only way the other guests can shut him up is to give him a large glass of wine. He makes as if to sit down but then gets up again and taunts the bride that she is incapable of bearing a son with as fine a body as his – and proceeds to reveal more of it than is decent.

Now, as the wine goes round, things really start to get out of hand. The Peripatetic, Kleodemos, attempts to seduce a pretty slave boy. Aristainetos, the host, notices and adroitly shifts the boy aside, replacing him with a servant who looks like a mule. The rhetor starts declaiming but no one listens to him and only the servants politely applaud. The grammarian Dionysodoros sings a mixture of verses from the poets of classical Greece. Next a slave comes in bearing a letter for the host from another Stoic who has not been invited and is furious to find that Zenothemis has been. The slave reads out the long, pompous letter, which includes an insinuation that Zeno is having a relationship with his teacher, Diphilos. The guests, by now half-drunk, greet its contents with derision. The host is embarrassed and Kleodemos the Peripatetic gets so angry that he denounces all the Stoics for their empty philosophical ramblings. Before long he and Zenothemis are spitting at each other and throwing punches.

Ion, the Platonist, now tries to restore order by asking the guests to take a simple issue, marriage, and debate it in the style of a dialogue, the conventional way in which Plato discussed philosophical issues. Why not give up marriage altogether and hold women in common, as Plato had recommended, and embrace pederasty instead? After all, young boys are the most beautiful. The rhetor intervenes to criticise Ion's over-sophisticated use of language. Now the main course arrives, and everyone sits down to eat. The Stoic Zenothemis has been positioned next to the Epicurean Hermon and they have to share a plate of meat. Already at odds over the table placing, they disagree over which one of two roast birds is fatter than the other, and soon they are pulling each other's beards and fighting. A goblet aimed by Zenothemis at Hermon hits the bridegroom instead and Kleodemos tries to gouge out one of Zenothemis' eyes. The Stoic, supposedly above feeling physical pain, howls in anguish. The women, outraged by Ion's suggestion that they should be held in common, run around the room in a state of distress and the Cynic Alkidamas shows his contempt by urinating in front of everyone. He then knocks over all the lamps so the room falls into complete darkness. When the lamps are relighted, Alkidamas is found undressing one of the girl flute-players and Dionysodoros has been quaffing the wine. The party disintegrates, the wounded are carried off, the damaged bridegroom in the very coach he had reserved for his bride, and Alkidamas stretches out on a couch to sleep.

This satire, the work of Lucian of Samosata, a Syrian who wrote in Greek, shows the resilience of the main schools of philosophy in the second century AD and provides evidence of how lively philosophical discussion remained in this era. This will be the subject of *The Children of Athena*, although my overarching theme is Greek intellectual life in all its breadth and variety from the conquest of Greece in the second century BC to the end of the Roman empire in the fifth century.

I

Introduction: Greece Becoming Roman

There are certain epochs in European cultural history that many historians choose to ignore, leaving a gap in the record rather than exploring important intellectual trends and developments and addressing the achievements of some remarkable intellectuals. One such is the period of Greek history between the point when Greece came definitively under Roman rule in the second half of the first century BC up to the time when Christianity became the dominant religion of the empire in the fourth century AD. The classical period (480–330 BC) and the subsequent Hellenistic period (330–30 BC) are well covered in the textbooks and other studies but the next centuries still suffer from Edward Gibbon's derisive judgement in *The Decline and Fall of the Roman Empire* (1776–89): 'If we except the inimitable Lucian, this age of indolence passed away without having produced a single writer of original genius, or who excelled in the arts of elegant composition.' A century and a half later, in that fine poem *Autumn Journal* (1939), Louis MacNeice echoed Gibbon: 'And Athens became a mere university city… And the philosopher narrowed his focus, confined his efforts to putting his own soul in order and keeping a quiet mind.' However, if one includes the geographer and astronomer Ptolemy, the physician Galen and the polymath and biographer Plutarch, as well as a host of other important philosophers and orators, Gibbon's age of indolence begins to look positively industrious. Another aspect of this era, and every bit as important, is that the early Christian theologians were brought up in this same philosophical climate that nourished the writers and thinkers just mentioned, and their works cannot be understood without some appreciation of the way it influenced them.

Why then have the achievements of these polymaths been ignored? Most histories of the period from 30 BC concentrate on the exploits of the Roman empire, and the Romans, inevitably, tend to be disparaging about the peoples they conquered – it is as if the Greeks have faded from the scene. The centuries after 30 BC saw long periods of peace on the Greek mainland and in Asia Minor, disturbances being confined to the empire's eastern borders with Parthia and, later, Sassanid Persia. Yet it was just this stability that allowed intellectual life in Greece to survive. The thinkers I will look at in this book were usually from wealthy, landed backgrounds and enjoyed a comprehensive and uninterrupted education in grammar, literature and rhetoric from an early age. An elite few might progress to study the various schools of philosophies that were still alive from classical times in Alexandria, Athens or, for orators, Rhodes. It is right to call them the 'Children of Athena', the Greek goddess of wisdom who can be traced back to the second millennium BC.

What now becomes extraordinary is the variety of pathways that the most erudite minds took. They could pick and choose from what was already a rich array of academic disciplines, many of them founded by the Greeks themselves. So a historian such as Polybius might look back to the classical period and take inspiration from Herodotus and Thucydides; an astronomer such as Ptolemy working in the second century AD draws heavily on Hipparchus who had discovered the precession of the equinoxes or Eratosthenes who had measured the globe; a Hellenistic philosopher such as Posidonius looks back to the early Stoics;

Galen is steeped in texts from Hippocrates, 'the father of medicine'. Most were invigorated by the dialogues of Plato, which left enough ambiguity for later thinkers such as Plotinus to develop Platonic insights in new directions. All revered Homer, who was quarried as much for his heroes and geography as he was as an exemplar for moral behaviour. These individuals were imbued with a powerful sense of an intellectual heritage that was believed to be superior to any other. Thus they radiated self-confidence. It must not be forgotten that the great buildings of classical Greece were still intact; their enduring presence in Athens, Alexandria, Delphi or Olympia further strengthened the notion of being part of a great cultural tradition. Pausanias, another of my subjects, links his survey of such buildings to the libertarian instincts of the Greeks.

While many educated Romans spoke Greek, Greek was a subtle language and hard to translate into Latin. Lucretius (*c.*99–55 BC), whose elegant poem *De rerum natura* ('On the Nature of Things') drew heavily on the Greek philosopher Epicurus, complained that his task was 'difficult on account of the poverty of the [Latin] language and the newness of my subject matter'. Many of the more sophisticated works of the period never reached Roman ears. Those that survived became embedded in the archives of the Byzantine empire and many lost their status after the coming of Christianity by dint of being pagan. Some were translated by the Arabs, who appreciated the quality of the Greek intellect during the period of Islamic cultural flowering that began in the eighth century, and only arrived in the West in the medieval period in cumbersome Latin retranslations. When they were rediscovered in the Renaissance it was at different times and in a variety of different contexts. Galen and Dioscorides, with his extensive herbals, remained influential as authorities for many centuries. Ptolemy's *Almagest*, his great work on astronomy, was first translated into Latin in the twelfth century, his influential *Geographike* in the fifteenth, fifty years before a single copy of Strabo's *Geography* was brought in by the Greek intellectual Plethon when he visited Florence in 1439. Lucian was championed by Erasmus in the sixteenth century (as was the 'heretic' Origen whom Erasmus had rediscovered in the original Greek), Plutarch by Montaigne and Shakespeare at the end of that century. The Neoplatonist Hypatia, murdered by a Christian mob in Alexandria in 415, became a subject of intense interest again during the revival of philhellenism in the eighteenth and nineteenth centuries. So the common tradition that these Greek-speaking writers and thinkers inherited and exploited was fragmented. One of my aims in writing this book is to restore the integrity of that tradition through bringing these lives together without neglecting the immense variety of their achievements.

The thinkers and writers we will encounter in these pages share a common educational background, an absorption in centuries of classical texts and a confidence in their cultural superiority. They not only knew the sources but could manipulate them to create original texts. However, this process sometimes had a negative impact – Ptolemy's *Almagest* drew so heavily on previous astronomers and was seen as so authoritative that the chronological sequence of advances and the works of earlier important astronomers went missing. City life – so intrinsic to ideals of Greek civilisation – was the essential context for their lives and work, not least in providing audiences for their learning and disputations. During our period, Greek cities continued to be embellished in sophisticated ways, creating an elegant backdrop to the achievements of their most intellectually gifted inhabitants. In short, what might be seen as a ragbag of unconnected lives deserves to be seen as a single, unified and vibrant intellectual culture in which debate was possible across the disciplines.

The conquered Greeks had to accommodate themselves to the reality of Roman hegemony. There was tacit acceptance that Roman rule was impregnable and acquiescence inevitable.

Opinions varied on the quality of the Roman mind. (Remarkably, many of the Greek elite did not speak Latin at all.) But some, such as Polybius and Plutarch, were prepared to seek out kindred souls and establish friendships. Before we explore these interactions further, however, the story of the coming of Rome to Greece needs to be told.

In the great days of Greece, the classical period of the fifth and fourth centuries BC, Rome would hardly have registered in the Greek mind. The city's reach went no further than central Italy and Rome did not even possess a navy until the Punic Wars in the second half of the third century. These wars extended Rome's rule across the defeated Carthaginian empire in northern Africa and Spain. During the third century Rome had also encountered, and in some cases sacked, the Greek cities of southern Italy and Sicily. So began the entanglement of the austere and disciplined Romans with the more sybaritic cultures of the opulent Greek elites. It was some time before Rome came to accept and tolerate traditions so different from their own: in the second century BC the conservative senator Cato the Elder expressed his implacable opposition to the supposed decadence of Greek life and its threat to traditional Roman values.

The Punic Wars shifted the Roman gaze towards the east. Hannibal, the last great Carthaginian opponent of Rome, had made an alliance with Philip V of the Antigonid dynasty in Macedonia in northern Greece. Under its earlier monarchs, Philip and Alexander the Great, Macedonia had had a formidable military reputation although this had never threatened Rome. Once Hannibal was finally defeated at Zama in 204 BC, Rome was set on revenge for Philip V's antagonism. In 198 BC, sheltering under the pretence that the freedom of the Greeks needed to be defended from Macedonian expansionism, the Romans sent a brilliant young commander, Titus Quinctius Flamininus, to resist it. Over his three years of command Flamininus destroyed the armies of Philip and, asked to preside at the Isthmian Games of 196, he proclaimed the freedom of the Greek cities, both of the mainland and those along the coast of Asia Minor, from the threat of Macedonian rule.

While there was initial rejoicing among the Greeks – Plutarch in his *Life* of Flamininus reports that the shouts of joy from the spectators could be heard from the isthmus of Corinth as far as the sea – Rome now considered Greece to be within its sphere of interest. So, when Antiochus III of the Seleucids, the dynasty that had succeeded Alexander in his Asian conquests, hoped to expand his territory by moving westwards across the Aegean, Rome reacted violently, defeating his armies both on the Greek mainland and in Asia Minor (192–188). Antiochus was forced to withdraw as far as the Taurus mountains (in what is now central Turkey), a further step in the erosion of his kingdom, and pay a vast indemnity. Rome took no territory from Philip V, who had finally allied with Rome against Antiochus, and peace was restored for twenty years.

It was Perseus, son of Philip V, who attempted to revive the ancient glories of Macedon by moving southwards into Greece after his succession in 179. Again Rome reacted. At the Battle of Pydna in 168 Perseus' army was destroyed by the Romans, Macedonia divided up and the Molossians of Epirus who had supported Perseus sold into slavery. The victorious Roman general, Aemilius Paullus, appropriated the royal Macedonian barge and sailed it up the Tiber into the city. He stunned the Roman citizenry with the fantastic loot – gold, tapestries and art treasures – that he had plundered from Pella, Perseus' capital. Macedonia was made into a Roman province, and so fell under the direct rule of Rome.* To celebrate his conquest, Paullus

---

* 'Province' originally described the sphere of legal competence of a Roman magistrate. The term was then expanded to refer to a territory outside Italy under direct Roman rule via a Rome-appointed magistrate. The first was Sicilia (Sicily). The proclamation of a province was the final, and irrevocable, step when a client king or ally of Rome failed to be sufficiently subservient or, as in this case, became hostile.

erected a victory monument of himself on a column in front of the temple of Apollo in Delphi, a column that Perseus had intended to carry a statue of himself.

Roman imperialism now became more aggressive in mainland Greece. Rome indulged in a strategy already honed in the Italian wars of siding with one city, in this case Sparta, against its rivals. Two years later, 146 BC, the trading port of Corinth was sacked as an example to others – so effectively in fact that the site lay abandoned for a hundred years. Further expansion came in 133, when King Attalus III of Pergamum in north-west Asia Minor bequeathed his kingdom to Rome. This would become the province of Asia with its capital at Ephesus on the west coast. Back on the Greek mainland, Athens was brutally sacked by the Roman ex-consul Sulla in 86 BC after it had unwisely allied itself with an independent king, Mithridates VI of Pontus, who claimed he would liberate the city from Roman hegemony. Posidonius records that the Athenian envoy, an Aristotelian philosopher called Atheneion, was hopelessly gullible in believing these promises and the city paid a devastating price. While Sulla does not appear to have imposed a 'Roman' constitution on Athens, it seems clear that the ruling magistrates, the archons, were now expected to be pro-Roman. Large indemnities were imposed on other Greek cities, especially in Asia. This was followed (in 27 BC) by the creation of the province of Achaia covering most of Greece, with its capital not at Athens, as might have been expected, but at Corinth, which had been refounded in 44 BC by Julius Caesar and settled with Romans.

In 63 BC the Roman general Pompey the Great brought the remnants of the Seleucid dynasty in Asia Minor to an end. He too created a new province, Syria, to fill the vacuum. Roman control of the east was now complete if still unsettled by invaders and the civil wars of the late Roman republic. The defeat of Mark Antony and Cleopatra at the Battle of Actium by the ambitious Octavian, adopted son and heir of Julius Caesar, in 31 BC led to the annexation of Egypt, whose capital Alexandria was a centre of Hellenic civilisation, and where other Greek communities were settled among the local population. Egypt too became a Roman province, distinct in that its wealth was kept under the direct control of the Roman emperors. Gradually other provinces were added across Anatolia to provide a patchwork of control in the east.

Two Greek lives that unfolded during the process of Rome's conquest, which shed light on the ways in which the Greeks responded to Roman rule, are those of Polybius and Posidonius. Polybius served as a cavalry officer during the Third Macedonian War and, after the defeat of his forces, was taken as a hostage to Rome in 167 BC. He was socially flexible enough to become part of a Roman aristocratic circle and, in his *Universal History*, to explore the reasons why the Romans had been so successful as conquerors. By the first century BC the Stoic philosopher Posidonius was already known to members of the Roman elite for his learning and he is a good example of the growing respect educated Romans had for Greek intellectuals.

By the end of the first century BC, under the emperor Augustus, Roman rule had become a comparatively frictionless process. While prejudices remained stubborn – the Romans ridiculed the lack of fighting qualities among the Greeks, the Greeks saw the Romans as boorish and uncultured – the elites of both cultures recognised the advantages of collaboration. The Romans had absorbed most of the western Greek settlements and were used to employing Greeks as slaves, who often possessed skills that were lacking in Rome. The more educated Romans were attracted by Greek philosophy, especially Stoicism, and science. Greeks provided the most respected doctors, as we shall see in the case of Galen, and the Roman elite spoke Greek. As the Roman statesman and orator Cicero wrote to his brother Quintus: 'Even as we govern that race of men in which civilisation is to be found, we should certainly offer to them what we have received from them... for we appear to owe them a special debt.' The poet Horace remarked that 'captive Greece took captive her savage conqueror and brought the arts to rustic Latium'. 'Remember', wrote Pliny the Younger to a colleague about to take up office in the province of Achaia, 'that you are sent to the pure and genuine Greece, where civilisation and literature and agriculture too, are believed to have originated… Pay regard to their antiquity, their heroic deeds, and the legends of their past.' The lure of a Greece that once was remained strong. Roman visitors to Athens sought out Plato's Academy, the tomb of Pericles and the beach on which the orator Demosthenes had perfected his oratory. The term 'imperial Hellenism' has been used to describe this trend.

Above all, the memories of the Roman conquest and the way that the rigours of the Roman civil wars had been partly fought on Greek territories meant that the Greeks were ready to accept peace. Polybius, who, after all, had direct experience of war with Rome, counselled them to do so. Shrewd commentators such as Plutarch knew Roman retaliation against unrest would be brutal, especially as nowhere in the Roman mentality could there be found any doubts over the Roman right to rule. As Virgil put it in the *Aeneid*, 'Roman, remember by your strength to rule Earth's people – for your arts are to be these: to pacify, to impose the rule of law, to spare the conquered, battle down the proud.'

In fact, Roman administration was remarkably light, and this allowed Greek cities to run their own affairs and prosper. Despite the suppression by Sulla, the Assembly in Athens is recorded as issuing its own decrees again as early as 49 BC. After his defeat of Antony and Cleopatra at Actium in 31 BC the shrewd Octavian (from 27 BC known as Augustus) visited Athens and, according to Plutarch, 'after reconciling with the Greeks, he handed out the grain left over from the war to the cities, which were in a terrible state, having been stripped of money, slaves, and working animals'. In his *Rituals and Power: The Roman Imperial Cult in Asia Minor*, Simon Price showed how the cults of the emperors were integrated into Greek religion, the terminology and practices of worship being comprehensible and mutually beneficial to both cultures. After its refounding by Julius Caesar in 44 BC, Corinth became the centre of the imperial cult while in Athens a small temple to Roma and Augustus was placed prominently in front of the Parthenon. As the Greek orators told their audiences, while before they had been wasting resources in mutual antagonisms, now it was a case of competing to be the most beautiful. The two civilisations compensated for each other's strengths and weaknesses. In the words of the geographer Strabo: 'While the Greeks are thought to have been successful in the foundation of cities because they paid attention to the beauty and strength of their sites, their proximity to some port, and the fineness of the country, the Romans took great care of the things that the Greeks neglected, such as road paving, aqueducts and sewers.' The Romans possessed more technical expertise than the Greeks when it came to building. The vast span of the *odeion* donated to Athens by Augustus' colleague Agrippa needed Roman architects to construct it. More than a century later, Hadrian put in hand a 100-kilometre aqueduct to bring water to Corinth, a challenging construction needing to cross mountains and valleys and certainly requiring advanced technological skills. As it passed through the territories of several different cities, it needed Roman supervision to maintain its security.

Discounting cities founded as Roman colonies (usually for discharged veterans) of which forty are recorded in the Greek east – the most notable of which was the refounded Corinth which quickly became the centre of a trading network – Roman immigrants to Greece seem to have experienced few difficulties fitting in. Studies have shown that Roman immigrant families had adopted Greek after two generations, largely as a result of marrying locals. They were even competing in Greek games. Corinth appears to have been largely Latin-speaking in 44 BC, but by the second century AD the citizens had adopted Greek. Cicero's intimate friend Titus Pomponius was so well accepted in Athens that he gave himself the name Atticus. Yet as a result of the ensuing stability, many Greek cities turned inwards and became obsessed with their status in relation to their neighbours, quarrelling even over 'an ass's shadow', as one orator, Dio of Prusa, put it. These disputes had to be carefully managed by city councils so as not to arouse the suspicions and antagonism of the Roman authorities.

In the period following the Roman conquest of Greece, there existed many other flourishing cultures in the east. After the destruction of the Persian empire by Alexander, Greek communities had settled in cities as far east as present-day Afghanistan. Throughout much of the Near East, Aramaic, the first language of Jesus, was a *lingua franca*. Languages such as Syriac (a dialect of Aramaic), Phrygian, Pisidian and Galatian Celtic are known from written survivals, many of them in inscriptions or texts. (Syriac was used by many eastern Christians to record theology and it spread east in Christian communities as far as India.) Under the Ptolemies, Greeks had established themselves as an elite in Egypt, but Egyptian culture remained intact and there was comparatively little interaction between Greeks and the native population. There were also large Jewish populations, not only in Judaea and Jerusalem but also scattered throughout the east as a result of the diaspora that followed the destruction of the Temple in Jerusalem by the Babylonians in the sixth century BC. Alexandria, for instance, was the home of an important Jewish community, one of the many that had adopted Greek through translations of their scriptures, the Septuagint. It was understandable that a charismatic Jewish teacher, Jesus of Nazareth, who lived during the reigns of the emperors Augustus and Tiberius, would be written about in Greek even though he was not Greek-speaking.*

Overall, there were many more speakers of Greek than Latin in the Roman empire. As Cicero admitted in 62 BC in his oration in defence of the Greek poet Archias, who had been accused of

---

* One of the challenges facing New Testament scholars is to ascertain what might have been lost by the translation of Jesus' oral Aramaic into Greek prose.

claiming Roman citizenship: 'Greek literature is read in nearly every nation, but Latin only within its own boundaries, and these we must grant are narrow ones.' It is extraordinary to find that, as late as the fifth century AD, few Greeks, even the bishops, spoke Latin. However, the degree to which local populations mastered Greek is difficult to assess. One intriguing source of evidence is tomb inscriptions from Anatolia, many of which are in faulty Greek. This suggests that Greek had a formal status, and that even those populations whose first language was not Greek aspired to use it for their memorials. Clearly a knowledge of Greek would help in dealings with a Greek-speaking local administration and with fostering trading relationships with Greek communities. But the Greeks prided themselves on their superiority and made it difficult for outsiders to be accepted into their culture. The following words, by the physician Galen writing in the second century AD, are a classic expression of Greek cultural arrogance. 'Greek is the most pleasant language… and the most fitting for humans (sic). If you observe the words used by other peoples in their languages, you will see that some closely resemble the wailings of pigs, others the sound of frogs, others the call of the woodpecker.' In the following century the sophist Philostratus criticised the Cappadocians for their poor Greek, mocking them for their mixing up of consonants and mispronunciation of vowels.

By AD 140, a number of the educated elite, notably those in mainland Greece or Asia Minor, were adopting Attic, the dialect of classical Athens, as a means of isolating themselves from *koine*, the Greek of the streets.* It required a rigorous training to master, much as it would if one was to learn to speak Latin today. Dictionaries of Attic words and texts explaining how it

---

* *Koine* varied according to the context in which it was spoken or written so could be adapted for official documents or narratives, such as the texts of the New Testament. *Koine* in Attica, where it was a direct derivative, was different from *koine* as it evolved in Egypt.

should be spoken were available for the committed. The satirist Lucian of Samosata, who knew the Attic texts well, ridiculed those whose attempts to learn Attic were so clumsy that no one could understand what they were trying to say. In Lucian's *Professor of Public Speaking*, a sham teacher of rhetoric advised his student, 'Pull together fifteen but no more than twenty Attic words and practise them well; have them on the tip of your tongue – "sundry", "eftsoons", "prithee", "in some wise", "fair sir," and the like – and in every speech, drizzle on a few as a sweetener.' In another satire, *Lexiphanes*, Lucian portrays an orator who strings together so many meaningless phrases that a medical man has to be summoned to give him an emetic to purge them from his system. He can then be taught to speak Attic properly by studying the ancients – the poets first, then the orators, next Thucydides and Plato, and finally the playwrights, both comic and tragic.

Aelius Aristides and Herodes Atticus, about whom there will be more to say in Chapters 16 and 17, were probably the best exponents of Attic; others spiced up their texts with Attic words or avoided certain elements of *koine* as unworthy of an educated man. It was easy, as Lucian suggested, to be seen as pretentious.

2

Scrolls, Education and Travel

As the Roman empire consolidated its rule across the Mediterranean, Greeks were also encouraged to travel and to satisfy the curiosity that had been such a prominent feature of their culture. The geographer Strabo used Homer's *Odyssey* to argue that 'the wisest of the heroes was the one who travelled and wandered in many places, considering it important that "he saw the cities and knew the minds of many men"'. Plato had travelled for some ten years – mainly in Sicily and southern Italy – after his shock at the execution of Socrates in 399 BC. Many Greek intellectuals of the period after the Roman conquest spent time in Rome – the physician Galen practised there for many years and the Neoplatonist Plotinus taught there – and some went even further west. Posidonius passed through the Straits of Gibraltar to study the rise and fall of the Atlantic tides and Lucian toured Gaul to show off his rhetoric. Many visited Egypt, travelling up the Nile as far as what is now Ethiopia. According to a biography by Philostratus, one Apollonius of Tyana and his companions made an extensive survey of Egypt: 'In several places they took boats across the river [Nile] in order to visit every sight on it: for there was not a city, temple or sacred site in Egypt that they passed without discussion.' Hundreds of inscriptions for the period survive, especially in southern Egypt. In AD 191, three visitors from Alexandria, Serenus, Felis and Apollonius 'the painter', left their names on the wall of the temple to Isis as far south as Philae. A visit of the emperor Hadrian in AD 130 is recorded on the 'singing' statue of Memnon. Plutarch tells of one Cleombrotus of Sparta who had made 'many excursions in Egypt and about the land of the Cave-dwellers, and had sailed beyond the Persian Gulf – his journeys were not for business, but he was fond of seeing things and of acquiring knowledge'. Plotinus had hoped to travel to Persia with the Roman armies in order to converse with native philosophers. One is reminded of the words of the twentieth-century Greek poet George Sefaris (1900–71) that 'Greece is travelling, always travelling'.

By the first century AD conditions were settled under the imperial administration and new roads were being built which opened up economic opportunities (as we shall see in the case of Sagalassos in Interlude Three, p. 197). Among the fullest accounts of travel are those of Paul of Tarsus whose letters describe his missionary journeys to spread the news of Christ. It may be that Paul exaggerates the perils when he tells the Corinthians (2 Corinthians 11:26) that 'during my frequent journeys I have been exposed to dangers from rivers, dangers from brigands, dangers from my own people, dangers from Gentiles, dangers in the town and in the country, dangers at sea, dangers at the hands of false brothers'. Yet the journeys were made and, despite many misfortunes, Paul survived until his presumed but unrecorded martyrdom in Rome in the mid-6os AD. His maritime adventures – when he was arrested in Jerusalem he insisted, as a Roman citizen, on being taken to Rome to appeal to the emperor – are detailed in the Acts of the Apostles.* They include delays due to unfavourable winds, the skilful exploitation by the ship's captain of wind and currents, and even a shipwreck on Malta

---

* There has been much debate about Paul's Roman citizenship. The Pauline scholar, the late Jerome Murphy O'Connor, speculated that Paul was descended from a freed slave.

after his captain had lingered so long that the autumn gales had begun. (Winter sailing was dangerous in the Mediterranean and shipping ceased for several months until calmer spring weather returned.)

Some travellers, as we have seen, were merely curious to see ancient sights such as the pyramids, but others saw 'seeing' as a vital part of their researches, whether to study medicinal plants (Dioscorides and Galen), geography (Strabo) or the sites of the past (the historian Polybius and Pausanias). There is a famous passage from the second- and third-century theologian Clement of Alexandria which describes his intellectual restlessness before he became a Christian:

> Of these teachers [that I followed], one, an Ionian, lived in Greece, two others who came from Coele-Syria [a region of the province of Syria, including the Bekaa Valley] and Egypt respectively were in Magna Graecia [southern Italy]. Others were in the east – one was from Assyria, and the other a Hebrew from Palestine. I found the last of them where he was hiding in Egypt. Here I came to rest.

Clement's travels in the search for knowledge emphasise the impulse for learning among the Greeks in these centuries. One of the most extraordinary features of this culture is the multitude of texts that the educated elite were able to access in an age when papyrus rolls had to be copied by hand and were vulnerable to damp and fire. A recently discovered letter from the physician Galen describes a fire in Rome in AD 192 that swept through the libraries on the Palatine Hill and even down into the Forum where it destroyed another library in the Temple of Peace. Galen was devastated as he had deposited the only copies of some of his works in these libraries. Among the other losses he records were works by Aristotle, Theophrastus, Aristotle's successor at the Lyceum, and the Stoic philosopher Chrysippus. Galen also mentions in passing that the papyri in another library had been rendered unreadable as damp had stuck the sheets together. As soon as a text was out of the hands of an author anyone could deface it. The poet Horace tells one bearer of his poems not to drop sweat over the words while he was carrying them or let them fall into the mud. Copies were not always done well. The philosopher Seneca used the word *mendosus*, 'blemished', to describe a text that had been so badly copied that the writing was illegible or so full of errors as to be useless. The works of Aristotle appear to have been neglected after his death and by the time they were recovered in the first and second centuries there were immense problems of interpretation of the corrupted texts. So this was a world where the survival of literature was precarious, and many important works have not survived. As a result we are left with a distorted and diminished view of intellectual life in the classical world.

Yet, despite the vulnerability of their contents, libraries across the Greek world were important features of any civilised city. The most famous was that of Alexandria, which had, as its original aim, the acquisition of a copy of every 'published' Greek work, even some in translation from other languages (such as the Hebrew scriptures in its Greek translation, the Septuagint). It is not clear to what extent the library was damaged by fire in fighting between Julius Caesar and Cleopatra against Cleopatra's brother in 48 BC, but records suggest that it was still functioning into the Roman period before its final disappearance in about AD 270.

It is in Alexandria that one finds the best evidence of textual expertise. In a remarkable feat of erudition, the poet Callimachus (*c.*310–240 BC) assembled a bibliographical catalogue of the library in 120 rolls. The poetry section, for instance, was divided into tragedies and comedies, epic poems, lyric poems and so on. Prose works were similarly divided and even cookbooks were indexed, under 'miscellaneous'. Authors were listed within their section in alphabetical order with a brief biographical sketch for each. The first line of a text was often used as a 'title'. In the second half of the third century BC the director of the library,

Eratosthenes, was another polymath. While he is mostly known for his scientific works, such as carrying out measurements of the globe from Egyptian sites, he wrote on poetry, mathematics, philosophy and produced a *Geography* that would later be heavily drawn on by Strabo for his own *Geography*. Callimachus' catalogue has not survived but an inscription has been found in Rhodes which details books in much the same way. Among standard reference works were texts analysing obscure or obsolete words. The library had many copies of the Homeric epics and they were collated to compose a standardised version. The leading scholar in this enterprise was the chief librarian Aristarchus of Samothrace (*c.*220–*c.*143 BC) who worked through the epics line by line and rejected any doubtful lines. It is said that he marked duplicates with a star sign, *asteriskos*, which has survived as a marker in printing to this day.* Then there were commentaries on Homer and the major Greek poets and a succinct grammar of the Greek language by one Dionysius, a native of the city, which survives. The finest of the grammarians, Herodian, who worked in the second century AD, was born in Alexandria and must have made considerable use of the library's resources before he ended up in Rome during the reign of Marcus Aurelius. His work on Greek accents is still useful. In short, this was an age of sophisticated linguistic studies.

A number of libraries of the ancient Greek world can still be visited, even though they are all now bereft of their rolls. It is moving to find oneself at the library high on the citadel of Pergamum – placed, appropriately enough, next to the temple to Athena, the goddess of wisdom – and stand by the shelves where rolls of papyrus were once consulted. Skins were also used here as a writing material – the word 'parchment' is derived from 'Pergamum'. The Attalid rulers of Pergamum (third and second centuries BC) competed aggressively with the Ptolemies

---

* Such was the rigour with which Aristarchus worked that the word 'aristarch' survives to describe a severe critic.

in Alexandria and this may well have been why they resorted to parchment after papyrus supplies from Egypt became harder to obtain.* Visually, the most spectacular library is that in Ephesus, founded in memory of one Celsus by his son, Aquila. Celsus had been governor of Asia between AD 105 and 107. Aquila financed a sumptuous building which doubled as a library and a mausoleum for his father. The whole complex took some twenty years to build and was only completed in AD 135. Its façade, now reconstructed, is particularly magnificent, with three entrances originally graced with statues personifying Wisdom, Virtue and Knowledge. The niches within suggest that it housed a collection of 3,000 rolls with an underground chamber containing the body of Celsus.

The contents of these celebrated ancient libraries have perished. There is, however, one remarkable survival from a villa in the resort town of Herculaneum, destroyed in the eruption of AD 79 which also engulfed Pompeii. The heat of the blast must have reached 300 degrees Celsius and so only the charred remains of papyrus rolls were found when the villa (now known as the Villa dei Papyri) was located in 1750. Unlocking their secrets has been challenging. Many disintegrated as a result of inappropriate handling by those determined to access the thoughts of the authors and it is only recently that some of the texts have been deciphered. The library appears to have housed a private collection placed there in the first century BC by the Epicurean philosopher Philodemus (c.110–c.40–35 BC) who enjoyed the patronage of Calpurnius Piso, the villa's owner. The majority of the texts are by Philodemus but he appears to have founded the library with works of Epicurus, notably his text *On Nature* of which there are many copies, some with marginalia by Philodemus himself. After Philodemus' death, further texts by Epicurus were added to the library. Despite the villa being

* It is said that the library's 200,000 rolls were given as a gift by Mark Antony to his lover Cleopatra and so may have been moved to Alexandria.

in Italy, the vast majority of the works are in the original Greek. This may be a reflection of the fact that Greek was a language in which the educated master of the villa was fluent (in itself a sign of the growing respect of the Romans for Greek culture), but it is likely that this collection was kept separately from a Latin library or a second Greek library with a wider range of texts (which will be found one day when the villa is fully excavated).

Another large cache of papyrus fragments (some 100,000 of them) has been found in a rubbish dump beside Oxyrhynchus in Middle Egypt. They date from Hellenistic and Roman times and provide a superb survey of what was being read by literate Greek communities. Remarkably, the twenty most common authors represented in Oxyrhynchus, headed by Homer and the playwright Euripides, all date from before 200 BC, providing a fascinating glimpse of the works that were considered 'classics' at the time. Among the fragments are letters complaining of the boredom of being without books. One of the most important findings from Oxyrynchus is that while codices, texts in book form, are comparatively rare in the first century AD, by AD 300 half of the recovered texts were in this format. The codex appears to have originated in Rome but it was appropriated by Christian readers who found texts easier to find in a codex than in a roll.

So there is good evidence that intellectual life continued at a sophisticated level even after Greece was politically and militarily eclipsed by Rome. Athens still retained its aura as a major cultural centre (and in AD 132 the emperor Hadrian added yet another library to those that were already there). Many of the individuals explored in this book were educated in one of its schools. Alexandria had enormous prestige as the focal point of Greek science and mathematics and was, as seen, home to its own outstanding library. The geographer Strabo spent some time there and Ptolemy composed his texts on geography and astronomy there. Virtually every serious Greek scholar appears to have visited Alexandria at some point in their lives. However, even those outside the big cities appear to have access to a wide range of texts. Plutarch, living on his family estate in a small community in Boeotia, was able to quote from an extraordinary range of sources for his essays and *Lives*.

This can be seen by looking at one such essay, his *On the Apparent Face in the Orb of the Moon* (composed around AD 100). As the title suggests, this is an erudite discussion concerning not only the surface of the Moon as it can be perceived from the Earth, but its place within the universe and whether it might be inhabited. The essay ends with an exploration of the mythology surrounding the Moon. It stands as a testament to the intense curiosity of the author and his quoted participants. (Plutarch uses a variety of characters, each arguing from their own philosophical perspective.) Some of the essay's 'scientific' speculations are not found elsewhere and are ahead of their time.

In the text the participants between them mention or quote thirty-five named individual sources. They include poets, ranging from Homer, as would be expected, through the seventh- and sixth-century lyric poets to the fifth-century Pindar, famous for his odes to the victors in the games. From the same period there are the pre-Socratic philosophers Heraclitus, Parmenides and Anaxagoras and the Sicilian Empedocles. By the fourth century we have the Athenian playwrights, Aeschylus, Sophocles and Euripides. Then come the great philosophers of the fourth century, Plato, Aristotle and the atomist Democritus. The botanist Theophrastus provides information about the variety of plant life and the extreme climates in which it can survive (thus raising the possibility of life on the Moon). They are followed by the Stoics, including the founders of this school of philosophy and its distinguished later exponent Posidonius, and the astronomers Aristarchus of Samos, who suggested that the Earth went round the Sun, and Hipparchus, who was the first to spot and measure the speed of the precession of the equinoxes. Mathematicians include Menelaus of Alexandria, a contemporary of Plutarch, who was obsessed with defining the attributes of triangles placed on a sphere. Cosmology is represented by the sixth-century BC Pherecydes of Syros and the fourth-century BC Metrodorus of Chios, who was known for the earliest theory of the origins of the universe. Among the diplomats are the fourth-century BC Megasthenes, an expert on India, and Hegesianax, Seleucid ambassador to Rome in the 190s BC, who was also a grammarian and poet. Plutarch's mastery of a variety of sources from across the centuries is impressive but he is not untypical. Strabo was able to draw on two hundred authors for his *Geography* and Galen quoted from a large range of texts attributed to Hippocrates. In his surviving writings Clement of Alexandria makes over a thousand references to other writers, embracing 348 different classical authors; he cites Plato 600 times and Homer 240 times (from virtually every book of the *Iliad* and *Odyssey*). Libanius, a prominent orator of the fourth century AD, is still steeped in the classics, including Homer, Plato and Demosthenes, as well as Plutarch (the *Moralia* and the *Lives*) and the speeches of Libanius' rhetorical model and inspiration Aelius Aristides from two centuries earlier.

The Greek word for these scholars was *pepaideumenoi*, 'men of culture', able to understand material from across the disciplines. (Those outside this elite were termed *idiotai* (singular *idiotes*) and usually treated with contempt by the *pepaideumenoi*.)* These men felt a strong loyalty to their place of birth, an intimate relationship with the language itself, and were certain of the value of eloquence and knowledge of the classics. This was a closed class, confident of its superiority and dismissive of those who did not belong.

Inevitably the programme of education was a long and demanding one for the aspiring man of culture. Once basic literacy had been achieved the student would progress to a grammarian. The first task would be to understand how a

---

* The word *idiotes* in Greek meant a person who did not involve themselves in public affairs. The Latin adopted the word as *idiota* to mean an ignorant person and so it came eventually into English.

text was correctly structured and the pronunciation of key words. Then a canon of authors would be introduced and the grammarian would go through each highlighting important passages. By now the student was ready to compose his own essays and develop techniques of argument. Disputations were an excellent way of grounding a career in rhetoric. So the student might take a subject such as 'Why did Medea kill her own children?' and work out all the various motivational possibilities, even to the extent of challenging Euripides' version in his celebrated play.

The next stage was to move on to study with a teacher of rhetoric. Typically the boy being taught would now be about fourteen, though older pupils were taken on, some even when they had children of their own (and the younger students would join the older ones in classes so that they would have a taste of the further demands of the curriculum). Libanius, himself a notable orator, describes the pleasures of teaching: 'How great it is to rule over wellborn young men and see them improve in rhetoric and proceed to the various paths of life. And what honours one receives from them and their fathers, from citizens and foreigners.' There were many genres of oratory, depending on the audience and the context in which a speech might be delivered.

The students would first listen to the teacher's own speeches to become conversant with the conventions of each genre. The aim was for them to become capable of presenting a well-structured oration which used knowledge from earlier Greek culture in an original way. As Lucian of Samosata put it in his text 'You are a Prometheus in Words', it should include 'excellent vocabulary in accordance with ancient standards, penetrating thought, perceptivity, Attic grace, harmony and the skilfulness of the whole'. The elite orators became famous and moved from city to city as performers. Aelius Aristides boasted that when visiting Pergamum he was greeted with an audience of thousands (doubtless an exaggeration, as was typical of the man), while a rival Egyptian orator could attract only seventeen. Presentation was, of course, important but giving a speech in public was also about showing off one's social status. As Galen explains: 'In any of the well-regulated cities it is not permitted for everyone to speak in public. Only if one is a person of distinction and can display pedigree, upbringing, and education worthy of addressing the public do the laws allow him to speak in public.'* Orators were men from families with the wealth to provide them with many years of education and they wanted their audiences to acknowledge this. On the other hand, they could charge fees for their appearances and many orators became wealthy enough to donate buildings to their native cities.

It was an arduous training. One year Libanius started with fifty-seven students but by the end of the second year as many as thirty-five of them had dropped out. The culmination of this course was the *dokimasia*, a ritual in which the successful student had to return to his native city where he would be officially welcomed and then make a speech, normally one glorifying the city. These were major occasions, a welcoming home of a young citizen who, it was hoped, could represent his city in the future. No wonder that many a student viewed the event with trepidation, since it provided an opportunity for people to assess whether his family had spent their money wisely. It was an important moment for the teacher as well; his reputation would depend on a successful *dokimasia*.

The student could also move on to a school of philosophy. It is known from Athenian records from that some students simply enrolled as passive listeners and were thus able to go from one philosophical school to another. This gave them sufficient understanding of philosophical principles to be seen as educated and to be able to converse with other members of the elite. Others formed a more intimate connection with a teacher and would not only master texts in detail but also undergo a moral training.

* From his *On the Therapeutic Method*.

Here there were rivalries. In his famous dialogue *Gorgias*, where he uses a real-life Sicilian rhetorician, Gorgias, as one of the disputants, Plato challenged the rhetoricians for putting the contrived art of persuasion above true knowledge. Following Plato's example, the dedicated philosopher – easily recognisable by his garb and demeanour – tended to think himself superior to the mere orators, who in their turn would be quick to point out unworthy behaviour among the philosophers. However, as we will see in the next chapter, there was a fluidity between intellectual traditions. Philosophers valued the art of speaking well while rhetoricians would inevitably absorb some philosophy with which to infuse their orations. The fourth-century Roman poet and rhetorician Ausonius claimed that education led to 'good living, sound learning and forceful speaking'.

The educated elite were connected to an extensive network of relationships. There were official contacts, of course – everyone depended on favours for the advancement of themselves and their protégés. The best example is provided by Libanius in the fourth century AD. His many surviving letters reveal him to have been busy recruiting new students to his school in Antioch and then seeking to place them after they had 'graduated' (see pp. 304–7). Good *personal* relationships also existed between members of the elite, as can be seen in the coterie of intellectuals surrounding Plutarch. The noun *philos* meant 'a dear one' and it could be used flexibly to denote not only an intimate friendship but love of entire groups such as poets or rhetors or even one's fellow citizens. Describing the qualities that make someone a good friend, a *philos*, Libanius writes, concerning one Apellio, of his 'gentleness, his sincerity, his capacity for friendship, his ignorance of dishonest gain'. Loyalty and a reciprocal desire to support each other in the challenges of life consolidated the relationship.

Very few studies of this period mention the environment in which these intellectuals thrived. In many respects, they remained firmly in the grip of classical tradition: they continued to hark back to Homer as their hero and the model for correct moral behaviour, and they were surrounded by the architectural showpieces of the classical period. In Athens, the buildings of the Acropolis dominated the city as they still do today. Despite the damage the city had sustained in Sulla's sack of 86 BC, it had escaped the complete destruction inflicted on Corinth. In the second century AD, the orator Aelius Aristides displays, in his *Panathenaicus*, delivered at the city's ancient Panathenaic festival, a profound knowledge of Athens' buildings and history. Pagan cults were still being celebrated – they would only be closed down in the AD 390s – so the temples would still have been hosting rituals and sacrifices. The drama festival, the Great Dionysia, held each year in March since at least the sixth century BC, continued to be held here. Records suggest that Athens sponsored the restoration of eighty sanctuaries and their cults in Attica in the early imperial era. One reconstruction of the Acropolis in late antiquity (the fourth or fifth century AD) suggests that nearly a thousand dedicatory statues were still in place. Extraordinarily, six hundred years after the Battle of Plataea, delegates from Athens and Sparta were still meeting each year at the scene of the final defeat of the Persian invaders in 479 BC, to commemorate the victory at the festival of Eleutheria ('Liberty'). The great games, held at Olympia, Nemea and the Isthmus of Corinth, together with the Pythian Games at Delphi, were still drawing crowds to their extensive sanctuaries. In his influential *Natural History* (AD 70s), Pliny the Elder claims that there were at least 3,000 statues in Athens, Delphi and Olympia, a massive display of heroes, victors of the games, patrons, politicians and philosophers.

The Romans added two more Panhellenic Games, one in Nicopolis, the city founded by Augustus to commemorate his victory at Actium, and the Heraria (in honour of Hera, the wife of Zeus) at Argos in the Peloponnese. Magnificent additions were still being made to existing buildings. Each year Ephesus, capital of the province of Asia, would welcome the new governor of the province in an extravagant ceremony along a grand colonnaded avenue leading from the harbour to the centre of the city. Libanius talked of the colonnaded streets of Antioch as if they were flowing rivers. In short, the lives described in this book were lived against a backdrop of magnificent settings, many of them already centuries old. Appreciation of the Greek architectural heritage is evident in this description of an auditorium by Lucian of Samosata. 'Anyone who sees it and is trained in the arts of rhetoric would surely have an equal longing to make a speech in it, fill it with shouting and become himself a part of its beauty.' This harmony between speaker and architecture is also well evoked by Aelius Aristides in a speech to the citizens of Cyzicus in Anatolia: 'Then is perfection achieved, truly like a gift from some god, when due proportion in your souls and your buildings chime together... we must believe living by the standards of beauty is possible when harmony and order rule everywhere.'

3

Philosophy and its Schools

Philosophy, as pioneered by the Greeks, concerned itself with making the Earth and the universe surrounding it intelligible and considering the possibilities of spiritual dimensions beyond its observable reality. Intrinsic to it was the elaboration of methods of assessing certainty in argument, so logic comes to play an important part. Some assertions clearly trumped others but it took time to evolve standards of proof in various disciplines. These concerns added up to a wide-ranging intellectual project with different issues predominating as times changed. For the individual, the search for wisdom and its relationship to virtue was predominant. This extended to relating individual virtue to good governorship, a point stressed by Plutarch in his essays on effective leadership.* One analogy expressed by Stoic philosophers compared philosophy to a garden, logic as its enclosing wall, physics (the constitution of the visible world) as its soil and ethics as its fruit.

Argument was vital to make this a living tradition. Aristippus, a pupil of Socrates, saw the benefit of philosophy as giving the individual the ability 'to consort confidently with everyone'. 'Philosophy must convey to its devotees the ability to remain

* See pp. 119–21.

superior to others in debate,' noted the Roman Stoic philosopher Musonius Rufus, 'the Roman Socrates'. His Greek contemporary, the orator Dio Chrysostom, suggested, rather arrogantly, in a speech to the assembly of his native city of Prusa, that 'the business of the true philosopher is none other than rule over mankind'. While philosophers must often have irritated their listeners with their earnestness, philosophy involved public display and a play on the emotions of an audience. As Plutarch put it: 'The heart must feel such anguish at the philosopher's words that tears will flow.' Boundaries between areas of intellectual enquiry were fluid and it was often hard to distinguish between philosophy and other disciplines pioneered by the Greeks – mathematics, the sciences, history and geography. Many philosophers were adept at ranging across the academic disciplines. The result was intense discussion among an educated elite across the disciplines in a way that is rare today. And these debates took place across the entire span of the Greek-speaking world. Even a remote centre of Greek learning, the city of Alexandria-in-Sogdia, now known as Ai Khanum, in Afghanistan, had a gymnasium where philosophy was taught.

It was within the fervent intellectual debates of fifth-century Athens that Socrates (470–399 BC), a native of the city, emerged to transform the purpose of philosophy by highlighting 'living virtuously' as the aim of the enterprise. For Socrates this involved suppressing natural desires and adopting an ascetic lifestyle but also stern questioning of received opinions. In contrast to the sophists, the intellectuals who dominated philosophical debate in fifth-century Athens, Socrates refused to charge for his teaching. Following the Socratic model, becoming a philosopher now involved a continuous programme of self-questioning and a refusal to allow material desires to divert one's search for truth. As Plutarch would put it: 'Observe also how, as far as independence and honour are concerned, material gifts fall far below those bestowed by literary discourse and wisdom.' Socrates was the ideal philosopher – a hero to later generations, even lauded as such by Christians despite his paganism. After Socrates a number of different schools and approaches developed. Plato and Aristotle both headed their own schools in Athens, the Academy and the Lyceum respectively, in the fourth century. In the third and second centuries BC, the Stoics appeared as did the followers of Epicurus, who believed that the gods did not influence human life and that the cultivation of a peaceful mind was most important. Sceptics and Cynics challenged the conventions of philosophical debate. Most of the figures discussed in this book adhered to one or the other of these philosophical schools and usually had some understanding of the central tenets of each of them. They will be explored more fully in the rest of this chapter.

One of the intellectual currents that has attracted me to the Greek thinkers of the Roman period is their continuing commitment to virtue and wisdom for their own personal satisfaction and peace of mind. The period is full of relevant texts for what is now known as 'mindfulness'. *Paideia* was the term used to denote a culture of learning with a focus on the search for virtue. A second-century AD philosopher, Albinus, who attempted to integrate the different philosophical schools, sets it out beautifully:

> Since it is necessary for us to become contemplators of our own soul and of divine things and of the gods themselves and to attain to intelligence, which is most beautiful of all, we must first purify our thinking from false opinions. And after the purification we must awaken and call forth our natural intuitions, and purify these and make them shine out distinctly, to be our first principles. After this, when the soul has been made ready, we must plant the appropriate doctrines in it, by which it is brought to perfection; and these are doctrines of physics and theology and ethics and politics.

Paideia included the appreciation of fine literature and the leisure to enjoy it. Typically for his generation Albinus assumes that a spiritual element should be included. The traditional idea that Greek religion and philosophy were distinct from each other is not supportable.*

The commitment to personal virtue extended to the ambition of bringing concord to city life. 'City before self' was deeply ingrained within the Greek mind with loyalty to one's city often predominating over any form of shared Greekness. In his *Guide to Greece*, Pausanias refers to 'betraying one's ancestral city and its inhabitants for personal profit as the most impious of sins'. A fine example of the expression of this pride comes in the funeral oration of Pericles in fifth-century BC Athens as recorded by the historian Thucydides. Here Pericles associates Athens with civilised values and enhanced cultural achievements and even presents it as a mentor to other Greek cities. The political stability of the cities within a settled empire of the first centuries AD allowed the ideal to be developed to its fullest extent. In fact, as Plutarch argued, it was peace and constancy of mind which translated into good leadership. 'Those who govern must first achieve governance of themselves, straighten out their souls, and set their character aright, and then they should assimilate their subjects to themselves.' Crucial to the politician's success was oratory and so this became the most important medium of the age for the transmission of knowledge to the illiterate. The young man with *paideia* has, according to the fourth-century orator Libanius, 'installed Demosthenes in his soul [i.e. mastered classical rhetoric]... He will think it his duty to make the cities happy; he will rejoice when the executioner's sword lies idle; he will make the citadels beautiful with buildings; and he will remain throughout the servant of the Muses.' Libanius is so deeply immersed in Greek culture that, in his orations, he is

---

* See the chapter on 'Philosophy' by Rick Benitez and Harold Tarrant in Esther Eidinow and Julia Kindt (eds.), *The Oxford Handbook of Ancient Greek Religion*, Oxford University Press, 2015.

hardly aware of any other culture (other than the rising power of Christianity) but his own.

Yet there were tensions between love of city and the philosophical life. The Stoics claimed to believe in a universal humanity that transcended one's city or ethnic group and the Cynics rejected any ties to individuals or institutions. The philosopher Favorinus, a friend of Plutarch and intimate of Herodes Atticus, noted the existence of barriers, both geographical and artificial, and the problems they could cause: 'They separate Asia, Europe and Libya from one another with rivers; neighbouring peoples with mountains; local inhabitants with city walls, fellow citizens with houses; cohabitants with doors; and even those who share the same ceiling with coffers and boxes. This is the reason for wars.'

As we saw in the breadth of references to earlier writers and scholars in Plutarch's essay on the Moon, the cultural traditions established in the classical era of Greek history remained alive and vigorous over the centuries and this was particularly true of the schools of philosophy. There were underlying similarities between them, a commitment to finding truth, for instance, but they each had to provide a framework within which debate could take place. While Christianity increasingly relied on authoritative texts and prided itself on fidelity to these through an unbroken succession from the apostles, pagan philosophers accepted that divergence could take place so long as the ethos of a school was preserved. (This was the view of Diogenes Laertius, writing in his *Lives of the Philosophers* in the third century AD, and marks an important distinction in the history of European thought. Many Christian doctrines were expressed as creeds and thus became non-negotiable.) On the basis of the surviving sources, it is difficult to trace the rise and fall of different philosophies, but there is no doubt there were phases in which specific schools enjoyed greater prominence. Plutarch, for instance, is often given credit for reawakening an interest in Plato as against the enduring popular schools of Stoicism and Epicureanism.

Through the ages, the school founded by Plato (*c.*429–347 BC) was, indeed, the most pervasive, and his *Dialogues* continued to be much admired. 'Everyone, even those who do not accept their teachings or are not enthusiastic disciples, reads Plato and the Socratic school,' remarked the Roman orator Cicero. Plato saw the world around him as chaotic and human society vulnerable to the volatility of emotions. How far he was influenced by the Athenians who condemned their fellow citizen Socrates to death in 399 BC or the turmoil of the Peloponnesian War (the defeat of Athens took place when he was in his mid-twenties) is uncertain, but it left him with a profound distrust of human society and democratic politics, the theme of his dialogue the *Republic*. He even chose not to marry (as did other philosophers such as Epicurus). For Plato, it is in the immaterial world that certainty is to be found and only the most committed mind is capable of accessing it. Having dedicated himself to the search, Plato founded his Academy, a school in a suburb of Athens, in 387 BC. It became famous and, despite some periods of inactivity, would survive until closed by the Christian emperor Justinian in AD 529.

The *Dialogues* take an issue and, often using Socrates as a participant, question its contradictions.* A major attraction of the *Dialogues* is their exploration in depth of the chosen philosophical problem. While they often, but not always, lead to a conclusion which fits with Plato's ultimate aim of confirming that it is only in the immaterial world that certainty can be found, they provide a comprehensive and lively introduction to whatever is being discussed. A. N. Whitehead (1861–1947) characterised the European philosophical tradition 'as a series of footnotes to Plato' in that most of the underlying problems of philosophy are touched upon in the *Dialogues*. They benefit from Plato's distancing himself from the debate and their range

---

* Whether Socrates was portrayed as his true self or as Plato would have wanted him to be has been much debated.

suggests that over his long life he revised his stance on many issues. The ensuing ambiguities allowed the Platonic tradition to remain vibrant through phases of development known as Middle Platonism and Neoplatonism. As will be shown in later chapters, Plutarch was an undogmatic adherent, Plotinus developed Platonism in new directions, and Clement of Alexandria and Origen reconciled it with Christianity.

Plato believed that each individual had a soul which existed eternally in that it had a pre-existence and survived after death. The soul had three parts; the first, embedded in the head, was Reason or *logos*, which had the power to control the other parts. The second was a spirit which gave vigour and emotional impact. It was based in the chest. The third, situated in the stomach, contained its desires, sex and greed. The soul inherited knowledge from previous lives and this could be recovered by presenting an individual with a logical problem, usually a mathematical one, and seeing how they could recover it from a pre-existing life. This was the theme of the dialogue *Meno* in which a slave, Meno, is led through a series of logical deductions to show that even a slave had pre-existing knowledge.

The true Platonic philosopher enforced the dominance of Reason over the other parts of the soul. This would be achieved by developing an expertise in knowing, a process which required commitment and a breadth of learning. One of the dialogues, *Ion*, includes a discussion of expertise in understanding poetry. Ion, a rhapsode, a reciter of epic poems, who has won prizes in the competitions, claims to be an expert from his study of Homer alone. He is soon challenged by Socrates, who says that his supposed 'expertise' in Homer must be limited when he has no knowledge of any other 'inferior' poets against which to judge him. (*Ion* is a superb example of Socrates' exhaustive questioning.) Socrates goes on to point out that there are passages from Homer which a physician or a charioteer will be better qualified to assess than a rhapsode. It follows therefore that Ion, who prides himself on being the best interpreter of

Homer, is not as expert as he claims. Yet Plato does not condemn Ion's enthusiasm for Homer and so underlying philosophical questions are left open for further discussion, making *Ion* one of the most attractive of Plato's dialogues.

How could one embark on the quest for knowledge? Plato believed that one must begin with understanding the limitations of worldly knowledge. Not only was the material world unstable and largely unpredictable, the desires of humans, whether greed or sexual, inhibited the discovery of truths. The undisciplined masses were also part of the challenge in that they reinforced the volatility of the material world. Yet there were alternative ways of defining reality. Mathematics runs through Plato's works. It provided certainty through proofs which no one could challenge. Mathematics also encourages abstract thinking and the use of logic, and Plato emphasises that it provides a model that is more secure than one relying on empirical evidence.

If there are eternal truths, as illustrated, for instance, at an elementary level in a mathematical proof, where are they ultimately to be found? Plato claimed that they existed in the immaterial world. So, one takes a concept – Beauty, for instance. One could discuss what appears to be 'beautiful' in the world around us: a sunset, or a sculpture or a human face might qualify. Yet it is just this variety of experiences of 'the beautiful' which makes the concept unstable. However, if one contemplates these different experiences of beauty one might eventually find underlying truths that form a part of each one. This enables one to envisage what Plato called a Form or Idea of Beauty which has the essence and 'truth' of a mathematical proof. In a brilliant narrative in his *Republic*, Plato describes how characters chained in a dark cave with a flickering fire behind them might have only a shadowy vision of reality. As they progress towards the entrance of the cave, the light and their vision increase, they will eventually emerge into the sunlight and truth will be revealed. This is an analogy of an understanding of the Forms. Yet across the dialogues, Plato deals with these ideal Forms in different ways and he leaves many issues unresolved. He concentrates on 'positive' Forms – Beauty, Justice, Courage, and ultimately, at the top of a hierarchy, 'the Good' – leaving it unclear whether one can have a Form of Ugliness or Tyranny.

Those who reach a full understanding of the Forms achieve the culmination of philosophy and virtue itself. Here Plato runs into an enduring issue. In his *Republic*, he showed the chaos of democracy by describing a ship in a storm where there is a desperate need for one helmsman to take charge. Just as he allotted three parts to the soul, Plato divides society into three groups. There are the Guardians, who have reached an understanding of the eternal truths that might create a happy and virtuous state (and these could be the equivalent of a skilled captain who could bring the ship to safety). Then there are those such as the army (the spirited ones) who can be used as supporters of good order and defence of the state. And then there are the masses, swayed by their base desires. Plato believed that those who had, after many years of philosophical searching, found 'the Good' had a reached a true understanding of how a state should be run. In a last dialogue, the *Laws*, Plato lays down its rules. So important are order and discipline to the smooth functioning of Plato's state that his prescriptions for its preservation are austere in the extreme: poetry is to be banned and children brought up in common. It was on account of such apparent harshness and disdain for freedom that the twentieth-century philosopher Karl Popper would describe Plato as 'an enemy of the open society'.*
In fact, as with the Forms, Plato is more ambivalent about the way power can be administered and this gives scope for different interpretations by later thinkers. The range of the *Dialogues* is so wide that one can immerse oneself within the Platonic tradition without necessarily being dogmatic (Plutarch is a good example of this). What Plato provides, essentially, is a way of thinking

* The Austrian Karl Popper's *The Open Society and its Enemies* came out in two volumes in 1945.

philosophically. Knowledge of the dialogues appears to have been seen as part of the education of any cultured mind, much as some knowledge of the plays of Shakespeare might be today. The intensive questioning by Socrates provided a good model to follow.

How was Plato viewed over the centuries of Roman domination of the Greeks? In contrast with the works of Aristotle, to be discussed below, the body of the *Dialogues* seems to have survived intact. Yet there is little evidence to show how they were studied. Did students start with mastering the *Dialogues* themselves or did a teacher compile a course from them? A contributor to the discussions in Plutarch's *Table Talk* divides Plato's *Dialogues* into the narrative and dramatic. 'The easiest of this latter sort they teach their children to speak by heart; causing them to imitate the actions of those persons they represent, and to form their voice and affections to be agreeable to the words.' So this was an early part of a child's education.

One of the surviving texts, *Mathematics Useful for the Reading of Plato* by Theon of Smyrna, dating from the time of the emperor Hadrian (r. 117–38), suggests that students needed background knowledge in order to fully understand Plato. 'When someone is trained in all aspects of geometry and music and astronomy, making the attempt to read the Platonic treatises is a most blessed undertaking', as Theon puts it. In the middle of the same century, Albinus produced *An Introduction to Plato's Dialogues*, which may have been a summary of lectures Albinus had attended. Albinus stressed the importance of 'knowledge of divine matters, so that one who has acquired virtue can become assimilated to them'. A more ambitious work by Alcinous, a Platonist philosopher of the second century AD, *Didaskalikos* or *Handbook of Platonism* ('an introduction to the study of the doctrines of Plato' in the words of the author), is probably a manual for teachers. It contains material from every dialogue, but Alcinous has often rearranged phrases and introduced material from other commentators. It may even have been an introduction for those not prepared to assemble or buy the many rolls of each dialogue. Another text, the so-called *Timaeus Locrus*, reduces that dialogue to a précis of the original, eliminating what the teacher considers to be difficult philosophical points. It is a bit like boiling down Shakespeare's *Hamlet* to a mere narrative of its main events.

Once the student made it to the dialogues themselves, there was considerable debate over which of them should be read first. Diogenes Laertius (third century AD), who devoted a full chapter to Plato in his *Lives of Prominent Philosophers*, an important if often inaccurate assembly of material, records: 'Some begin from the *Republic*, some from the *Great Alcibiades*, some from the *Theages*, some from the *Euthyphro*, some from the *Timaeus*', and so on.* Other accounts, which appear to have been originated by the first-century AD Thrasyllus, the court philosopher to the emperor Tiberius, group the dialogues according to a specific theme – in Thrasyllus' case those surrounding the death of Socrates, for instance. Albinus suggested that they be read in order to 'purify the soul', in other words as a course in moral development. Some Platonists highlight a single dialogue, for instance *Timaeus* where Plato explores the possibility of a divine craftsman who creates the universe, which leads on to an intense discussion of that concept or *Phaedo*, which deals with the immortality of the soul. There is no doubt, however, that Platonic studies continued at a sophisticated level. The Roman grammarian Aulus Gellius (second century AD) describes his time in Athens as a student of one Taurus who had learned his Platonism from Plutarch. Taurus accuses Gellius of simply coming to Athens to study rhetoric and insists that if he is to continue in Taurus' class, he 'must penetrate to the inmost depths of Plato's mind and feel the weight and dignity of his

---

* Diogenes was obsessed with proving that Greek philosophy was pure, uncontaminated, even in its origins, from 'barbarian' sources and, in contrast to Posidonius and, later, Clement of Alexandria (pp. 256–66), does not believe in the recovery of an ancient wisdom.

subject matter, not to be diverted by the charm of his diction or the grace of his expression'.

Whatever introductory work needed to be done to set students up for more profound study of Plato, philosophical investigations inspired by his thought continued unabated in the centuries after his death. As late as the third century AD Plotinus would divert Platonic themes towards mysticism and monotheism. A later Neoplatonist philosopher, the Syrian Iamblichus (c.AD 245–c.325), highlighted the main subject of each dialogue and arranged them in thematic groups, those concerning ethics, logic and physics, and then, as the culmination of a course of Platonic study, theology (including the *Phaedo*) and finally the *Timaeus*. This order appears to have been followed in the Athenian schools in the two centuries before they were closed down in AD 529.

In 367 BC a new student from Stagira in northern Greece arrived to study at the Academy. Aristotle was a flamboyant and intellectually curious character, perhaps too worldly for the austere atmosphere of the Academy. While at first he followed Plato's doctrines, and was respected by Plato for his prodigious intellect, Aristotle's mind took him in such different directions that he ended up founding his own school in Athens, the Lyceum. In particular, Aristotle reacted against the way Plato depreciated the natural world and so ignored the philosophical methods needed to understand it. There was, after all, some sort of order in the material world. Why, if it were otherwise, was there constancy in the seasons and why could eclipses be predicted? And how did a chicken's egg contain only chicks and not baby pigeons? Moreover, Aristotle found Plato's conception of the immaterial world untenable – essentially it could not be proved to exist and, as presented by Plato, was filled with logical contradictions. Better, surely, to concentrate on what one could actually see before one.

Aristotle's breadth of researches and teachings was extraordinary. He was inspired by living creatures – 'inherent in each of them is something natural and beautiful' – and pioneered works on zoology and biology that contained acute observations of a vast range of organisms. He delved deeper in the hope of discovering the essence of living things, notably, for humans, the importance of the soul in providing a force that nourishes us to some higher form of existence. He conceived of the fullest state of being human, *eudaimonia*, 'a flourishing', where the rational mind is at its most effective. His studies on ethics were also profound. His central concern here involved integrating moral behaviour within rationally considered responses to changing circumstances. With so much empirical material available, Aristotle was also forced to think about organising it. In his *Prior Analytics*, believed to be the earliest formal study of logic, he investigated the validity of arguments. The *Posterior Analytics* defines the first principles from which one can demonstrate that knowledge about a specific issue or substance is hard to refute. These works were often placed alongside another text, the *Categories*, a vastly influential work in later Western philosophy which dealt with the distinctions between different substances. In his *Politics* Aristotle assessed different forms of government; he also explored an array of 158 constitutions existing in the city states around him but, regrettably, most of this element of the text is lost. The *Politics* would be drawn on by Polybius in his analysis of the Roman constitution. While Plato's political philosophy tended towards disciplined, and hence, hierarchical, order, Aristotle's instinct was towards some element of public participation so long as the focus was on the creation of a virtuous community.

In his cosmology, Aristotle envisaged an Unmoved Mover, with no emotional contact with the human world but as a setter in motion of the planets which circled the Earth, each within their own distinct sphere. The stars were in a further sphere beyond these. This simple arrangement would be challenged by later astronomers, including the polymathic second-century scientist Ptolemy. Scholars have debated the extent to which Aristotle believed in an Active Intellect associated with the Unmoved Mover which was related to each individual human soul. This implied that on death an individual's soul was absorbed back into the Active Intellect and had no independent existence after death. Meanwhile Aristotle's successor as head of the Lyceum, Theophrastus, continued with Aristotle's work, especially on plants, so earning himself the title of 'the founder of botany'.

So how was this extraordinary range of works and Aristotle's distinctive approach to philosophy to be transmitted to future generations of Greeks? While Plato's *Dialogues* existed as a coherent body of work, Aristotle was not so lucky. In contrast to the flowing prose of Plato, many of his texts appear to have survived only in the form of jotted-down lecture notes which lacked the clarity of Plato's *Dialogues*. Some may even have been distorted by revisions from lecture to lecture. Their survival was further hampered when Aristotle was eclipsed by the Stoics and Epicureans of the third and second centuries BC. By the time of Strabo, the geographer of the first century BC, his works had become difficult to find. Strabo tells a story of the texts passing from the Lyceum to editors who neglected them or allowed shoddy copies to be made. Even though the researches of Aristotle might have seemed essential for his purposes, in his *Geography*, Strabo used no more than twenty quotations from Aristotle and these only from two works.*

Eventually those of Aristotle's works that survived came into the hands of one Andronicus of Rhodes who brought them to Rome from Athens in the first century BC and produced a catalogue of some 1,000 titles. Andronicus created an ordered sequence of the texts with the works of logic first. (Other scholars started with the texts on ethics.) The text dealing with

---

* These were the *Meteorologika* and *On the Cosmos*.

the fundamental problems of human existence was placed by Andronicus after (*meta*, in Greek) the volume on physics, and the term 'metaphysics' has stuck. Yet many of the later Greek scholars and thinkers hardly mention the work of Andronicus and so, although his system of ordering Aristotle's works was widely accepted, there must have been other copies of the works circulating. By the first and second centuries AD there was considerable debate over which of the texts attributed to Aristotle were authentic.

The followers of Aristotle were known as Peripatetics, 'those who walk around'. They were now faced with the challenge of assessing the texts, exploring their consistency by comparing one with the other or analysing their style to try to establish those which were truly composed by the master. As a result of the challenges involved, the Peripatetics may have become the most erudite of the textual analysts. It was inevitable that many of them would become commentators, pointing out copying errors or interpreting passages that had been left unclear. Interpretations of the same texts could be so divergent that the final versions that emerged were incompatible. Despite this, Aristotelian scholars essentially worked in cooperation with each other, freely adding the suggestions of their fellows to their own commentaries. The commentaries varied in scope. Some were made up of comments alongside the included text, others assumed the reader would already be familiar with the texts and they did not need to be included. The physician Galen, for instance, provided a commentary on the *Categories* which he considered useful only for those who had already gone through the text with a teacher. In contrast, one Boethus of Sidon, a Peripatetic of the first century AD (not to be confused with the sixth-century AD philosopher Boethius), was exhaustive in commenting on one phrase after another and then providing his own interpretations with ripostes to Aristotle's opponents. Another Peripatetic commentator, Aspasius (*c.*AD 80–150), played a critical role in ensuring that the *Nicomachean Ethics* became the leading Aristotelian text on ethics. It remains so to this day.

The Peripatetic philosopher who is best known as an Aristotelian commentator is Alexander, originally from the opulent city of Aphrodisias in Caria, in what is now south-western Turkey. (He worked at the end of the second century AD and into the third.) Alexander considered that each work of Aristotle could be related to any other and the commentaries he provided were of such quality and covered so many of Aristotle's subjects – they included works of logic, physics, ethics and metaphysics – that they helped establish a coherent body of Aristotle's works that has survived.* Alexander elaborated Aristotle's critiques of Plato's Forms and challenged the Stoic concept of 'fate', stressing that individuals had the reasoning power to make choices. He argued that Aristotle did not believe in personal immortality of the soul, so setting up a later conflict with the Christian belief that each soul was distinct and immortal. He was involved in a lengthy feud with Galen over Aristotelian concepts of causality and time.

It is not known where Alexander's school was – it may well have been in Athens – or how he taught, but there is enough evidence to suggest that he worked from the original texts, explained them, and then opened up debate among his students. *Koinologia*, which could be translated as 'philosophical discussion', was the word he used to describe the technique. His status can be seen from the dedication of his work *On Fate* to the emperors Septimius Severus (r. 193–211) and his son Caracalla (r. 198–217). Other schools catering exclusively for Peripatetics existed and conducted debates with rival schools. The Neoplatonist philosopher Plotinus used some of Aristotle's texts and Alexander's commentaries on them alongside those of

---

* One scholarly criticism of Alexander's commentaries is that he was so immersed in Aristotle that he achieved an unjustified uniformity between the works and even went beyond them.

other philosophers but Alexander appears unique for his time in preserving a distinct Aristotelian tradition. His commentaries were adopted by the Arab philosophers, eliciting sophisticated commentaries from such luminaries as Avicenna (980–1037) and Averroes (1126–98). Translations of these commentaries began to circulate in the medieval West from the twelfth century and came to dominate the university curriculum. It was the Dominican scholar Thomas Aquinas (1225–74) who integrated Aristotle, 'the Philosopher', into Catholic theology.

Across the centuries of late antiquity, Aristotle stimulated a sophisticated study of the natural world and works on logic which would help classify its elements and establish methods of evaluating empirical experience. At a time when mysticism was becoming part of the intellectual landscape, Alexander kept a more empirical tradition alive. Galen, a contemporary of Alexander, provides a good example. While extraordinarily well read across a variety of traditions, Galen acknowledges the influence of Aristotle on his logic and methods of demonstration. Susan Mattern, a modern biographer of Galen, argues that, despite Galen criticising many of Aristotle's findings (in addition to the feud with Alexander mentioned above, Galen's meticulous dissections often challenged Aristotle's more cursory observations), the philosopher was, in fact, more influential to him than either Hippocrates or Plato. In matters of logic, Galen preferred Aristotle to the Stoics.

Among the systems of thought criticised by Alexander the most notable was Stoicism, which first appeared as a school in Athens some twenty years after Aristotle's death. The word Stoic originated in the discussions between philosophers as they paced up and down the Painted Stoa, the colonnaded passage adorned with frescos that ran alongside the marketplace and civic centre, the *agora*, in Athens. The traditional founder of Stoicism, in about 300 BC, is Zeno of Citium (a mixed Greek-Phoenician town in modern Cyprus) (334–262 BC), though virtually none of his works survive. Stoicism soon became an Athenian school, usually with a named leader, and its key tenets were subject to intense and evolving debate. Zeno's immediate followers were Cleanthes (*c*.330–230 BC) and Chrysippus (*c*.280–207 BC), although they were unlikely to have anticipated the diverse pathways that later Stoics would take.

The Stoics assumed that all elements in the material world were connected to one another and were part of a wider harmonious cosmos driven by some beneficial divine force. It was essential, they insisted, to understand the unity of the divine and the material world. Chrysippus, who did much to make the philosophy intellectually coherent, argued that 'the heavenly bodies, and all those that possess some sempiternal regularity, cannot be fashioned by man: therefore that by which they are fashioned is better than man, but what would you call this if not God... God is mixed with matter and pervades the whole of it and in this way shaping it and forming it and creating the universe'. According to Chrysippus the ordered procession of the planets was an observable feature of a cycle in which the cosmos would dissolve into fire but would be reborn. The fertility of the Earth, which enabled humankind to live fruitfully, was a sign of its essential benevolence.

In contrast to those philosophies, such as Epicureanism, that advocated a withdrawal from the world, the Stoics expected to find a role in it for themselves.* Their ethics required the individual to seek a harmonious relationship with the cosmos, in which they were fully integrated. It was acceptable to be wealthy (and most leading Stoics were wealthy enough to have the leisure to philosophise) but material goods should not disturb one's peace of mind. Self-discipline was vital but there was a tension between accepting there were forces in the unfolding of

---

* In my Prologue, we saw representatives of the two philosophies clashing with each other.

the cosmos that were inexorable and could not be resisted* and the belief that one could act creatively alongside the evolving cosmos. It is telling that the Stoic philosopher Epictetus, working in the first and second century AD, headed his first recorded discourse with the title 'About things that are within our power and those that are not'.

Stoics talked of a steady accumulation of wisdom. Children required food, warmth and security. As they grew towards adulthood these became less immediately important; instead the intellect searched for virtue, the highest state of being. The Stoics adopted the four virtues expounded by Socrates in Plato's works: temperance, courage, justice and practical wisdom. Although there was much discussion as to how these virtues related to each other, together they provided an ideal. Zeno, the founder of Stoicism, was said to have achieved it by being open to all and presenting his arguments in witty and pithy observations rather than intricate and elaborate argumentation. He lived modestly on bread and honey with the odd cup of good wine. So, despite being an outsider in Athens, Zeno became a celebrity who was honoured with a statue and buried with acclaim in a tomb in the Kerameikos cemetery just outside the city walls. Musonius Rufus, a first-century AD Stoic from Rome, provided a model for self-discipline by taking his students out in the fields so that they could observe him undertaking manual work. Musonius was highly influential, recorded as a teacher of a number of Stoic students and, according to one of Plutarch's informants, offered guidance on how 'to get through life safe and sound'.

In contrast to the Sceptics, the Stoics believed that it was possible to observe the material world accurately and that logic could be used to further develop this process so as to understand how each object was linked to each other in the

---

* It was this approach that Alexander criticised in his *On Fate*: he wished to stress the importance of individual responsibility in line with Aristotle's work on ethics.

chain of being. Chrysippus was renowned by later thinkers, such as Clement of Alexandria, as a fine exponent of rational thought. Unfortunately his most important work, *Logical Inquiries*, has been lost. If Chrysippus' works had survived in anything more than fragmentary form, we would understand a great deal more about the foundations of Stoic logic. The idea of taking personal responsibility for one's actions was pervasive in Stoicism and Seneca, a civil servant in the court of the emperor Nero, exemplified this by the calm and dignified way in which he committed suicide after he was ordered by the emperor to do so. He was much lauded (and represented in Renaissance art) as a result. Yet the ideal Stoic, wise and continent, unprejudiced and rational, an avid searcher for truth untroubled by material or physical desires, would be hard to find. In practice, the rigidity of early Stoicism was moderated through the decades by the experience of living in the real world.

It goes without saying that Stoicism provided a feast of issues for intellectuals to debate. What was the nature of the divine force and could it be understood through observing the celestial universe? If everything was connected, what was the relationship between events in the natural world and the stars? If events moved in an ordered cycle, how could logic help to find an explanation for the course of the cycle? Where was the scope for the exercise of free will in a universe of inexorable cycles? Were there underlying rules for human behaviour, 'natural law' as it would later be termed, that should be sought out, and how could agreement be reached on what they consisted of? What explanation was there for the presence of evil in what was believed to be a harmonious and ultimately benevolent universe? How could one find a place for human emotions? The Stoics distrusted unrestrained feelings as they disturbed rational thought, yet they were aware that there had to be some kind of feeling or care for those around us.

This was another area where Stoicism came into conflict with Aristotle's ethics. Aristotle had believed that anger, for instance, should be expressed when appropriate, the Stoics that it should be controlled.* There was much discussion as to whether, ethically, one should search for personal fulfilment if this could only be achieved at the expense of others. Did one have a duty primarily to oneself, to one's immediate family, one's city or to humanity as a whole? One shadowy second-century AD Stoic, Hierocles, acknowledged the different circles of kinship, extending from family to city, and from ethnic group to all humanity, but argued that one should attempt to bring the outer edges of the circle inwards and extend the natural feelings of affection for one's family outwards.

It was Seneca who claimed that 'we Stoics are not subjects of a despot: each of us lays claim to his own freedom'. Thanks to this determination to decide for themselves how and when to act, Stoics wrote voluminously and the school remained vibrant. Debates among the Stoics were profound and ongoing. One of the most important elements of the philosophies discussed in this chapter was the relationship between the respect shown to the original founding texts and those contributions by later teachers and commentators.† Although the works of the founders of Stoicism were read (one scholar boasted of owning 700 rolls of Chrysippus' works) there was not the same adulation of founding texts as existed in other schools. In short, Stoicism seems to have struck a good balance between tradition and innovation in that it continued to evolve in ways the original founders might not have recognised.

While Stoicism originated in Greece, the Romans were also drawn to it. The Stoic philosopher Panaetius of Rhodes (*c.*185–110 BC) spent long years teaching in Rome and did much to make

---

* Many centuries later, the essayist Michel de Montaigne wrote (1580) that for 'the Stoics, pity is a vicious passion: they want us to succour the afflicted, but not unbend and sympathise with them'.

† It goes without saying that giving too great a 'sacred' quality to a text constrains the development of a lively intellectual tradition.

the philosophy respectable. The first two books of one of Cicero's most influential works, *De Officiis*, 'On Duties', were largely a paraphrase of Panaetius' thoughts. No other Greek philosophy resonated as much with the Roman mind as did Stoicism, and so it provides one of the matrices within which the relationship between Greek and Roman was consolidated. The culmination of this came with the emperor Marcus Aurelius (r. AD 161–80), whose Stoic *Meditations* (its original title was *To Himself*) were actually composed in Greek.

In contrast with the Stoics, the followers of Epicurus (who taught in Athens from 307 until his death in 271 BC) saw the avoidance of mental anxiety and physical pain as the prime aim of philosophy. Diogenes Laertius, writing some 500 years later, in the third century AD, knew of some 300 rolls of Epicurus' writings (and he quoted from three letters of Epicurus to which he had access) and notes that they are remarkable in that Epicurus does not use quotations from other philosophers or poets. Of all the Greek schools, there was none that revered the texts of its founders more than the Epicureans.

Epicurus rejected the power of the gods. He accepted that they existed as real beings (as atomic compounds) but believed they could have no impact on human life. Instead, he followed an earlier materialist, Democritus (*c.* 460–*c.*370 BC), who believed that the world was composed entirely of atoms and that when an individual died the atoms making up his body dissolved and reassembled themselves in new forms. In his view, the world had always existed and the universe was without limits. Epicurus believed that the senses were reliable sources of knowledge, and that all that could be known could be perceived through experience and observation of the world. If an object was not clearly seen, it could always be subject to further observations over time.

If the gods had no power over human life, there was no reason to fear death. This was one, important, element in the cultivation of a tranquil mind. The distinction between pleasure and pain was not absolute – it was rather that they were on a spectrum. So one might feel lonely (a cause of moderate pain), meet up with friends (moving towards pleasure) and then actively enjoy their friendship (pleasure itself). The achievement of pleasure might also be through contemplation of past pleasures or those to come. Once the mind was calm, the highest pleasure could indeed be achieved through companionship with others rather than through public achievement. Epicurus made the distinction between the impulse towards companionship, which is a natural human inclination, and a desire for fame which, he argued, is an unnatural desire created by society. The search for pleasure did not mean hedonism (in the modern sense of the word). 'The pleasant life is produced not by a string of drinking bouts and revelries, nor by the enjoyment of boys and women, nor by fish or other items on an expensive menu, but by sober reasoning,' as Epicurus put it. In this he was close to other philosophic ideals. Epicurus had no place for abstract virtues. Justice is certainly an Epicurean ideal but only in so far as it creates a stable society within which pleasure might be enjoyed. One should obey the law because punishment will cause pain; even the thought of being caught in commission of an illegal act will bring anxiety.

An extraordinary survival from ancient times is the summary of Epicurus' philosophy inscribed on a portico wall in his native city by one Diogenes of Oenoanda (a Greek settlement located in south-eastern Asia Minor). The vast construction, which is now in fragments, may have stood 4 metres high and some 80 metres long, making it the longest inscription surviving from the Greek and Roman world. It is dated to AD 120 or shortly afterwards. Six thousand words have been recovered of an original 25,000. Diogenes included in his inscription some of his own writings in addition to those of Epicurus and proclaimed that this monument was a philanthropic endeavour, a rare form of public benefaction. The text includes other tenets of Epicurus. Simplicity was always to be preferred. It was better to sleep on a straw mattress than be diverted by 'an elaborate house with fretted and gold-spangled ceilings'. Another Epicurean conviction was that the iconography of the gods should be designed to show their benign nature. 'We ought to make statues of the gods genial and smiling, so that we might smile back at them rather than be afraid of them.'

Epicureanism was another philosophy that was attractive to Romans. In fact, one of the most eloquent expressions of Epicureanism was by a Roman, the *De rerum natura* of Lucretius from the first century BC. The presence in Herculaneum of a library dedicated to Epicurus suggests a living tradition that remained part of any philosophical debate. The Platonist Numenius of Apameia, writing towards the end of the second century AD, tells of 'the Epicurean sect resembling a true and harmonious state which is of one mind and sharing a common point of view'. Epicureanism also had its critics, however. Plutarch and the Stoic philosopher Epictetus wrote against the Epicureans complaining of their withdrawal from public life that had been such an essential part of Greek society. If it had not been for the record of Diogenes Laertius' positive support for Epicurus, we would not have known that it was still an active philosophy as late as the third century AD.

Central to the philosophical enterprise is the search for criteria by which one can judge what is true. Yet the investigation and definition of truth is problematic in itself. It was Socrates who said he knew nothing but the extent of his own ignorance. Each school was forced to confront the problem, with perhaps the Peripatetics, with their stress on classifying empirical evidence, having the most elaborate and effective forms of proof, but the Stoics and the Epicureans also claimed it was possible to 'know' the material world. The Greek word for investigation is *skepsis* and those who concentrate on the problems of knowing to the extent of questioning whether any belief is true are termed the Sceptics. It is hard to see the Sceptics as a defined school as among their number there were varying degrees to which the possibilities of truth were acknowledged, and contradictions were present within this movement which made it philosophically unstable. 'How can one know for certain that there is no such thing as certain knowledge?' is the obvious one and was exploited as such by the Sceptics' opponents. The fundamental challenge for the Sceptics was how to live well in the absence of certainty.

One of the schools where Scepticism found a home was Platonism. As we have seen, the Platonists rejected the order of the material world so they had every incentive for doubting the validity of what could be said about it. The sixth leader of the Academy, Arcesilaus (c.318–243 BC), revived the questioning techniques of Socrates. He targeted the Stoics, especially its founder Zeno who had argued that one could confidently make empirical judgements about the material world. Arcesilaus replied that sense impressions were always unreliable – there were many ways in which the eyes could deceive. There could be dreams or hallucinations and similar objects (identical twins, for instance) could be confused one with the other. At the very least there should be a suspension of judgement.

A later leader of the Academy, Carneades (c.213–129 BC), followed Arcesilaus in using Socratic questioning to destroy the apparent certainties of his opponents. He carried on the feud with the Stoics, this time targeting Chrysippus. Carneades became notorious when he visited Rome in 155 BC as one of a group of philosophers pleading to be let off a fine imposed on Athens. (One of the crucial roles of Greek orators/philosophers under Roman hegemony was to petition the Roman magistrates – and later the emperors – for privileges for their native cities.) To the consternation of his audience, Carneades defended the concept of justice one day and then ridiculed it the next. His purpose was to stress the unstable nature of such concepts and in his writings he went further to show – contrary to what Stoics and Epicureans believed – that one could never define what the best way of living could be.* Yet Carneades had to live in the real

* This was the first recorded instance (and noted by the historian Polybius, who was probably there) of Romans being confronted by Greek philosophy, though, in this case, through an interpreter.

world and he appears to have accepted that some knowledge could be regarded as provisionally true. If nothing could be seen as true, how could one decide what to eat or when there was a need to escape from a fire? The solution was perhaps to assess the immediate importance of an issue to oneself as an individual and then to carry out extra observations to raise the level of certainty, even if one still retained an element of doubt. So Carneades proposed a hierarchy of assertions, from the most to the least certain. As a result, some have seen him as the creator of probabilism, the science of knowing how probable any assumed truth might be.

There was a separate school of Sceptics (and technically this is the true home of Scepticism) founded by Pyrrho of Elis (c.360–270 BC).* Virtually nothing is known of Pyrrho but he was claimed as an inspiration by a later Sceptic, Sextus Empiricus. It is said that, having stopped worrying about what it is possible to know, Pyrrho was able to find tranquillity of mind, even remaining calm when his ship was caught in a storm. Yet legend told otherwise: that he doubted the reality of the material world so completely that his friends had to guide him around to stop him falling off cliffs or not getting out of the way of carts.† Sextus Empiricus' work *Adversus Mathematikos*, 'Against the Academics', deals with each of the subject disciplines in turn, from geometry to music, from rhetoric to logic. Another work, *Against the Rhetoricians*, deals with the problem of the purpose of making speeches and the authority of speechmakers.

So little is known about Sextus' life that one has to suspend judgement even about the period in which he was living. (The last datable figure in his work is the emperor Tiberius, who had died in AD 37, but Sextus is usually seen as having being active in

---

* Plutarch noticed the distinction between the two schools in his *On the Difference between Pyrrhonists and Academics*.
† One is reminded of the story of the pre-Socratic Thales of Miletus (sixth century BC) who was so busy looking at the stars that he fell down a well.

the second century AD.) If his aim was to achieve 'tranquillity', then it is understandable that he chose to avoid public life. He argued that one did not start by being a Sceptic, but as one delved more deeply into philosophical issues, the problems of 'knowing' became more obvious and unsettled the mind. Sextus' target is dogmatism, and he accuses both Stoics and Epicureans of this. The dogmatic thinker, if he is honest, must realise that elements of what he claims to know are untenable, and thus he cannot have tranquillity of mind. Somehow one must find a way of living that leaves the mind open to continuous investigation of the world around one with a reasonable acceptance that one must make provisional judgements about the nature of existence. 'Because of the equal strength in opposing objects and accounts, we come first to suspension of judgement and then to tranquillity.'

Further evidence of a resurgence of interest in the Sceptics in the second century AD comes from Epictetus and Galen who are known to have written on the subject. Within the Pyrrhonist School (and there is little record of individual thinkers other than Sextus taking the school forward), there was a great deal of fertile and ingenious thinking. It might be seen as a Sceptic mantra that one must keep on searching to the extent that one reaches a dead-end or realises that one has to suspend judgement. Even the epics of Homer were quarried for evidence that the great poet understood the limits of knowledge. While it was obvious that human beings might differ in their assessment of an object – is this picture beautiful or not? – the school also found a place for the sensory world of animals. If a dog can smell something that a human cannot, on what grounds could one say that the smell exists? How could the Epicureans be certain that everything is made up of atoms when the senses cannot see them? If it is impossible to believe anything for certain, how can one know that one is a Sceptic? If a perfume has an attractive scent but is bitter to taste, what does this say about the coherence of the senses? The state of mind of the observer will affect what is experienced; the same event will be interpreted differently from person to person and from mood to mood. One glass of wine is satisfying, ten glasses of the same wine might be damaging. Something we believe to be unique may be thought valuable, but if we come to realise that there are many examples of the same object then the value is lost. So how to define value? The achievement of the Sceptics was to raise these questions and so invigorate debate.

The most uncompromising and visible way of being a philosopher was to become a Cynic. Anecdotes suggest that the term Cynic comes from the Greek *kuon*, a dog, as the more outrageous behaviour of the Cynics was canine, not least in their unruly barking. As Lucian puts it in his text *Runaways*, 'it does not take much effort to throw on a cloak, hang a wallet from your shoulder, carry a staff in your hand and shout – or rather bray or bark – and abuse everyone'. In fact, the term covers a wide variety of behaviours but usually involved abandoning all possessions and taking to the road. Notable was the rejection of one's native city in order to become *kosmopolites*, 'a citizen of the world', a phrase born at this time. Diogenes Laertius, who devotes a whole book of his *Lives of the Philosophers* to what he terms a 'school' of Cynics founded by Diogenes of Sinope (404–323 BC), a contemporary of Plato, records that they 'live frugally, eating only for nourishment and wearing only a cloak [in this case a rough garment worn against the skin] and despising wealth, fame and noble birth'. Most were vegetarians and drank only water. They regarded certain academic disciplines, among them mathematics, music and astronomy, as superfluous to the life of the philosopher. Although writing many centuries later, Diogenes Laertius records that Diogenes of Sinope insulted passers-by, urinated and masturbated in public. Plato regarded him as 'Socrates gone mad'. In a celebrated encounter, recorded by Plutarch and Diogenes Laertius, Diogenes demanded that Alexander the Great get out of the way of the Sun.

Diogenes of Sinope was an extreme case. In contrast, Zeno,

the founder of Stoicism, was seen as a Cynic as regards his exemplary ascetic lifestyle. (The ancient commentators disagree as to whether Cynicism was compatible with Stoicism or was a school that was antagonistic to all other philosophies.) To show the range of the term, when two uninhibited Cynics, Crates and Hipparchia, husband and wife, were having sex in public, it was Zeno who rushed up to conceal them with a cloak. Likewise Dio Chrysostom, a writer and thinker of the first century AD who regarded himself as a Cynic during his period of exile from Rome and his native province of Bithynia, appears to have been seen as respectable, mixing easily with those he met. In contrast, the satirist Lucian, who despised the Cynics, describes one Peregrinus as a Cynic who had killed his father and then wormed his way into Christian circles.

Opponents argued that Cynicism was merely a way of life and did not deserve to be called a 'school', yet there were important philosophical dimensions to Cynicism in that it called into question the nature of conventions and status. Diogenes of Sinope went so far as to argue that morality came from within oneself and not from following religious ritual or accepting subservience to the gods. In effect, Cynicism rejected all forms of traditional philosophy. By throwing off convention, social as well as intellectual, one would truly find oneself. In Christianity it found an echo in the work of the Franciscans, who renounced any form of ownership and, originally at least, denigrated learning as a form of corruption. The Cynics have also had modern followers, especially on the hippy trail of the 1960s.

It should be clear from this rich tapestry of debate that the Greek-speaking culture that continued to flourish under Roman rule was an intellectually highly sophisticated one, whose leaders had an extraordinary range, not least in mastery of their cultural heritage. They displayed an excellence in virtuoso performances in whatever discipline they adopted. 'One of the most striking features of Hellenistic culture is that many branches began to detach themselves from the philosophic tree. More and more specialised scholars, mathematicians, astronomers, physicists, medical doctors, scholars and philologists began to appear – learned men who were not philosophers and did not wish to be considered as such.' In the case of certain individuals, it can be difficult to see which philosophy exerts a dominant influence on their work. Galen, for instance, prided himself on keeping up with all schools. It was also a combative world. Geoffrey Lloyd, the pre-eminent historian of Greek science, notes that 'one could touch on almost every aspect of Galen's work, in logic, moral philosophy, psychology, physiology, anatomy, pathology, pharmacology and therapeutics by way of an analysis of his reactions to others'. Without this cut and thrust of debate the intellectual world of this period would be as sterile as Gibbon claimed that it was.

A new 'philosophy' was to enter Greek intellectual life in the first century AD. Jesus of Nazareth, a charismatic Jewish teacher with a large following in Galilee, came to Jerusalem where the Roman authorities and Jewish priesthood collaborated in having him executed by crucifixion, probably in AD 30. His followers soon claimed that, despite his dead body being buried, he had appeared alive three days later and had remained on Earth until he 'ascended' into heaven forty days later. Increasingly he was talked of as *Christos*, the messiah long hoped for in Jewish tradition. Although Jesus had spoken Aramaic, his literate followers, a Jewish apostle, Paul, and the authors of gospels ('the good news') outlining his life and teachings, wrote in Greek.*

When Christian communities spread outside Judaism they had to reconcile Jewish tradition with the wider Greek world. So how did Greek intellectuals who had been brought up within the philosophical milieu described in this book cope with this? As will be shown, Platonism fitted well with Jewish conceptions of an absolute Jewish God and so became integrated with an

---

* It is difficult to know which of Jesus' teachings have been lost in translation.

emerging Christian theology. A role had to be found for Jesus but, as Clement of Alexandria and Origen, also of Alexandria, argued, he was Reason (*logos*) itself and marked the culmination of Greek philosophy.* Much further work had to be done to reconcile the apparently entirely human nature of Christ with his role as the Son of God.

The theological debates of the fourth century AD were every bit as sophisticated as those conducted in earlier centuries, but by this time the emperors, beleaguered by their enemies, barbarian and otherwise, were impelled to impose absolute definitions of Christian belief and debate was quelled. The final resolution created a very different intellectual and cultural world from that of classical antiquity and the Hellenistic centuries. It would involve giving a sacred status to an agreed canon of scriptures with a clerical hierarchy determining how they should be interpreted. A church was in the making.†

* In this book these two theologians will be treated as parallel, rather than antagonistic, intellectuals.
† See the transition explored in Charles Freeman, *AD 381*, Pimlico, 2008.

4

The Historian: Polybius (c.200–c.118 BC)

The Battle of Pydna in 168 BC marked a turning point in the relationship between Rome and Greece. For two centuries the Macedonian phalanx, created by Philip of Macedon, father of Alexander the Great, had dominated Greek military strategy. By now, however, the phalanx had become a rigid formation constrained by memories of its own victories. At Pydna, on the Macedonian coast, Perseus, king of Macedon, was confronted by Roman legions under the command of the veteran Roman general, Aemilius Paullus. Despite a terrifying Macedonian charge, the legions stood firm and were able to infiltrate the phalanx and slaughter its soldiers so effectively that Macedon ceased to exist as a military power.

The Romans exploited their position to extend their hegemony in Greece. In the Peloponnese the Achaean League of cities, centred on Megalopolis,* had benefitted greatly from the support of Rome in an earlier war against Macedon (200–196 BC) and now dominated most of the peninsula. The official stance of the League was to recognise Roman influence

---

* As its name, 'the big city', suggests, Megalopolis had been founded as a conglomeration of Greek cities in the fourth century BC – to resist the power of Sparta.

but 'within the strict conditions of Achaean laws', a position which maintained its dignity as an independent political entity. Despite the apparently friendly relations with Rome the League had, however, shown signs of hesitation in the years during the rise of Perseus. The League assembly passed and then withdrew an offer to provide troops to Rome in support of the war. The Romans always expected a sycophantic and submissive attitude from their allies and they were taking no chances. After the victory at Pydna, it was decreed that a thousand hostages from the leading ranks of the Achaeans were to be taken to Rome.

Among them was Polybius, the commander of the League's cavalry. Polybius had been born in Megalopolis, around 200 BC. His father, Lycortas, was a wealthy landowner, deeply involved in the politics of the League. Polybius grew up enjoying typical aristocratic pursuits, riding and hunting, and listening to political debates that were focused on sustaining a workable relationship with the growing power of Rome. He had been appointed commander of the cavalry when he was thirty, the youngest age at which it was permissible.

In contrast with most of the exiled Greek hostages, who stagnated in remote areas outside the city, Polybius remained in Rome. He quickly attached himself to Scipio Aemilianus, the eighteen-year-old son of the victor of Pydna, later to be a general in his own right. Polybius had met Scipio through the 'loan of some books and conversation about them'. Scipio in return relished the company of the older man, and his intense interest in politics. They also bonded over their shared love of hunting. Polybius would idealise Scipio as the best of the Romans, his discipline and honesty marking him out from others who had been corrupted by the wealth of looted cities. Gradually Scipio gathered around him a circle of intellectuals, both Greek and Roman, among them the Greek Stoic philosopher Panaetius, who probably influenced Polybius with his ideas.

Polybius remained part of Scipio's circle for more than twenty years, even after all restrictions on the Achaean hostages were rescinded in 150, and this civilised ambience may have influenced his positive attitude to Roman imperialism. (He must have ignored the murderous rivalries between the leading Roman families of his day!) During the Third Punic War, he went on campaign with Scipio and was present with him at the sack of Carthage in 146 BC. In the same year, the Achaean League had finally achieved its ambition of subjugating Sparta but this extension of the League's power led to Roman retaliation. The Achaean forces were in decline and were easily defeated. It was now that Corinth was thoroughly sacked – Polybius records that the plundered art treasures were piled up outside the city walls. The defeat of the League marked the moment when Roman domination of Greece was unambiguously sealed.

Polybius was now so deeply embedded in the Roman aristocracy that he was employed to establish settled conditions in what was now a defeated country. He was so successful in conciliating the members of the League that they honoured him with an inscription in his hometown that records its thanks that he 'had quenched the anger of Rome'. Thus did Polybius play a crucial role in the Greek acquiescence in Roman hegemony. He lived into his eighties and it seems a fitting, if abrupt, end for such an active man that he died after falling from a horse.

Polybius had begun writing early. Even before he reached Rome, he had compiled a biography, now lost, of the celebrated Achaean *strategos*, or general, Philopoemen (see also pp.188–9). Yet he now set himself a challenge that went far beyond this. He was astonished by the success of Rome in conquering, first, the western Mediterranean and then the Greek east. He would have realised that in Rome he had access to the sources that would enable him to construct a coherent narrative of these events. In the 150s BC he began to write the *Universal History** (often referred to as *The Histories*) for which he is famous.

Writing history was, for Polybius, a serious endeavour. There

* Polybius defined his project as *ta katholou graphein* – a universal history which culminates with the subjugation of almost the whole world (*oikoumene*) to Rome.

were relevant precedents in the great Greek historians of the fifth century BC, Herodotus and Thucydides. Polybius followed Herodotus in creating an expansive (hence 'universal') history that did not condescend to his audience. Perhaps, although Polybius hardly mentions him, Thucydides, historian of the Peloponnesian War, was the most important model. They had much in common. Both were writing contemporaneously, within fifty to seventy years of the events they described; they had both been soldiers and had known defeat and exile. Above all, Thucydides was a realist: he had no illusions about the horrors of war and the complex motivations of those fighting them. This must have appealed to Polybius, who was fascinated by the forces that impelled the Romans to power.

Polybius was well aware of a number of histories, both Greek and Roman, written since the fifth century which are now lost to us. He was critical, sometimes contemptuously so, of their limitations. In particular he decried histories where events had been embellished solely to make them more attractive to the reader. He gave short shrift to any accounts that dwelt on the miraculous, stories of a statue of Artemis on which rain never fell, for instance. He believed that his fellow Greeks – his primary audience – needed to be aware of the significance of the rise of Rome as a turning point in world history in which they had to acquiesce. In a meditative introduction to his Book Nine, he refuses to deal with 'genealogies and myths, the planting of colonies, the foundation of cities and their ties of kinship', all of which had been well covered in other histories. Instead, he will concentrate on the 'actions of nations, cities and rulers'. He admits that this will 'appeal to only one type of reader and will scarcely make attractive reading for the majority'. He is writing for an educated elite and he is the first historian we know of to suggest that a secure knowledge of the past is essential for political life. Rather than discussing the events of individual wars, he sets himself the task of exploring the nature of warfare generally and its relationship with politics. In this he considers himself to be breaking new ground. He certainly did not lack confidence in his ability to achieve this.

So what intellectual background did Polybius bring to his project? It appears that he had had a conventional Greek education in literature and rhetoric. In his work he quotes several philosophers, including Heraclitus,* Plato and Aristotle, and there are elements of Stoicism in his view of *Tyche*, 'Fate', as the force which drives the universe onwards. While he appears to have read widely and critically from earlier studies and must have had access through his contacts to the archives, especially those kept in Rome, one cannot imagine him enjoying spending long hours there. Whatever education he had had, his training had left him with a passion for military technology and strategies. He makes it clear that the outcome of a battle can only be understood if one has walked over the battlefield, or the achievement of Hannibal in crossing the Alps assessed unless one had taken the same tortuous path (Book Three of the *Universal History*). He certainly explored sites as far as he could. He tells of travels 'through Africa, Spain and Gaul, and voyages on the sea which adjoins those countries on their western side'. Later he visited Alexandria and Sardis on the Asian mainland.

Polybius was also an avid interviewer. Sociable and inquisitive, he met a wide range of contemporaries and prided himself on his skills in eliciting the information he wanted. In Book Twelve of the *Universal History* he lays into a historian called Timaeus for relying too heavily on documents and hearsay. He had good contacts. There was the intellectual circle around Scipio and then his fellow Greeks who were in exile around Rome. Many of these had been prominent members of their own communities and Polybius would have been able to put their knowledge and insights alongside those of his Roman contacts. He also appears

---

* The philosopher Heraclitus (active about 500 BC) was fascinated by the process of change, which he believed was constant. He is famous for his aphorism that one never steps in the same river twice.

to have had access to other high-ranking sources. When he was researching the life of Hannibal, for instance, he learned much from Masinissa, the elderly king of Numidia (Book Nine). And he was able to interview members of the court of Perseus, some of whom had known Philip V. By this time too Rome had become the centre of the Mediterranean world and there would have been many envoys visiting the city who could further fill out the background.

So this was to be an expansive history, not only dealing with the Mediterranean as a whole but with the characters of its peoples, their political systems and the geographical background. The core of the *Universal History* would be the fifty-three years from the outbreak of the Second Punic War in 220 BC to the Battle of Pydna and the defeat of Perseus in 168 which Polybius believed to be a crucial turning point in world history. The *Universal History* is prefaced by two background books introducing Rome and extended with books dealing with the twenty years after Pydna leading up to the destruction of Carthage and Corinth in 146 BC.

Polybius makes digressions in which he analyses issues he considers to be of importance. In Book Three, when he begins the section on the outbreak of the Second Punic War with Hannibal, he deals with causation in history. He describes immediate causes, such as an attack by one party on another, but Polybius feels one must provide a broader perspective. In the case of the invasion of Persia by Alexander the Great, for instance, he believes this event to have been signalled by Greek incursions into Persia seventy years earlier. In considering the 'causes' of the conflicts he narrates, he dwells on the institutional framework and moral character of the antagonists and this becomes perhaps the major underlying theme of the *History*. Above all Polybius was obsessed with creating a narrative which is accurate. 'It is not the historian's business to show off his ability to his readers, but rather to devote his whole energy to finding out and setting down what was really and truly said.' The motives of both sides need impartial evaluation. Praise and blame must be distributed without favour. Even patriotic feelings of the historian should never bias him towards peddling falsehoods.

His chosen dates – and the wars fought within this timespan – give Polybius ample scope to display his strengths as a historian. His knowledge of military affairs and technology serves him well. In Book Six, he deals in depth with the arrangements, the training, the order of command and deployment of the Roman army. There is even a section on the psychology of new recruits in battle and how to ensure they fight with the required courage when they go into battle for the first time. Describing the siege of Syracuse (214–212 BC) during the Second Punic War he delights in the ingenuity of Archimedes' defensive weapons.* In his account of Hannibal crossing the Alps in Book Three, he distinguishes the role of resolute leadership, logistics and sheer human endurance as the Carthaginian army winds its tortuous way through the mountain pass with the snowfalls of winter coming on. Once the army has come down into the Po Valley and is heading southwards towards Rome, Polybius gives a gripping account of the manoeuvres of Hannibal and his Roman opponents as they exploit the terrain to achieve the perfect position from which to counterattack. It is Hannibal who triumphs in the devastating Battle of Cannae (216 BC) where the Roman army is completely destroyed. The survival of Rome after this catastrophe is used by Polybius to demonstrate the underlying strengths of the city. 'Although the Romans had beyond any dispute been worsted in battle and their military reputation annihilated, yet through the particular virtue of their constitution and their ability to keep their heads, they not only won back their supremacy in Italy and later defeated the Carthaginians, but within a few years had made themselves masters of the whole world.'

---

* A mathematician, physicist, engineer and inventor, Archimedes (c.287–212 BC) took part in the city's defence and was killed when Syracuse finally fell.

The most influential part of the *Universal History*, not least so far as Polybius' Renaissance readers were concerned, related to his treatment of the Roman constitution. The nature and comparative merit of political systems had been discussed among the Greeks for centuries. In 510 BC Athens had thrown off tyrannical rule and set the city on the path of democratic government for its citizens. The advantages and dangers of (direct) democracy were hotly debated by both politicians and philosophers. Plato in his *Republic* had denigrated democracy, arguing instead for the rule of a few wise men who had studied the underlying concepts of law and justice so that they could impose them on the citizen community. A much more open-minded discussion could be found in Aristotle's *Politics* where the philosopher provides an extensive survey of different forms of government, exploring the strengths and weaknesses of monarchies, oligarchies and democracies and even suggesting that a constitution based on a mix of these was possible. There has been debate over the extent to which Polybius knew these texts (and others now lost) but they had undoubtedly become part of educated discourse by the time Polybius was writing. The scholarly consensus is that he moved beyond them to provide an original analysis of his own.

Polybius considers the Republican constitution of Rome in Book Six of the *History*, describing the relative powers of the consuls (which he classifies as 'monarchy' or rather kingship, as there were two consuls), the Senate (classified as the 'aristocracy') and the people (who represent 'democracy') and the checks they placed on each other. Crucially he did not see these relationships as inflexible but able to adapt to changing circumstances. Yet, and here Polybius differs fundamentally from Aristotle, he envisaged a cycle of politics that would lead from the original autocracy of a primitive society to oligarchy and then democracy. Polybius uses the term *democratia* to describe a society in which the will of the people matters but one in which they obey the laws and respect the gods. He believed that the ritual of religion provided a powerful binding force for any society. Such a 'democratic' society would, Polybius believed, inevitably degenerate into mob rule (here he used an obscure term *ochlocratia*, derived from *okhlos*, 'mob', to describe the degeneration), so requiring a single man to take charge again and initiate a new cycle. Even though the Romans had achieved a balanced constitution that was particularly effective in its time, there would be an eventual decline and fall. Polybius accounts for the defeat of the Carthaginians as the result of the degeneration of their constitution just at the moment when the Romans were at their strongest.

In what sense did Polybius place his *History* within a wider philosophical context? He notes how victories are often thrown away and how defeats, especially those of Rome by Hannibal, can be the catalyst for later success. Constancy and resilience in dealing with the inevitable setbacks of life are the virtues here and Polybius may have absorbed these values from Stoicism. Again, Polybius, in line with the philosophers whom he had absorbed, appears to favour moderation and restraint – he certainly expects rulers and generals to engage in considered strategic thinking. There is no place for impulsive actions or dependency on the gods. 'Rashness, excessive audacity, blind impetuosity, vanity or foolish ambition are all easily exploited by the enemy... for a general with such defects in his character will naturally fall victim to all kinds of stratagems, ambushes and trickery.'

Polybius' identifying of *Tyche*, Fortune or Chance, as a driving force in the unfolding of history has generated much scholarly debate. In Polybius' time *Tyche* was personified as a goddess yet he is ambivalent about her role. In some passages he portrays her as an essentially benign force that, for instance, watched over Rome's rise to power. '*Tyche* steered almost all the affairs of the world in one direction and forced them to converge upon one and the same goal.' This is close to the Stoics' conception of history being driven inexorably forward. It has been suggested that for Polybius this provides some justification for Roman rule and why it should no longer be resisted by the defeated Greeks. In other passages *Tyche* appears more capricious, able to unexpectedly shift the course of events, perhaps when Polybius, who prefers to find rational explanations, can find no other cause for them. He notes for instance that no one would have predicted that the Persian empire would fall so easily to a virtually unknown opponent, Macedon, and then that Macedon would in its turn be so easily defeated by Rome.

Polybius was well aware that many conquerors saw victory as an end in itself but he wished to evaluate the Roman conquests within a broader moral perspective. He could hardly have dealt with such cataclysmic events, many of which had involved the deaths of thousands, without some emotional involvement. Was the Romans' imperial mission fundamentally ameliorative, and should it therefore be accepted by the Greeks? By the time he was writing the bulk of his history around 150 BC Polybius considered that it was, although he had some concerns about the rapacity of the Romans. Discussing the sack of Syracuse by the Roman general Marcellus in 212, for instance, Polybius reflects on whether the taking of so much loot does any more than arouse jealousy and encourage sympathy for the losers. And Polybius describes an increase in Roman ruthlessness. By the end of his extension of the *History* to 146 BC, a year when Roman armies sacked both Carthage and Corinth, he seems less convinced of the merits of Roman rule. When, having accompanied Scipio to north Africa, Polybius witnesses the destruction of Carthage, he records, in a passage that would resonate among later generations, that

> Scipio, when he looked upon the city as it was utterly perishing and in the last throes of its complete destruction, is said to have shed tears and wept openly for his enemies. After being wrapped in thought for long, and realising that all cities, nations, and authorities must, like men, meet their doom; that this happened to Troy, once a prosperous city, to the empires of Assyria, Media,

and Persia, the greatest of their time, and to Macedonia itself...
the brilliance of which was so recent, either deliberately or the
verses escaping him, he said:

'A day will come when sacred Troy shall perish, And Priam
and his people shall be slain.'

So too would Rome fall as Macedon had done.

Having explored the nature of war so thoroughly, Polybius
pleads for restraint and humane conduct.

Violent and gratuitous destruction of temples, statues and all
such gear, since it offers absolutely no advantage to one's side in a
war, and does nothing to cripple an enemy, can only be described
as the act of a deranged mind and attitude. Decent men should
not make war on the ignorant and wrongheaded with a view to
stamping them out and exterminating them, but should rather
aim to correct and remove their mistakes. Nor should they lump
the innocent and guilty together, but rather treat those they regard
as guilty with the same merciful compassion that they extend to
the innocent. Wrongdoing as an instrument of terrorisation, to
coerce unwilling subjects, belongs to the tyrant, who hates his
people as much as they hate him, but a king's business is to treat
everyone well, to win men's love by his humane and generous
conduct, and thus to rule and preside with the consent of those
he governs.

One of Polybius' Renaissance readers, Alberico Gentili (1552–
1608), Italian-born Regius Professor of Civil Law at Oxford,
who was steeped in Roman military history, would come up
with much the same rules for the conduct of war.

Polybius died around 118 BC and his works soon became required
reading for Greek-speaking intellectuals. Plutarch (who read
everything!) refers to Polybius twenty-six times in his surviving
works and used his life of Philopoemen as the basis for his own
(which may well be why Polybius' version was not recopied).
Yet what survives of Polybius' work is fragmentary. Originally

the *Universal History* comprised forty books but only the first five survive intact. By the ninth century AD much had been lost from the later books. Some, such as Book Thirty-Four, devoted to geographical matters, exist only in a few fragments in later quotations, notably in Strabo's *Geography*. In its original form the *Universal History* must have been a massive work. Enough of it remains to show that Polybius not only wrote an informative and coherent history that dealt with an extraordinary period in human history but also encouraged its Greek audience to recognise that Roman hegemony could not be reversed.

5

The Polymath: Posidonius (135–51 BC)

In 63 BC, the Roman general Pompey was at the height of his powers. After a brilliant campaign in the eastern Mediterranean in which he had annexed Syria and the cities of Pella and Damascus, he had forced Mithridates VI of Pontus, one of the most formidable enemies of Rome, to commit suicide, and had moved into Anatolia where he reorganised the remnants of the Seleucid kingdom. He added three provinces to the empire, Cilicia, Bithynia and Pontus, and Syria, and two client kingdoms, Armenia and Judaea. He arranged for censuses to be carried out in the provinces so that taxes could be collected and sent to Rome. Pompey himself had accumulated great personal wealth and, of course, immense prestige from his achievements.

On his way home, Pompey stopped on the island of Rhodes. He had decided to visit an old acquaintance, Posidonius, whom he had first met in the mid-80s BC when Posidonius had been part of an embassy to Rome from Rhodes and then, for a second time, in Rhodes itself in 66. Posidonius was a Greek Stoic philosopher, now elderly, in his seventies, and riddled with gout. Pompey arrived at Posidonius' house in full regalia, his attendants bearing the *fasces*, the traditional axe with rods bound around it. Finding Posidonius too ill to leave his bed, Pompey divested himself of all these symbols of his authority before entering. Later generations would marvel at the spectacle of a Roman general, with so many achievements behind him, paying such homage to an intellectual. Posidonius proceeded to deliver a lecture on the theme 'There is no good but moral good', during which, good Stoic that he was, he pointed to his gouty leg and claimed nothing could persuade him that the pain was evil. It was to be stoically endured.

Nearly two decades earlier, another Roman statesman had visited Posidonius to learn the art of rhetoric and to pick up the elements of Stoic philosophy. This was Marcus Tullius Cicero, then in his twenties and already on his way to becoming one of Rome's greatest orators. In his later letters Cicero would refer to Posidonius as his teacher and 'dear friend'. Posidonius was ready to recognise the Roman aristocracy – which in the first half of the first century BC was still running a republic – as a moral elite. This was, to say the least, optimistic; even by the 80s BC Roman politics was being corrupted by unscrupulous and populist politicians. However, one could argue that the ethical tradition, exemplified by Cicero's famous condemnation of Verres, the fraudulent governor of Sicily, in 70 BC, was influenced by Stoic values of honest public life. In his old age, Cicero would compose a work on public duty, *De officiis*, whose content owed a significant debt to Posidonius' teacher Panaetius.

Posidonius was a Syrian Greek born in the city of Apamea* on the Orontes river in northern Syria in 135. It was an unstable region, still part of the Seleucid kingdom but vulnerable to conflict with the Ptolemies of Egypt, and the young Posidonius left home to study, as so many wealthy Greeks did, in Athens. It was here that he joined the school of Panaetius, an old man, but now head of the Stoic school and influential as a teacher. While Posidonius is seen as a Stoic, his mind ranged more widely, and he was well versed in Plato and Aristotle, both of

---

* The city was named after the wife of Seleucus I, a Sogdian (Sogdia was part of Iran) noblewoman whom the king married in 324 BC.

whose schools were still active in Athens. Like all Stoics, he was a believer in the essential unity of Earth and the universe. Once, in a far-distant Golden Age, there had existed a pure and universal wisdom from which each culture had developed its own philosophy. Reaching back to rediscover this heritage was the true task of the philosopher. Stimulated by Aristotle's interest in the natural world, Posidonius sought to understand the relationships between aspects of this world more fully. Like Polybius, he was no armchair theorist (he had a nickname – 'The Athlete') and he was soon off exploring and observing. His travels took him through much of western Europe and north Africa as he followed his ambition to understand the natural world and its peoples. Determined to tabulate the connection between the Moon and the tides, he travelled through the Straits of Gibraltar so that he could observe a greater discrepancy between high and low tides than he could find in the Mediterranean.

It is frustrating that so little of Posidonius' work survives because it would appear that his wide-ranging erudition matched that of Aristotle, and he was acclaimed as an intellectual superstar by his contemporaries, 'the most learned scholar of my time', according to the geographer Strabo. As the Roman Stoic philosopher Seneca put it: 'Live with Chrysippus [the revered Stoic philosopher] and Posidonius: they will make you acquainted with things earthly and heavenly; they will bid you work hard over something more than neat turns of language and phrases mouthed forth for the entertainment of listeners.'

In the 90s BC Posidonius moved to Rhodes, which had established itself as a major cultural centre after the conquests of Alexander. The island's prominent position in the eastern Mediterranean and two fine harbours made it a perfect entrepôt for trade and its shipbuilders became famous. It had strong links with the Ptolemies, the dynasty that ruled Egypt from Alexander's foundation, Alexandria. Politically it involved its citizens in government at a time when popular participation was fast disappearing as monarchies established themselves across the east. By the second century BC, however, Rhodes could hardly ignore the rising power of Rome and, after the defeat of Perseus in 168 BC, it was forced to become a dependent Roman ally. Its commercial wealth remained (wine from Rhodes was favoured in Rome) and it became a cultural magnet for elite Romans – such as Cicero and Julius Caesar – who wanted to study rhetoric with the best Greek teachers.

Rhodes was also an important centre for sculpture. Three sculptors from the island were said to have created the famous statue of Laocoön and his sons, rediscovered in Rome in 1506 (and now in the Vatican). A variety of exuberant sculptures found in the seaside grotto of the emperor Tiberius at Sperlonga* – and now on display in a museum there – also came from Rhodes. It is said that there were 3,000 statues in the port city of Rhodes alone. After Sulla's sack of Athens in 86 BC, many Athenian intellectuals fled to Rhodes, boosting still further its prestige as a cultural centre. By this time Posidonius was respected enough to be elected as one of its 'presidents' and it was in this capacity that he was part of the island's embassy to Rome in 86 (where he had met the young Pompey for the first time).

Some two hundred years after its birth, Stoicism was a vibrant and still-evolving philosophy. By this time Roman rule over the Mediterranean was well embedded and Posidonius credited this emerging empire as further evidence of a harmonious universe. The climate and fertility of Italy confirmed that it was intended as the centre of the world. Posidonius was determined to integrate other philosophical traditions with Stoicism even though more conservative Stoics criticised him for insisting that Plato and Aristotle had something to offer. Plato had highlighted the potency of natural desires, such as anger, sexual passion, greed and the impulse to dominate, which needed to be held in check if the mind was to be free to search for philosophical truths. In contrast, the Stoics had

---

* Sperlonga is a coastal town between Rome and Naples.

traditionally seen such desires as judgements which were faulty but which could be corrected. Posidonius sided with Plato rather than with Stoic tradition: desires were a natural part of the undisciplined soul. Taking one of Plato's examples, he described the emotions as two unruly horses driven by a charioteer who would have to learn to control them. One of his recommendations was that music should be used as part of the education of children in moral behaviour (the lyre was said to calm adolescent passions) and that food and drink should be restricted from an early age so that they did not cause emotional disturbance. In short, Posidonius saw emotions as having a physical foundation that could be manipulated. Adopting ideas from Aristotle, Posidonius also emphasised the importance of developing good habits so that when emotions were aroused they were recognised and moderated.

Posidonius was an innovative thinker. Rather than being simply a dry and remote philosopher, he was intrigued by technology and empirical science, one reason why the works of Aristotle were attractive to him. While more traditional Stoics regarded such interest in practical matters as unworthy of an intellectual, Posidonius believed that some understanding of the workings of the natural world could only amplify Stoic beliefs. Much of his work was concerned with finding connections, between humans and the natural world, between the Earth and the heavens, between climate and geography. He spotted, for instance, that the tides appeared to relate to phases of the Moon and this was why he set off to the tidal waters of the Atlantic to check this out. He plotted the relationship between the phases of the Moon and its position at the equinoxes and when the tides were at their height, although he assumed wrongly that the Moon became warmer and cooler according to its phases and that the seas expanded or contracted correspondingly.

Posidonius followed earlier traditions, set by mathematicians and astronomers, in attempting to measure the universe. He computed the distance of the Moon and the Sun from the Earth and the circumference of the Earth itself.* He is also credited (by Cicero) with creating an orrery, a mechanical model of the solar system. If this orrery bore any resemblance to the Antikythera Mechanism,† an instrument dating from much the same period (150–100 BC), with a complete set of dials, it could have been very sophisticated. Posidonius appears to have believed that the future movements of the planets and thus predictions for life on Earth could be divined from studying the skies.

There has been much debate about how successful Posidonius was in achieving accurate measurements. The problem lies in understanding his units. While his attempt to measure the distance of the Sun from the Earth may have been too small by half (although probably more accurate than any of his competitors), he may have had more success in measuring the circumference of the Earth. An attempt to do this had been made by an earlier astronomer, Eratosthenes (c.276–c.194 BC), who had measured the different angles of the Sun on the same date and at the same time at two separate locations on the Nile. His calculations may have led to roughly the right result (modern scholars estimate that they were at the most 17 per cent out). Posidonius' calculation survives in a much later (?fourth century AD) work on astronomy by one Cleomedes. In his workings, Posidonius observed the difference between the elevation of the star Canopus just above the horizon in Rhodes and, to the south, Alexandria where it reached seven and a half

---

* At this date the Earth was believed to be at the centre of the planets. Only Aristarchus of Samos (c.310–c.230 BC) had suggested otherwise.
† The Antikythera Mechanism, an instrument for measuring the stars, was retrieved from a sunken Roman cargo ship off the coast of the Greek island of Antikythera in 1901. Its complexities are only gradually being unravelled but they have shown that Greek technology was far more advanced than once believed.

degrees.* Yet his estimations were inaccurate, and it was only by chance that the errors cancelled each other out to reach what appeared to be close to the actual figure of the circumference, 24,901 miles (40,074 kilometres).

If, as the Stoics argued, every component of the universe, including the weather, acted on the others, then a study of the effects of climate was essential. Greek thinkers from a variety of disciplines, including Herodotus, Hippocrates and Aristotle, had argued that climate defined the behaviour of societies. Posidonius went further in his determination to explore every aspect of the weather, from rainbows to winds (he noted the regularity of the east winds between Spain and Sardinia), and from lightning to clouds. He was also fascinated by sudden changes in the Earth's surface caused by volcanoes and earthquakes even though in his time, there was little chance of understanding their causes.

If these wide-ranging interests were not enough, Posidonius also wrote history, starting a history of the Roman empire just at the point where Polybius had left off, in 146 BC, and continuing to 88 BC. Although this work is now lost, fragments suggest a very different tone from Polybius. Posidonius focused more on the psychology of the main characters and ethnography of the peoples surveyed, in contrast to the narrative approach that was the predominant feature of Polybius' *Universal History*. One of Posidonius' most fascinating assertions is that civilisation is driven forward by wise men and philosophers, rather than by generals and statesmen. The fragments of his history that survive include as 'wise men' Moses, who taught the Jews that there was only one divine force, King Minos of Crete, and Lycurgus of Sparta, who was responsible for devising the constitution of the city. Among the Celts he accorded a high status to the Druids, praising them as philosophers and theologians.

* Greek mathematicians and astronomers had adopted 360 degrees as making up a circle, possibly as this equates approximately to the number of days in a year.

Enough of Posidonius' study of the Celts is known from later sources to make some assessment of his success as an ethnographer. His account proved useful to later generations of historians and Roman generals such as Julius Caesar so, while the original is lost, extracts are preserved in their works. Posidonius had only a shadowy understanding of the different tribes and peoples of northern Europe, something that has only become clearer with modern archaeological research, but there is no doubt that he was an accurate and thoughtful observer. He made a distinction between the tribes through their language, way of life, their physical characteristics and their location.

In an extract reproduced by a later source, he talks of how the Celts feast together and shows that he has a good eye for social distinctions.

> When many of them sup together, they all sit in a circle and the bravest sits in the middle, like the leader of a chorus, because he is superior to the rest either in his military skill, or in birth, or in riches, and the man who gives the entertainment sits next to him. Then on either side the rest of the guests sit in regular order, according as each is eminent or distinguished for anything. And their armour-bearers, bearing their large oblong shields, stand behind and their spear-bearers sit down opposite in a circle and feast in the same manner as their masters. And those who act as cup-bearers and bring round the wine, bring it round in jars made either of earthenware or silver... and the liquor which is drunk is, among the rich, wine brought from Italy or the country around Massilia [modern Marseilles] and is drunk unmixed but sometimes a little water is mixed with it... Among the poorer classes what is drunk is beer made of wheat prepared with honey...

Despite his gout, Posidonius survived for another ten years after his meeting with Pompey. Like Polybius he lived into his eighties. An active life infused with Stoicism clearly had its benefits! While other writers, among them Strabo, Julius Caesar, Plutarch and Galen, used Posidonius as a source, it is very difficult to make a definitive assessment of his contribution to the many fields which absorbed him: philosophy in its broadest sense, history, geography, meteorology, astronomy and even, according to some fragments, a challenge to the mathematical proofs expounded in Euclid's famous *Elements*. In this sense he represents the breadth of enquiry enjoyed by Greek intellectuals of this period – an eclecticism virtually unknown among the Romans. By following his teacher Panaetius in expounding Stoicism to the Romans, he consolidated the relationship between the two cultures through a philosophy that fitted well with the more austere features of the Roman mentality.

One of the most important of Posidonius' works was entitled *On the Ocean*. We know of it because parts of *On the Ocean* are summarised in one of the most accomplished texts of this period, by Strabo, a Greek from Pontus, in what is now north-eastern Turkey. So far we have considered a historian and a polymathic philosopher. Now we turn to a geographer.

6

The Geographer: Strabo (c.63 BC–c. AD 25)

One of the enduring features of the Greek intellectuals of the Roman period is their immense respect for earlier authorities. The influence of these authorities pervades one of the most complete surviving Greek texts from antiquity, the *Geography* (in Greek *Geographike*, 'writing about the Earth') of Strabo. While Strabo uses some two hundred different sources for the *Geography*, he applauds Homer as the founding father of his discipline. It was now 700 years since Homer's epics had been first written down but to have knowledge of them continued to be regarded as the pinnacle of a Greek cultural education, and they were seen as providing models of correct moral behaviour.* Like most educated Greeks, Strabo had known his works from childhood.

The Homeric epics provided a portrayal of the Mediterranean at what was, for Greeks, the beginnings of their civilisation. In the *Odyssey* in particular, Odysseus travels across a Mediterranean that is in transition. He moves from a leisured sojourn with the nymph Calpyso to the settled community of the Phaeacians after he is washed up on their shore. Here he is welcomed as a

---

* The German philosopher Hegel claimed that Homer was for the Greeks what air was for humans.

guest, bathed and feasted, and his story is respectfully listened to by the assembled company. In between these experiences he and his men are confronted by the Cyclops Polyphemus, a man-eating giant who represents the anarchic savagery when there is no effective law. Gods either help or impede Odysseus as he makes his tortuous way across the sea to his wife Penelope who has faithfully waited for him in their palace on Ithaca. In the *Iliad*, the range and origins of the Greek participants again show how diverse were the communities from which these warriors came. Strabo absorbed from Homer the example of societies experiencing change and he would have seen the spread of Roman rule in his time as providing similar challenges. Yet Strabo went far beyond this in establishing Homer as an authoritative geographer in whose footsteps he was following, citing him no fewer than 700 times. He interprets many communities he describes as the descendants of peoples mentioned in the epics. The value of Strabo's idealisation of Homer lies partly in its revealing just how strongly the epics still resonated in the Greek mind in the first century BC.

The *Geography*, written and continually revised from the late 20s BC to the early 20s AD, aimed to provide a survey of the Mediterranean world. At a time when educated Roman readers were taking an increasing interest in works written in Greek, it must have been directed at both Greek and Roman readers. It is noticeable, however, that the section on Italy (which may have originally been composed as a separate work) appears designed for a Greek audience who might not know much about the region, while Strabo's description of his native Anatolia is rather aimed at Romans who, he feels, might not appreciate its illustrious history, not least as the site of the Troy of legend. He names some 200 famous Anatolian men and women, many of them his contemporaries.

Today philosophy and geography are distinct disciplines. Strabo did not see it that way. He believed that the integration of philosophy would enrich the *Geography*. As he put it in his introduction: 'Wide learning, through which alone it is possible to undertake this work successfully, is the characteristic of no one other than the man who surveys the divine and the human, and philosophy, as they say, is the knowledge of these very things.' Strabo was drawn to Stoicism and he accepts that the Earth is subject to a divine providence that ensures that it is a harmonious world for humans to live in. While the land and the seas are separate, the universe is designed in such a way that there are cavities in the earth in which drinkable water may gather for the benefit of humans and animals. Similarly, like Posidonius, Strabo believes that the stability of Roman rule is perhaps the result of providence. Yet, faced with the variety of terrains and societies that he encounters on his travels, one feels that Strabo would have benefitted from reading more texts by Aristotle. If, as he tells us, there had not been so many errors in Aristotle's works, he would have used them. He makes fewer than twenty references to the philosopher's works, and these are largely from a single work, *On the Cosmos*.

The *Geography* begins with two books in which Strabo discusses the nature and purposes of geography. He assumes that his study will be useful for statesmen, and thus an educated elite, but the reader does not need to know more than that the Earth is a globe and some elementary mathematics. Among the topics Strabo discusses in Book One are the problems in assessing the formation of the oceans, how water flows, the accumulation of silt in riverbeds and determining where waters once covered the Earth. (Strabo uses the presence of seashells far inland as evidence.) In Book Two, he deals with the ways in which locations on the Earth's surface might be measured. Here he uses the contrasting methods of two outstanding Hellenistic scientists, Eratosthenes (276–194 BC) and Hipparchus (*c*.190–*c*.120 BC), in determining latitude, and thus the links between similar societies on the same latitude – the discussion involves conflicting accounts of whether India is on the same latitude as Meroe, a civilisation on the Nile south of Egypt.* Throughout these two books, Strabo uses a wide range of different sources and it is his determination to get to the heart of a problem that impresses.

In general Strabo is interested in the relationship of peoples with their environment and how far they are able to transform it, for instance by exploiting its fertility or resources such as minerals. He is also aware of the importance of space, the distances between places and their relationship with each other. In this he is one of the founders of topographical scholarship. Overall, however, the text of the *Geography* varies in scope and while it contains much information on political systems, the differences between peoples, and their economic resources, this is not presented consistently. Later scholars have found the *Geography* to be frustrating to use, especially as Strabo often fails to make clear that the material provided by his sources does not always relate to the same period of history. He had, for instance, written a history of Alexander's campaigns from many original sources, now lost, and it is thought that in the *Geography* he presents the east as if it had not changed since the fourth century BC.

Strabo's survey of *oikoumene*, 'the Earth as a whole', is structured so that it begins at the south-western corner of Iberia and then works its way round the Mediterranean in a clockwise direction, with a diversion to India in the east, to the Libyan coast, concluding with the Greek settlement at Cyrene. The peoples to the north of Rome, in western Europe, some of whom had already been incorporated into the empire in Strabo's time, provide another diversion. Strabo uses material from Posidonius and others who have travelled in the Celtic lands. He goes further than Posidonius, however, by distinguishing between Celtic and Germanic tribes.

---

* Recent scholars have argued that Strabo's analysis is flawed as he did not have the expertise to understand Hipparchus' combination of location with astronomical phenomena.

One major source for Strabo was the *Geography* of Eratosthenes, now lost and largely known from Strabo's use of it. Strabo was in difficulties here. Eratosthenes did not share Strabo's adulation for Homer. As a scholar entrenched in the scientific thinking of the Hellenistic period, he believed the poet was a 'fable-prattling old wife', whose epics were largely mythical. In contrast, Strabo distinguishes between fact, for which he considers Homer reliable, and myth and poetic licence, which he accepts that Homer uses. It was a mark of the sophistication of Strabo that he can criticise Eratosthenes for his views but still exploit his researches. Eratosthenes, for instance, appears to have been the first scientist to grasp that the annual flooding of the Nile derived from rainfall in Ethiopia and from further south in Africa, a view repeated by Strabo. Cyrene, the final staging-post in Strabo's journey round the Mediterranean, was Eratosthenes' hometown.

The complexity of the *Geography* is shown when Strabo makes use of the work of Hipparchus, who directly criticises Eratosthenes in *Against the Geography of Eratosthenes*, a work known only through Strabo's use of it. Strabo also contrasts information from the histories of Polybius and the works of Posidonius. As with Eratosthenes and Hipparchus, he is never afraid of pitting sources against each other and making critical judgements. So while Polybius tells of the Roman general Tiberius Gracchus destroying 300 cities in western Iberia (Spain), Strabo draws on other sources to show how poor the land is, how uncivilised its inhabitants and how limited city life must have been, so suggesting that Polybius had exaggerated Gracchus' achievement. Yet with so many of the original sources now lost (some authors are completely unknown other than their mention by Strabo), reconstructing the framework of the *Geography* and assessing its accuracy has proved challenging.

★

Virtually nothing is known of Strabo's life other than what can be gleaned from comments in his *Geography*. Strabo is a Roman cognomen, here the name given to a distinct branch of a Roman clan, and it is assumed that he must have been born with a now-lost Greek name. As he later served under Aelius Gallus, a prefect of Egypt during the 20s BC and a member of a Strabo lineage, it is assumed that this was how he picked up the name. Strabo, as he tells us in the *Geography*, was born at Amasia in Pontus, a region running along the Black Sea coast of what is now north-eastern Turkey. Pontus had been part of the kingdom of Mithridates VI (r. 120–63 BC), a vigorous opponent of Rome who, as we saw in the last chapter, committed suicide after his defeat by Pompey in 63 BC. This was probably around the time that Strabo was born. Despite Strabo's Greek family being distinguished it had risked its status by opposing Mithridates' brutality. His grandfather had gone so far as to lead a revolt against Mithridates and so the family met with favour from the Romans after the extinction of the Mithridatic dynasty. Strabo is able to draw on his family's records to provide details of both Mithridates VI and his father, Mithridates V, who was assassinated by poisoning in 120 BC (a fate that weighed heavily on his son and successor).

The family soon moved across Anatolia to the city of Nysa, east of Ephesus in the Roman province of Asia, where Strabo received his early education. It was a good choice for an intelligent boy. The city prided itself on the study of Homer and epic literature and this must have been where Strabo absorbed his love of the poet. There were well-known teachers here. One of them, Apollonius, was regarded by Strabo as the leading pupil of Panaetius. Among other teachers Strabo mentions the grandson of Posidonius, Aristodemus, as a 'distinguished philologist'. Aristodemus may also have taught the children of Pompey and so probably gave Strabo an introduction to teachers in Rome where Strabo moved in the late 40s BC when he was about twenty. It was a tumultuous time. Julius Caesar had been assassinated in the city in March 44 BC and the Roman world was soon racked by civil war.

Strabo may have stayed in Rome as long as ten years. He must have been a lively and sociable character as the names of intellectuals he met in the city are scattered throughout the *Geography*. Stoicism was probably the philosophy to which he was most drawn, but he mixed with historians and geographers as well as philosophers. His early works were historical ones, a life of Alexander the Great (whose campaigns in Persia were drawn on for the *Geography*) and the *Historical Commentaries*, forty-three books surveying Roman history from 146 to probably *c*.29 BC, so ending with the civil wars in which Octavian had triumphed. The *Commentaries* were twice the length of the *Geography* and, if any more than a few fragments had survived, Strabo might well have been better known as a historian than as a geographer.

As the previous generations of his family had experienced the turmoil of the Mithridatic Wars, Strabo welcomed the stability brought by Augustus, though he made clear in the *Geography* that he expected his native Anatolia to be honoured by Rome for its prominence in the Greek world. Despite his acceptance of Roman hegemony in Greece – 'since they have surpassed all former rulers of whom we have records' – he had reservations about the severity of Roman domination. But Strabo's essential embracing of Roman rule paid him rich dividends since it led to his adoption within the aristocratic family of Aelius Gallus. Aelius was appointed prefect in Egypt in 27 BC and Strabo moved to Alexandria as part of his retinue. He seems to have stayed on after Aelius had left three years later. Here again was a wealthy city bustling with intellectual activity and achievement but Alexandria does not seem to have been his permanent home as Strabo records many visits to Rome. In a work which details the scattering of cities across the empire, Rome and Alexandria are selected for special treatment. Strabo emphasises the status of Rome in particular, citing its long history and impressive monuments. He does, however, remain a typical Greek when he states that the Romans borrow their texts from the Greeks but do not have the learning to fill in any gaps. (He may have been thinking of the 'philosophical' works of Cicero, which were heavily reliant on original Greek philosophy.)

Strabo certainly travelled widely. 'You could not find another among the geographers who has travelled over a much farther extent than I have'; not least, he went on, because, unlike most of his contemporaries, he knew the west of the empire as well as the east. He claimed to have reached as far east as Armenia and as far south as the Ethiopian border with Egypt. In fact, his detailed description of his voyage up the Nile with Aelius is one of the most memorable parts of the *Geography*. He tells how he was present with Aelius to hear the famous moaning sounds of the Colossi of Memnon beside the Nile.* He did not, however, travel further west than Italy and he had to rely on the researches of others, especially military commanders, to record western Europe. Some of his sources tell stories not known elsewhere. The Greek geographer Pytheas of Massilia appears to have made a circumnavigation of Britain, for instance, but his original account is lost and we are dependent on Strabo for including fragments of it, even if he thinks much of the narrative is fictitious. Strabo may well have had enough private resources to finance his travels, but his knowledgeable interest in mining and geology suggests that he may have had a professional background in those subjects.

Strabo lived on to probably AD 25 (he mentions the death of Juba II of Mauretania in AD 23) so experienced the long years of comparative stability of the reigns of Augustus and Tiberius. It was during these fifty-odd years that he worked on his *magnum*

---

* These were two enormous stone statues of the Pharaoh Amenhotep III erected in c.1350 BC. After damage from an earthquake a sound was emitted from one statue, possibly as it expanded in the sun. Strabo's was the first written account of the phenomenon.

opus. The *Geography* appears to have been subject to constant revision, although this cannot have taken up all his time and much of his day-to-day life remains a mystery. Like Polybius and Posidonius, he is another of my subjects who lived well into his eighties.

So far as ethnography is concerned, Strabo is Greek and consciously assumes that becoming Greek is a mark of civilisation. However, he is too sophisticated to draw a rigid distinction between Greeks and 'barbarians'.* The Mediterranean world of his day was in flux as it was in Homer's epics. For Strabo, the boundaries remained fluid. So-called 'barbarians' could become Hellenised while Greeks could degenerate into barbarians.

It is worth exploring Strabo's attitudes further as they tell us a lot about the cultural perspectives of his class. Strabo takes three factors as defining the nature of a people: their geographical position, their climate and their native attributes. Strabo, like other Greeks such as Herodotus and Aristotle before him, sees the central Mediterranean, Greece and Italy, as having the ideal climate, which their peoples are able to exploit along with the natural resources of these regions. Among these are the sea, which greatly facilitates trade. As these societies grow wealthier, they learn to appreciate the fruits of discipline and hard work and, crucially, they become morally and politically superior. In order to live peacefully together they evolve laws and constitutional governments. The *polis*, the city, is the highest form of community and a mark of true civilisation. Strabo talks of the ideals of self-restraint and moderation and displays a sophisticated understanding of the importance of *eleutheria*, liberty. In contrast, in outlying regions of the *oikoumene*, such as Ethiopia and Germany, extreme conditions of heat and cold and geographical handicaps such as mountains or deserts impede

* The term 'barbarian' was used by Greek speakers in classifying those who did not speak Greek (or the correct dialect of Greek). The word derives from the apparent 'babbling' of other languages as it came across to Greek ears.

any form of development. So here there is poverty, a lack of any form of trade and hence a degeneration of character. The peoples of these parts of the world are prey to their impulses and live, accordingly, in a state of lawlessness.

In between these areas of ideal and extreme climate are terrains that can be developed through the active intelligence of their inhabitants, at least when Greek colonisers have migrated to these areas. While Strabo assumes that the values of his own class and ethnic identity are the best, he does not translate this into a racially exclusive identity. When he describes the Greek settlement at Emporium* in Catalonia in what is now north-eastern Spain, he notes that Greeks and the native population 'in time came together under the same administration, a mixture of barbarian and Hellenic customs, something that has happened in many other places'. There are those who can claim Greek descent from earlier founding figures (and Strabo recognises different Greek tribes with their distinct dialects) and those who have adopted Greek customs. His account of the Carians of Anatolia, for instance, suggests that they either chose to adopt the Greek lifestyle or settled among Greek communities and were assimilated. Strabo is also aware that the Greeks have learned much from other peoples: the alphabet and mathematics from the Phoenicians, geometry from the Egyptians, and astronomy and science from the Babylonians. Yet it is the Greek communities who have transformed and developed this knowledge. While the Greeks have spread their culture peacefully, however, the Romans have been much more brutal and intrusive. They have, for instance, destroyed much of Greek culture in Italy, pushing it back towards a more barbaric past. The Celts of Gaul have simply been enslaved. So, although Strabo accepts Roman rule and the peace it brings (as he experienced in his own lifetime), he is convinced that the Greeks do culture better.

* This was a Greek colony founded by the Greek city of Massilia, modern Marseilles.

*

There are resonances of the *Geography* even today. It is intriguing to find the Mausoleum of Augustus, 'a great mound on a high foundation of white stone' with evergreen trees surrounding a bronze statue of the emperor, in Strabo's description of the monuments of Rome. After many years of neglect, and the looting of its marble by the Goths, the Mausoleum has just been restored. The translator of Strabo, Duane Roller, mentions other survivals from Strabo: ham from Serrano,* wildflower honey from the Hybleian mountains in Sicily, wine from the slopes of Mount Falernius on the borders of Latium and Campania (whose vineyards are said to have been founded by Bacchus himself!). The marble quarries Strabo names as Luna are those of Carrara in north-western Italy, used by Michelangelo and still exploited today. The mines of Rio Tinto in Spain that Strabo describes in detail, drawing on material from both Posidonius and Polybius, were active until recently. The British Isles still experience the fogs mentioned by Strabo in his *Geography*.

After Strabo's death the text of the *Geography* seems to have vanished. Later writers such as Plutarch, who used the *Historical Commentaries*, which was still then intact, did not appear even to know of it. Several of Plutarch's *Lives* would have been enriched by it. Only a single copy is known from the second century AD when it was copied out, so that by Byzantine times several editions were known and survive today (see Chapter 24, p. 329).

* What is now Jamón Serrano cured ham is mentioned by Strabo as being produced in his own day by the Cerretanians close to the slopes of the Pyrenees.

Interlude One

The Res Gestae of Augustus and the Sebasteion of Aphrodisias

Since Providence, which has divinely disposed our lives, having employed zeal and ardour, has arranged the most perfect culmination for life by producing Augustus, whom for the benefit of mankind she has filled with excellence, as she had granted him as a saviour for us and our descendants, a saviour who brought war to an end and set all things in order; and since, with his appearance Caesar [Augustus] exceeded the hopes of all those who had received glad tidings before us, not only surpassing those who had been benefactors before him, but not even leaving any hope of surpassing him for those who are to come in the future.

This text, significantly in Greek, was promulgated by a community of Greek cities in the province of Asia (they termed themselves 'The Hellenes in Asia'). It dates from 7 BC – twenty years into the era of peace instituted by Augustus – and provides an excellent illustration of how Greek communities in the province were responding to Roman rule. Divine Providence, it says, has acted to produce just the man needed for his times.

After his defeat of Mark Antony and Cleopatra at Actium in 31 BC, Octavian, revered by the Senate as Augustus from 27 BC, had tightened his grip on Egypt and commanded that senators could only visit the province with his approval. Its wealth could now be diverted to him personally and the conquest was the culmination of Roman control of the east. Augustus also defined the boundaries of the existing provinces of the Greek world, Achaia and Macedonia in mainland Greece (with Thrace added as a province in AD 46), Asia, Pamphylia, Cappadocia, Cilicia and Galatia in Anatolia, and then Syria and Judaea to the south towards Egypt. This took the empire in the east up to the boundaries of the Parthian empire. The Parthians were the most formidable of Rome's enemies but Augustus achieved a major coup in 20 BC when he negotiated the return of standards that the Parthians had captured in earlier campaigns against the Romans. The achievement was trumpeted throughout the empire, notably in a large issue of coins bearing images of a kneeling Parthian offering up the standards. Augustus sustained Armenia as a buffer state between the two empires.

The allegiances of the Greek cities that had been directed towards the Hellenistic monarchs were brilliantly manipulated by Augustus so that they were transferred to Rome. The process can be seen in the embassies received in the imperial capital. At the beginning of his reign, Augustus would often send these embassies on to the Senate but as his rule was consolidated they would plead directly with him in a practice that fitted more easily with the conventions established by his Hellenistic predecessors. In the cities themselves new cults, of Augustus and Roma, took the place of the old. An idealistic statue of Augustus, the Prima Porta statue,* shows him as a youthful conqueror in military dress, the breastplate decorated with traditional symbols of victory. The emperor is presented as a typical Greek hero, his face more reminiscent of the Greek Classical age than with 'the warts

---

* This famous statue, originally in bronze, was named after Prima Porta, the villa where Augustus' widow Livia lived, after a copy of it was found there in 1863.

and all' features of heads from the Republican period. Copies of the statue were sent across the empire.

In one Anatolian city, Ancyra, capital of the province of Galatia, there is a temple to Rome and Augustus which bears a long inscription in both Greek and Latin on its walls.* This is the most complete text of the *Res gestae divi Augusti*, 'what has been achieved by the "divine" Augustus' in his reign. It appears to have been composed by Augustus himself and it lists his military achievements and the way that he has spent his plunder, embellishing the city of Rome, restoring temples and hosting games. As a conqueror Augustus considers himself even greater than Alexander in that, unlike Alexander, his conquests are spread both to the west and to the east. He stresses that he has maintained the republican values of Rome by restoring power to the Senate, which had been sidelined in the civil wars of the later republic. The dominant theme is that he has brought stability to what is now an empire.

This was the message that was also broadcast by another monument, in the city of Aphrodisias, a free city in the province of Asia. With its capital at Ephesus, Asia was becoming the most sophisticated of the Greek provinces of the empire – 'by general consent superior to all others, both in the judgment of the rulers and virtually everyone else' in the words of the orator Aelius Aristides. As its name suggests, Aphrodisias was home to an ancient shrine to Aphrodite, the goddess of love, the Roman Venus. Julius Caesar had claimed descent from Venus and during the civil war with Pompey the city had played on this connection. Once Caesar had triumphed he lavished patronage on the city and his great nephew Octavian did the same. Aphrodisias prospered, with its own constitution and its leading aristocrats being granted Roman citizenship. It had the

---

* Ancyra is now Ankara, the modern capital of Turkey.

advantage of a good supply of local marble and its school of sculptors became known throughout the empire.

The link with the Julio-Claudians, the successors of Augustus, was enhanced by a flamboyant temple building, the Sebasteion (*sebastos* is Greek for 'saviour'), dedicated jointly to Aphrodite and the imperial dynasty. It was constructed over a forty-year period, from AD 20 to 60. Essentially it was a Corinthian temple whose façade was approached via a colonnaded processional way. This style had been used in temples dedicated to Julius Caesar and Augustus in Rome, so its use looks like a deliberate choice. The families who financed the temple building in Aphrodisias were in fact not Roman, but Greek. Two sets of brothers each donated funds for the building of one side of the colonnade.

The most spectacular feature of the colonnade was the 180 reliefs that lined the walls on two storeys. Aphrodisias went into decline in the middle of the first millennium and was hit by earthquakes, one of which detached the reliefs so that they lay face down in the earth until they were rediscovered by excavators in 1979. Remarkably, the sequence of images on the reliefs was still intact. These images contain an astonishing array of 'imperial' themes highlighting the integration of Greek and Roman culture as the Greek city of Aphrodisias welcomes the coming of Roman rule. The emperors are shown as semi-divine, and the Julio-Claudian dynasty as protectors of a Mediterranean-wide empire against barbarians who threaten it.

The reliefs that depict Augustus show him as the ruler of settled land and safe seas – a reaffirmation of the propaganda of the *Res gestae*. Those of his successors stress their role as conquerors. The emperor Claudius is shown in the very far west of the empire defeating Britannia, depicted as a woman surrendering to him. His successor Nero is represented as the conqueror of Armenia, although in the event it was never subdued by him. Yet history moved on. News must have reached Aphrodisias of Nero's murder of his mother Agrippina, his suicide in AD 68 and the subsequent damnation of his memory by the Senate. The most important of the reliefs, one that showed the emperor with his mother, was taken down and, turned upside down, was used as a pavement slab. Another portrait of Nero was defaced.

The propaganda of conquest is shown by reliefs of peoples across the empire that Augustus had brought into order. There are thirteen of them, including the *Callaeci* of northern Spain, several along the Alps and the Danube and even a tribe of *Bospori* from the Black Sea. In the east, the *Judaei*, *Arabi* and *Aegyptii* are recorded as well as the islands of Sicily, Crete and Cyprus. Each people is depicted as a statuesque female figure in bold relief with an inscription below describing their provenance.

The images on other reliefs are of similar interest. One cluster tells the story of the foundation of Rome: Aeneas flees from the burning Troy to Italy where he founds the dynasty that will itself give birth to Rome. The legend of Romulus and Remus with their wolf is shown and another relief depicts Aphrodite herself, the patron goddess of the city, being crowned by a personification of Rome. Then there are the gods of Greece, Heracles, Apollo and Dionysus, with a sequence of legends depicting the heroes of Greek mythology, so linking them to 'hero' emperors of the Julio-Claudian dynasty. The point is made by one of the inscriptions: *Theoi Sebastoi Olympioi*, 'The Olympian Emperor Gods'.

The Sebasteion, its reliefs now displayed in a museum on the site, is a stunning example of how visual propaganda was creating a narrative of a widespread, peaceful and prosperous empire which all its subjects could enjoy. Many of the lives that follow were able to exploit the comparative peace of city life in the Greek east.

7

The Botanist: Dioscorides (c.AD 40–c.90)

In his dedication of *De materia medica** to Areius, a fellow physician, Dioscorides assures his recipient that it is not for vanity that he is publishing his herbal, the most complete to survive from the classical world. His dedicatee was always a generous friend to anyone who shared his passion for knowledge, and Areius would appreciate the care taken by Dioscorides in examining his plants carefully, using only authoritative sources and seeking the advice of locals. Dioscorides goes on to describe the importance of observing a plant from its first appearance, through its maturity and to its eventual decline,[†] and of collecting samples at the right time and locality so as to maximise its strength as a medicine. Describing the plant's pharmacological efficacy was, after all, the main purpose in compiling such a work.

The Greek word *pharmakon* (whence comes our modern word 'pharmacy'), originally applied to any 'drug' whether it had a healing or harmful effect, dates back over three thousand years

---

* This is the Latin title by which Dioscorides' herbal is best known. The Greek original was *Periules iatriches*.
† In the famous Vienna *De materia medica* (Chapter 24, p. 321), some of the illustrations show a plant at different stages of its life.

to Mycenaean times.* In Homer's *Iliad*, heroes use ointment to soothe the pain of wounds. In the *Odyssey*, Helen, the daughter of Zeus, adds to wine a drug known as *nepenthe* that causes 'forgetfulness of pain and strife'. The goddess Circe is even able to use drugs to turn humans into animals but Odysseus is given an antidote, 'a black root with flowers like milk', which makes him impervious to it. So the idea that drugs can be powerful but that one drug can subdue the effects of another was already well established in the Greek world by the eighth century BC.

In the fourth century BC Hippocrates, the 'father of medicine', taught that substances had some form of power (he used the word *dunamis*, the root of the English 'dynamic') and, when integrated with the Hippocratic and Aristotelian theory of the four humours, blood, phlegm, yellow and black bile, a particular drug could help keep the humours in balance.

In the third century BC a text later (though wrongly) attributed to Aristotle emphasised the distinction between food and drugs. 'Healing drugs are the contrary to food. For what is by nature being digested, grows into the body and is called food. But what is not overpowered in this way goes into the blood vessels and disturbs them through its excess of heat or coldness, and this is the nature of a drug.' It was believed that a drug could add heat or cold or dryness or moistness and so be used to supplement or reduce the effect of any humour. Crucially two or more substances could be mixed so as to alleviate one or more elements of a particular drug. This approach reached its peak in the lifetime, *c.*AD 40–*c.*90, of Pedanius Dioscorides (Pedanios Dioskourides in the original Greek).

The mixture of drugs that were supposed to have a cumulative effect on each other reaches its most extreme form in a concoction known as theriac (the original Greek

---

* The Mycenaean civilisation, named after the citadel of Mycenae in the north-eastern Peloponnese, flourished across the Mediterranean between 1500 and 1100 BC. Its language was an early form of Greek.

word means 'pertaining to animals'). Theriac was said to have originated with Mithridates of Pontus who created an antidote to poison so effective that his attempts to commit suicide by poison in 63 BC failed because of the immunity he had developed. Pompey brought the recipe to the Roman world and theriac was perfected during the reign of Nero (AD 54–68) by the imperial physician, Andromachus the Elder. Andromachus substituted viper's flesh for an original ingredient, Nile lizard, so confirming that the primary role of the mix was to offset snake poison. It was said that the effect of the poison was to cool an organism and that the viper's flesh countered this by restoring warmth. I will have more to say about theriac when we encounter the physician Galen in Chapter 13.

Dioscorides and Andromachus were contemporaries, Andromachus in Latin Rome and Dioscorides in the Greek east, but there is no evidence that they communicated with each other. Another of Dioscorides' contemporaries was the Roman Pliny the Elder who compiled his voluminous *Natural History* before his curiosity took him too close to the eruption of Vesuvius in AD 79, with fatal results. The *Natural History* was a massive collection of material, the most complete 'encyclopedia' from the ancient world. Pliny's sources included Greek and Latin works, the results of extensive interviews with experts, and some personal observations which stretched to art (and valuably its history), astronomy, mathematics, geography and cultures of peoples as well as the natural world itself. When it came to information about plants and herbs, Pliny was heavily reliant on works by Aristotle and Theophrastus, Aristotle's successor at the Lyceum, who had written extensively on plant life. Unfortunately Pliny's knowledge of Greek was not reliable (there is no record that he ever even visited Greece) and in the Renaissance he was exposed for his many mistranslations and confusions between different plants. Dioscorides' work was much more 'scientifically' accurate, was soon translated into Latin and for centuries was considered authoritative.

Dioscorides was born about AD 40 in Anazarbus in the Roman province of Cilicia, now south-eastern Turkey. He appears to have had a traditional Greek education, probably at Tarsus, the capital of his province. His Greek is straightforward and precise and, like many of the Greek elite of this period, he has a broad and curious mind: 'I have had an unceasing inquisitiveness regarding knowledge of this subject [the healing power of plants].' He is often described as a physician in the Roman army. 'I was a soldier and travelled widely,' he records,* although the plants he writes about come mainly from the east – many of them from beyond the borders of the empire – so it may be that he collected them during the course of his independent travels rather than while he was serving in the Roman army. But he certainly organised his searches with military precision. The habitats of the plants he describes range from mainland Greece and its islands to Anatolia, Armenia, Persia, India and Arabia and Egypt including north Africa. Others come from Italy and Gaul, although it is often unclear which samples he has handled himself and which he has heard of by hearsay and added so as to make his compilation complete. He admitted only to 'knowing most herbs with my own eyes, others by historical relation agreeable to all and by questioning [and] diligently enquiring of the inhabitants of each sort'.

Dioscorides was also, like many of the Greek elite, supremely self-confident. He boasted that although he respected his predecessors in the field, his was by far the best survey of his subject. His ambitious aim was not simply to list plants but to explain the medicinal properties of each. Nature should be in the service of medicine; a knowledge of plant life, he insisted, had to be linked to their healing powers. The fact that *De materia medica* was endorsed by Galen, the greatest physician of the Greek

---

* I am very grateful for the 2000 translation of *De materia medica* by Tess Anne Osbaldeston from which the quotations are taken.

world, in the following century, and that it held its position for sixteen centuries, proved his point.

De materia medica was compiled in the AD 60s and 70s. It was divided into five volumes, each one taking a specific set of remedies. Dioscorides sets out the correct procedure for gathering the plants. It is important to assess when a herb is most powerful and when best to gather it. So a sunny day should be chosen for harvesting herbs as rain will weaken their healing power. Plants that grow in the open air, on mountains and hills where the winds reach them, will be of greater strength than those in dark and damp places. The physician should also be aware that the nature of a locale will condition when growth and flowering takes place. Generally a plant can be stored for three years without losing its medical strength. Dioscorides makes some recommendations for storage: 'Blossoms and perfumed materials must be kept in dry limewood boxes but certain plants are adequately stored in papyrus or leaf wrappings to protect the seeds.'

While Dioscorides accepts that some of his material comes from written sources, he prides himself on his hands-on expertise. He sorts out the different substances according to categories, a classification which proved particularly influential for later botanists. The first volume of *De materia medica* deals with aromatics and ointments derived from them; the second with sea creatures, land animals such as beavers, frogs and weasels, and vegetables; the third with herbs that may be applied or consumed raw and with roots and seeds. This large subject continues into book four, with the fifth and final volume dedicated to vines and wine and to minerals – not only those found in the earth but also metal compounds such as zinc and brass. *De materia medica* is among the first works of its kind to include 'animal, vegetable and mineral', covering some 600 plants, 35 examples of animal extracts and 90 different minerals. In contrast the texts by or attributed to Hippocrates listed only 130 medicinal substances. Dioscorides recommended many of the plants he described in

De materia medica as treatments for ailments; in all he makes an extraordinary 4,740 links between illnesses and conditions for which they were beneficial.

What stands out in Dioscorides' work is its thoroughness. Each entry lists the variety of names which describe each plant, where the plant is to be found and how its flowers, leaves and roots can be recognised. Then he describes the properties and uses of the drug, including how best to harvest and store it, the prescribed doses and any negative side-effects. Dioscorides even notes whether a particular drug can be used on animals. He often specifies whether the effects of a substance are heating or cooling, drying or moistening, so linking them to the doctrine of the four humours.

The first book of *De materia medica* includes many spices and the ointments derived from them. So cardamom – which, Dioscorides advises, is best if harvested in Armenia or along the Bosphorus, but is also found in India and Arabia – is good for sciatica, hernias and can also expel rectal worms. If added to the bark from the roots of a bay tree it can break down kidney stones. It is a warming spice, like cinnamon, of which Dioscorides lists several varieties. Cinnamon cleans away pus that darkens the pupils, can bring on periods and even cause women to abort. It also helps those who have difficulty urinating. To store cinnamon one needs to pound it into small pieces, soak it with wine and then dry it out.

One of the rarest shrubs is the tree balsam (*balsamon*) which Dioscorides claims only grows in one valley in Judaea and in Egypt. On the hottest day the tree is cut with iron nails to release a juice, which seeps out in such small quantities that it is sold for twice the weight of the equivalent in silver. 'The best juice is new, with a strong smell, pure and not inclining to sweetness, dissolving easily, smooth, astringent, and a little biting to the tongue.' The juice is the most effective part of the plant, followed by the fruit, while the wood has the least strength of all. Balsam is a strong 'heating' plant, counteracts fatigue, stimulates urination and helps with breathing problems, including pleurisy, pneumonia, asthma and persistent coughing. Naturally, considering the price, there are counterfeits but they can easily be spotted by dropping the juice on a piece of wool. If the balsam is genuine it will wash out without trace. Another test is to mix the juice with milk or water. The authentic juice will dissolve in the liquid while the counterfeit will drift to the top. Dioscorides warns the reader that the merchants of Petra, the Nabatean trading entrepôt in what is now Jordan, deal in a counterfeit but this can be spotted as the seeds are bigger and taste like pepper.

The second book contains a host of examples of medicaments that range from the testicles of beavers to spiders' webs. Dioscorides recommends the value of spiders' webs for placing on wounds. (It is now known that a clean and fresh web has antiseptic and anti-fungal properties that prevent bacterial infection.) The testicles of beavers, Dioscorides tells us, have many uses: as an abortifacient, to encourage sneezing and as an antidote to snake poison. Moistened with vinegar and then eaten they can help treat depression.* Meanwhile the hooves of goats burned and rubbed on the scalp with vinegar can reverse baldness. Viper's flesh has to be treated in a special way to be efficacious. The head and tail of the snake must be cut off and the intestines removed. Then the remaining flesh is boiled in oil and wine with salt and dill added. The resulting mixture makes the eyes 'quick-sighted', represses goitres and glandular swellings and calms the nerves. Claims that eating viper's flesh causes lice to grow inside the body are, Dioscorides confidently states, entirely mendacious.

In the same volume Dioscorides extols the value of honey, especially as a sealant. The best comes from Attica, but the Cycladic islands of the Aegean and Sicily also provide good

---

* To this day castoreum is extracted from the castor sacs of mature beavers and used for a variety of purposes, including aroma.

honey. Spring honey is to be preferred to honey harvested in summer. Winter honey should not be used as it causes weals on the skin. Avoid liquid honey, counsels Dioscorides; honey should be glutinous and firm and cling to the finger. It can be applied to ulcers and skin rashes but mixed with salt and olive oil it can be poured into the ears to cure tinnitus. It is also useful for healing the wounds of circumcision; the honey should be applied for the next thirty days. (Homer also mentions honey as a salve for wounds.) Honey from Sardinia, where the bees feed on wormwood, is good for sunburn.

In the third volume, which deals with roots, aloe is included among a section on prickly plants. Dioscorides recommends it for treatments of the skin: bruises, wounds, cuts, ulcers and itchiness. He even claims that it will stop blood oozing from haemorrhoids. Mixed with wine it stops hair loss. Aloe is still used today as an emollient for skin disorders and as an ingredient in moisturisers, shampoos and shaving creams. Dioscorides also cites a number of ways in which aloe is helpful if taken internally, as a laxative, as a cure for jaundice and for stopping the spitting of blood. It is also, he says, a good treatment for sore gums and mouth ulcers. (Recent research, it should be pointed out, suggests ingesting aloe can be toxic.)

Wormwood grows best, Dioscorides tells us, in the Taurus mountains and in Pontus and Cappadocia (in modern Turkey). As an aid to digestion, it can relieve pains in the intestines and stomach – and it also stimulates appetite. Mixed with vinegar it soothes indigestion caused by eating mushrooms and acts as an antidote to hemlock, 'the bites of the shrewmouse and those of the sea dragon'. Dioscorides goes on to talk of a variety of wormwood found in Thrace which is made into a wine called absinthe (he gives the Roman name *absinthium rusticum*). The locals meet to drink it during the summer in the belief that it gives them good health. This variety of wormwood is also used as an insect repellent and placed in chests to keep moths from eating clothes.

In the fourth book, Dioscorides describes a plant he names *periklumenon* – now known as the common honeysuckle or woodbine – as 'a single little shrub'. He provides a description of its leaves, flowers, seed and root. It grows in fields and hedges and winds itself around neighbouring shrubs. The seeds should be gathered and dried in the shade, though the leaves have the same strength. A small quantity of *periklumenon* taken in a drink for forty days will invigorate the body, 'reduce the spleen' and help those who have difficulty breathing or are plagued by hiccups. However, after six days of treatment it will cause blood to appear in the urine. Among its other effects, it induces childbirth and makes men sterile if they drink it over a thirty-seven day period. For those suffering from fever, the shivering can be relieved by mixing *periklumenon* with oil and rubbing it on the body. Dioscorides concludes by giving twelve alternative names for the plant including the Egyptian, Roman and African equivalents.

Hellebore (the name comes from the original Greek) is now known to be poisonous and animals leave it alone. Dioscorides seems to be aware of this and offers careful guidance for its harvesting. He knows that it can choke and he advises to choose plants from Cyrene (the modern Libya) rather than the more powerful variety from Cappadocia. 'It purges by causing vomiting, expelling matter of various colours' and can bring about abortions. Dioscorides cautions that it must be diluted either by taking it in small sips with food or with a large quantity of fruit juice. It has other uses: '[K]neaded with honey and polenta and boiled together with pieces of meat, it kills mice and decomposes them.'

In the fifth volume of *De materia medica* Dioscorides discusses wines and minerals. He is positive about the effects of wine: 'all unmixed and simple wine is warming, easily digested and good for the stomach'. Yet he is wary of drunkenness: 'too much drinking every day allows the entrance of sharp disorders'. It is better to drink water before and after drinking wine. Dioscorides goes on to compare different wines, from Italy (Falernian gets a good mention, as it does with Strabo), Sicily, the Greek islands of Lesbos and Chios and the region around Ephesus on the Asian mainland. Many wines benefit from being left for seven years before drinking. Always sensitive to his primary purpose of offering advice on healing, Dioscorides grades the wines according to the degree to which they aid digestion and other ailments. Old sweet-smelling white wines are good for those who sweat. Thick 'black' wines cause weight gain, 'thinner and harder' ones less so. Then there is a range of suggestions for adding honey to wine. Old wine can be mixed with half as much good honey and boiled up if needed immediately. At first it is filling but it later acts to increase appetite. If it is drunk after a meal it will cause stomach pains. Honey mixed with wine is also a restorative, recommended for those with weak pulses or a tendency to faint.

The second part of the final volume is devoted to minerals. Many of these need very elaborate preparations to make them effective. So brass, an alloy of copper and zinc, can be treated in different ways, some involving heating in furnaces, others by using vinegar, to create zinc or brass oxide which then can be used as a paste to put on the eyes. Brass from Cyprus (the home of numerous copper mines) can be mixed with vinegar (which can be diluted to double the quantity with 'old urine') to create a paste. To this is added alum, a chemical compound which was used as a dye or to fix a dye, and sea salt. Dioscorides advises that this should all be beaten together on the hottest part of a hot day until it becomes rusty in colour. Then it should be made into the shape of little worms and stored in jars. It can be used to treat many ailments of the skin, scars on the eyes, gangrenous ulcers and, mixed with oil and wax, to form an artificial skin over ulcers. The 'worms' can also be used as a suppository to cure fistulas. Alum comes in many forms but it is important to choose 'milky and juicy' samples which give out the smell of fire. It is suitable for 'things that darken the eyesight' and any abnormal growths including those on the eyelids. Mixed with honey, alum tightens gums (periodontitis) and strengthens loose teeth. Together with *brassica* leaves, alum is a good treatment for leprosy. If mined from the Aegean island of Melos and inserted by a woman before intercourse, it acts as a contraceptive.

De materia medica was immediately popular as it treated the subject matter in much more detail than its competitors. In practical terms, its usefulness was limited since each substance was accorded an implausibly high number of medical applications. And, as a general rule, it failed to make clear what quantity of a particular substance was needed to be effective. Having said that, Dioscorides was often aware, as was the case with hellebore, that ingestion needs to be limited. While he claims to have adopted a 'scientific' approach to his treatments, he would hardly have been able to evaluate the effectiveness of each 'cure' he proposes. Nonetheless, *De materia medica* remains as an example of the tenacity, curiosity and breadth of vision of the Greek mind.

8

The Philosopher and Biographer: Plutarch (c.AD 46 – after AD 119)

Plutarch is perhaps the most appealing of the figures covered in this book. He represents the best of the Greek cultural tradition, not least through his respect for public service. He accepts that he is a member of a privileged elite but counsels that this should never be exploited. (In his essay *On Inoffensive Self-Praise*, Plutarch is aware of how boasting about oneself can put an audience off – 'empty self-glorification is the opposite of glory'.) He comes across as a sociable intellectual who relished his friendships with eminent Greeks and Romans. He was extraordinarily well read – few Greeks had absorbed so much Roman history (and to do so he must have been highly competent, at the very least, in Latin). But Plutarch's learning was spread across many fields. While he remains best known for his *Parallel Lives* of prominent Greeks and Romans, he thought deeply about issues of ethics, including the attributes of a good ruler, and he reflected also, as seen in the discussion on *The Apparent Face in the Orb of the Moon*, on scientific matters. 'Our souls are by nature possessed of great fondness for learning and fondness for seeing', he says in his *Parallel Lives* and he deplores those who betray that nature. Stylistically speaking, he writes in an elegant literary *koine*, before the use of Attic became a mark of intellectual sophistication.

Plutarch was a Platonist by conviction but never a dogmatic one. As Plato had taught through dialogues with differing views put forward by the participants, Plutarch felt Plato had accepted that there were diverse ways of exploring philosophical issues and he responded to this. Although he hardly ever quotes Aristotle, recent scholarship has traced many elements of Aristotle's works in his essays. As a result he was measured in his judgements, always ready to suspend them when confronted by philosophical challenges. He was sensitive to the work of the Academic Sceptics such as Arcesilaus (see p. 56) but much more positive than the Sceptics. While he can hardly be called an original philosopher, he was immensely respected by those who followed him, especially the Platonists among them. In the sequence of 'Platonisms' he is firmly placed as a 'Middle Platonist' in that he stimulated a renewed interest in Plato's works.

Plutarch also provides us with one of the best descriptions of *paideia*. The essence of *paideia* for Plutarch is an understanding of fundamental virtues such as 'what is honourable and what is shameful, what is just and what is unjust… how a man must bear himself in his interactions with the gods, his parents, with his elders, with the laws, with strangers, with those in authority, with friends, with women, with children and with servants.' Plutarch must have learned this from an early age. Born in the early AD 40s he was a man with a strong attachment to family who could trace his ancestors back generations. ('I live in a little town where I am willing to continue lest it should grow less', as he put it in one of his *Lives*.) A letter to his wife on the death of a much-loved young daughter (the only girl after four boys) speaks not only of the loss of the girl's 'pure and simple gaiety… and affection and winning ways' but also expresses respect for how his wife has handled her grief. It is a moving letter written by a sensitive man who enjoys his home and the people in it. In his *Advice to Bride and Groom*, he offers conventional counsel, dwelling on the companionship of marriage and the importance of mutual respect between partners. But he is ready to accept that the wife may be superior in virtue and wisdom to the husband. While Plutarch travelled widely, across Greece and Asia Minor, southwards to Egypt and westwards to Italy where he had contacts with many leading Romans, he always returned to his native village of Chaeronea in Boeotia. He even established his own school there. Sadly only two of his five sons are known to have outlived him.

Yet, however peaceful the settlement seems today (and I have visited to pay respect to a memorial to Plutarch there), Chaeronea had a troubled past. In 338 BC, Philip of Macedon, with the aid of his son Alexander, had smashed an army of Athenians and Thebans and so set Macedonia on the path to dominance of Greece. Plutarch mentions the battle in his *Life* of Demosthenes. Demosthenes had urged on the Greek forces with impassioned oratory but fled in the actual battle.* Some 250 years later, in 86 BC, Chaeronea was the scene of another bloody battle, in which the Romans routed an army led by Archelaus, a Greek general serving under Mithridates VI of Pontus. The battle and the campaign around it are described at length in Plutarch's *Life* of the Roman strongman Sulla. 'The marshes were filled with blood, and the lake with dead bodies, insomuch that to this day, two hundred years after the fight, many bows, helmets, fragments of iron, breastplates, and swords of barbarian make continue to be found buried deep in mud.' Plutarch's great-grandfather told him that before the defeat of Mark Antony at Actium in 31 BC the people of Chaeronea were forced to carry grain down to the Gulf of Corinth to supply Antony's armies.

Plutarch was a deeply religious man and believed in a supreme and benign divinity. In this he had affinities with both Plato

---

* Philip erected a circular victory monument, the Philippeum, at Olympia to commemorate his victory. The foundations and remains of its Ionic columns can still be seen.

and the Stoics, but he was closer to Platonism than he was to Stoicism. While Plutarch had absorbed the work of Stoic writers and respected them, he had fundamental differences with them over the place of free will and the nature of their deity whom Stoics believed pervaded every element of the material world. Plutarch expounded these thoughts in his *On the Contradictions of the Stoics*. The Stoic deity could not be separated from evil and the passions, which Plutarch believed were the result of untamed irrational forces intrinsic within each personality. He also felt that the Stoics were too accepting of the influence of fate in their lives. Divine providence would reward virtue and so one should take responsibility for one's own behaviour and work towards perfection. Plutarch believed that the elimination of passions, which some Stoics advocated, would deprive individuals of the motivation to live active lives.

Plutarch's temperament must also have played a part in his rejection of these elements of Stoicism. In his essays he comes across as much less austere than the typical Stoic, well aware of what it is to be human in the real world in which order and chaos are still present. As for the Epicureans, he dismissed them for their refusal to relate to the gods. Indeed, he did not even regard them as serious philosophers.* Plutarch accepted the work of Aristotle in so far as it could be used in support of Plato. For instance, he valued the moderation expressed in Aristotle's *Nicomachean Ethics* over the austerity of more traditional Platonists. In short, it is Plutarch that we can credit for the emergence of a revivified form of Platonism in the second century AD that would gain precedence over the Stoicism and Epicureanism that had hitherto been popular.

Plutarch studied in Athens with Ammonius, Herald of the Areopagus, a prominent magistrate. In his public duties

---

* Plutarch's works arguing against Stoicism and Epicureanism are valuable in that they contain a great deal of original information about them and their adherents that would otherwise be lost.

Ammonius would have interacted regularly with Roman officials, thereby allowing his sociable pupil to build up his first contacts with agents of the occupying power. Plutarch would become intimately acquainted with the city of Athens. It was also Ammonius who introduced him to Plato's works. Plutarch came to know the *Dialogues* well, especially the *Timaeus*, Plato's account of the creation and Plutarch's favourite Platonic text.

Timaeus is the main speaker in the dialogue. While he may never have existed, Timaeus is imagined by Plato as a widely read and exuberant philosopher who appears to be a follower of the school of Pythagoras.* Socrates, while present, plays a limited role compared to those in other dialogues. Timaeus tells of a divine craftsman who brings order to a pre-existing state of chaos. The craftsman is benign and, even though the chaotic elements are not fully suppressed, the world he has created is essentially good. (Since the craftsman's work involved a distinct moment of creation, the *Timaeus* would prove acceptable to Christians.) The dialogue continues with a complex analysis of the created world and humanity's place within it. Human beings are a microcosm of the universe in that they encapsulate its main elements, including the remnants of the pre-existing chaos.

According to Plutarch, the individual soul contains the possibility of rational control of its more irrational (chaotic) parts and depending on how well it succeeds will be rewarded in an afterlife. Against the Stoics who believed that emotion could be tempered or even eradicated, Plutarch argued that the irrational was always part of the human soul and so the individual must struggle constantly to contain it. This was the theme of his *On Moral Virtue*. Vice was largely the result of ignorance which had to be combated. Education in virtue comes

---

* The followers of Pythagoras (*c.*570–490 BC) developed a variety of distinct beliefs. Prominent among these were vegetarianism and a belief in the transmigration of souls. Many also believed in the underlying mathematical structure of the universe. Plato was strongly influenced by Pythagoreanism.

from parents and teachers, from the example of those around us, from the laws of the cities and from the study of philosophy, the poets and history. It is essentially a training in *paideia*. Plutarch shares Plato's concern that poetry can be a corrupting force, but he believes that poems can be selected individually as a guide to virtue just as a bee picks and chooses among the flowers of a field for its honey.*

Plutarch valued philosophical discussion above oratorical flamboyance. He decried showing off or abstruse discussions about matters of grammar observing that drinking a medicine out of a fine Attic cup does not make the medicine more effective. He believed that a work of philosophy must have a purpose. Without being dogmatic, he wrote in order to reform his audience. Many of his essays, *On the Control of Anger, To an Uneducated Ruler, How One Might Discern a Flatterer from a Friend*, are in themselves educative texts and his best-known work, the *Parallel Lives*, used its subjects as didactic models for ethical behaviour. In *On the Control of Anger*, Plutarch argues that the expression of anger often makes a situation worse. Righteous anger may be justified but must be kept in check. (Plutarch puts forward the enduringly sensible idea that one should pause and reflect before expressing one's anger.) An optimistic and cheerful disposition helps subdue hostile attitudes. The ultimate goal lies in achieving happiness. In the afterlife, if the soul has achieved virtue, it will become divine and will have a role in overseeing the well-being of those humans left on Earth. On the other hand, the soul afflicted by evil may ascend to the Moon where it will be purified before returning to Earth. There is no eternal suffering in the afterlife in Plutarch's vision.

Plutarch was drawn to public service. He tells of how Epaminondas, the great Theban general-to-be who would break the power of Sparta in the fourth century BC, supervised the

---

* This analogy is taken up by Christian writers such as Clement of Alexandria; see p. 260 below.

clearing of dung from the streets of Thebes, a lowly job which a rival had forced on him, but which Epaminondas had endowed with such dignity that it was taken seriously. Plutarch humbled himself enough to supervise concrete and stone being unloaded in Chaeronea. ('I provide a good laugh for people visiting my town.') He found a more prestigious role for himself at Delphi. Delphi was not far from Chaeronea and the inhabitants of both communities had good relationships with each other. Plutarch seems to have visited the oracle and attended the Pythian Games as early as the reign of Nero (in the AD 50s and 60s) when he must still have been an adolescent or a young man. Here he may well have made contact with the entourage of the emperor and by the 70s he was visiting Rome. While he never felt his Latin was perfect, he was far more at home with Latin literature than his Greek contemporaries.

In Plutarch's time, the oracle at Delphi was still attracting visitors from across the Mediterranean world, some genuine petitioners, others attracted by the fame and history of the shrine. The oracle continued its traditional role of giving advice. Aulus Gellius, a second-century AD Roman grammarian, known for his *Attic Nights*, describes the games as 'a meeting of almost all Greece'. One of Plutarch's essays on Delphi, a discussion of the cult, mentions two typical visitors to the sanctuary – Demetrius, who is on his way from Britain to Tarsus in south-eastern Anatolia, and Cleombrotus, who has travelled from the Red Sea with Sparta as his ultimate destination. For those who were interested, there were guides available who would take visitors around the site, though Plutarch complained of their lack of understanding of the shrine's spiritual ethos. He also tells us that many oracles have closed down and that while Delphi used to have two priestesses, with a third in reserve, only one is now needed given the lower number of petitioners.*

---

* The oracle shrine of Apollo Clarios on the Ionian coast north of Ephesus was, in contrast, thriving during this period.

As a prominent local landowner, it is not surprising that Plutarch took on various roles at Delphi: as a priest of Apollo, to whom the main temple was dedicated; as one of the *epimetai*, responsible for overseeing the smooth running of the shrine; and as *agonothetes*, organiser of the Pythian Games. Plutarch relates how, on one occasion, there was conflict over new events being added to the games and that he argued in favour of keeping the music and poetry competitions.

The second of Plutarch's essays set in Delphi, *The E at Delphi*, focuses on monotheism, here in the form of the supremacy of Apollo. Plutarch regards Apollo as the founder of philosophy as he has left riddles which encourage humans to think philosophically. The work is made up of a conversation in which Plutarch himself, one of his brothers and his erstwhile tutor Ammonius, among others, take part. The problem they confront is the nature of the E which is inscribed on the temple of Apollo at Delphi. The work is interesting in itself as a discussion of how the Greek mind worked to solve an enigma. E (*epsilon* in Greek) is the fifth letter in the alphabet so the various ways in which five might be related to the symbol are discussed. According to Plato in his dialogue *Protagoras*, seven wise men had set up the maxims of 'Know Yourself' and 'Nothing in Excess' at Delphi, but if, the participants in Plutarch's dialogue decide, two of the seven are picked out as unworthy of wisdom this leaves five. There are five elements if one adds the heavens to the four on Earth, air, earth, water and fire. Ammonius provides a completely different explanation. According to him E can also stand for 'You are' with reference to Apollo, so designating the god as an eternal being. The distinction implicit in this interpretation of E, a distinction which is also discussed in the *Timaeus*, is between those things that are 'being' – the eternal truths – and those that are 'becoming', and thus subject to change in the material world. Apollo is 'being' and is talked of by Plutarch and his interlocutors as if he had the attributes of a single and supreme deity. 'He [Apollo] exists for no fixed time, but for the everlasting ages which are immovable, timeless, and undeviating, in which there is no earlier nor later, no future nor past, no older nor younger; but He, being One, has with only one "Now" completely filled "For ever".'

This theme is followed up in Plutarch's text *On Isis and Osiris*. Here Plutarch presents, in an address to Clea, a priestess of a cult dedicated to Isis in Chaeronea itself (Clea appears to have been a local landowner), a description and analysis of the myths of these Egyptian deities. The text gives Plutarch a chance to show off his intimate knowledge of Egyptian religion and culture but the underlying theme here is that, although they appear to be foreign deities, Isis and Osiris can be related to Greek philosophical thought:

> Nor do we regard the gods as different among different peoples nor as barbarian and Greek and southern and northern. But just as the sun, moon, heaven, earth and sea are common to all, although they are given various names by the varying peoples, so it is with the one reason which orders these things and the one providence that has charge of them.

The underlying assumption is that the Greeks understand the 'one reason' and the 'one providence' better than barbarians do. Plutarch reverses here the conventional belief, set out by the historian Herodotus five hundred years earlier, that the Egyptians were the origin of wisdom. With these two texts and his focus on Plato's divine craftsman in *Timaeus*, Plutarch represents the shift towards monotheism that can be found in both Christian and pagan culture, although it is not clear whether he considers Apollo, Zeus or the 'divine craftsman', who vanishes after the creation, as the Supreme God, with subsidiary deities such as Isis and Osiris related to them.

Plutarch also devoted a good deal of thought to the best way of governing cities. The most significant threat was *stasis*, civil strife, which could destroy a city or make it vulnerable to being conquered. In *Precepts of Statecraft*, Plutarch advises one Menemarchus from Sardis in Asia Minor who is just starting out on a political career. Menemarchus was wealthy and *Precepts of Statecraft* assumes that 'statecraft' is reserved to an elite. Menemarchus must not be swayed by the hope of material rewards or personal glory. 'There is nothing honourable or democratic in the love of holding office.' Respect should be won by the show of virtue rather than buying it through holding games or gladiatorial fights. (Plutarch abhorred these fights which, he believed, simply aroused the craving for blood and so disturbed the rationality of the soul.) Then, having ensured that he is motivated by virtue, the aspiring politician must consider how to influence citizens through oratory, which is the only true way of persuasion. He must have a strong, well-coordinated body and come across as gracious and courteous. If one cannot speak well for whatever reason, advises Plutarch, one should recruit a colleague. Plutarch counsels against emotional speeches lauding the past glories of the city. It is easy to inflame rivalries and arouse the suspicions of the Roman overlords, who will always dominate in any showdown. 'The boots of the Roman soldiers are just above your head,' he says, with lapidary concision. It is better to dwell on historic moments of civic magnanimity when your city has brought peace to itself and others.

When setting out, it is vital to approach even the most menial jobs with care.* It is also useful to have a mentor, in the form of a politician who has already won esteem for his oratory and virtue. Showing generosity in sharing tasks consolidates relationships and ends up achieving much more for the city. Plutarch tells the story of how, as a young man, he and a colleague were to be sent on an embassy. The colleague was late turning up so Plutarch went on his own and successfully completed the mission. When he got back, his father told him to say that the colleague had indeed gone with him so as not to humiliate the latecomer.

---

* This is the point at which Plutarch introduces the case of Epaminondas and the dung collection.

The primary aim is to 'ensure perpetual concord and friendship among one's fellows, and to remove all kinds of strife, dissension and hostility'. Tolerance of even the most difficult of citizens is preferable to social discord.

It is vital for those in public service to know and play to their strengths, Plutarch emphasises. There is a distinction between running an assembly and running a war; the Athenian statesman Pericles was wise in his decision to let his contemporary Cimon conduct the military affairs of Athens. Hannibal may have been a great general but he failed to be effective in the Carthaginian assembly. 'A good civic leader must keep everyone engaged in the political process, pacifying private citizens by ensuring equality and powerful citizens by allowing cooperation.' One must never expect to be rewarded. A decree in the assembly or a palm branch is sufficient. It is also important for a citizen of a Greek city to have good relationships with those in authority, in this case the Romans. Plutarch specifically mentions the way that Polybius used his friendship with Scipio in order to give benefits to his countrymen (see p. 65). Yet too great a dependence on the Romans, especially seeking their support for one faction against another, will only degrade a city's independence. In his work *Whether an Old Man Should Engage in Public Affairs*, Plutarch is rare for his day in arguing that old age should not be a bar to participation in public life.

One of the most celebrated of Plutarch's works is his *Table Talk*. Here a scholarly group of Greeks and Romans, Plutarch among them, recline at a *symposium*, the traditional Greek banquet of the elite, and discuss a series of intellectual issues. (One can imagine them sitting as devoted friends with wine and good food in the warm sun with a long afternoon ahead of them.) They are more than simply philosophers: at least one of them has been a consul, another the governor of Achaia, and the dedicatee of *Table Talk*, Sosius Senecio, is an intimate of the emperor Trajan. Plutarch plays a prominent part in many of the conversations. The discussions are unhurried and open-ended and they reveal the erudite atmosphere of the age as much as the *paideia* of the participants. The subjects explored are a wonderful mix: 'Why the middle of wine, the top of oil, and the bottom of honey is best'; 'Why women are hardly, old men easily, foxed'; 'Which was the first, the bird or the egg?'; 'What Plato meant by saying that God is always doing geometry?'; and, intriguingly, 'Why women do not eat the middle part of lettuce'. One suspects that Plutarch selected and shaped the discussions so as to show off his own breadth of interests. Many of the conversations come to no firm conclusion but they also make the point that even the most trivial issue can be the subject of philosophical debate.

One of the absorbing features of *Table Talk* is the flexibility and range of the debate: scientific explanations for natural phenomena mingle with mythical ones, the literatures of the past are quoted and pleasure taken in the absurdity of some of the questions. Medicine, music and mathematics are among the themes discussed. In Plutarch's late first-century AD *On the Apparent Face in the Orb of the Moon* (see earlier pp. 25–6), one can find a similar range of material; a discussion on astronomy showing that the theories of Aristarchus and Hipparchus were still being debated (as they were for Strabo), that there was serious consideration of how different environments, here the surface of the Moon, could support life, and how the Moon fitted into the structure of the cosmos. It is accepted that the Moon is solid, in opposition to Aristotle and the Stoics who had argued that it was made of some kind of ethereal mixture. Why, unless it was solid, would it block the Sun during an eclipse? While the telescope had not been invented, enough could be seen by sharp eyes of the ridges of the Moon to show that its 'face' was no more than the reflections of its rugged surface. The participants go on to discuss whether there can be life on the Moon. The work of the botanist Theophrastus, Aristotle's successor at the Lyceum, is brought in to show how plants can survive in extreme temperatures, in some cases apparently without rain, and in other cases under water in the oceans. Why then should there not be life of some kind on the Moon? If humans who had developed ways of sustaining themselves on the Moon actually looked at the Earth through the clouds, they, in turn, would be equally amazed that any life was possible there. In a discussion of the purpose of the Moon, it is accepted that many parts of the Earth, deserts or mountains, appear to be without purpose but serve to be a beneficial part of the whole. Here Plutarch steps outside of an anthropomorphic view of the universe and becomes a precursor of James Lovelock's Gaia hypothesis, proposing that the Earth is a self-sustaining organism. When discussing the myths surrounding the Moon, Plutarch surmises that souls may travel there after death and are dealt with according to their vices or virtues. *On the Apparent Face in the Orb of the Moon* is altogether a remarkable document and has led to Plutarch being honoured by the naming after him of a crater on the Moon.

For generations historians have debated at what point individualism begins in Western culture. In literature it may be said to be first glimpsed in the heroes of Homer or the agonised characters of the fifth-century tragedians, but certainly Plutarch's *Parallel Lives* of Greeks and Romans is part of the literary tradition of individualism.

In one of the most even-handed works of the period, Plutarch uses both Latin and Greek sources to present a sequence of paired comparative biographies. Alexander the Great is assessed alongside Julius Caesar and the Roman orator Cicero against Demosthenes whose rhetoric warned and stirred up the Athenians against the rising power of Philip of Macedon. Often Plutarch provides a summing-up, outlining the similarities and differences between the two characters he has discussed. It could also be said that the subjects of the *Lives* themselves provide compelling evidence of the extent to which determined individuals could influence society in the Greek and Roman world. In Plutarch's day, the possibility of his fellow

Greeks performing exploits of the magnitude of Alexander's had disappeared and even their Roman rulers (who, it appears, encouraged Plutarch to write the *Lives*) were constrained in the exercise of power.

The central purpose of the *Lives* is didactic. Plutarch uses his subjects as exemplars who are tested by every kind of political or military challenge. Plutarch imagines the man who is seeking virtue.

> With men of this sort, it has already become a constant practice, on proceeding to any business, or on taking office, or encountering any dispensation of Fortune, to set before their eyes good men of the present or the past, and to reflect: 'What would Plato have done in this case? What would Epaminondas have said? How would Lycurgus [the legendary lawgiver of Sparta] have conducted himself?'

Plutarch explains his approach to character: 'A portrait which reveals character and disposition is far more beautiful than one which merely copies form and feature.' And again, 'It is not Histories that I am writing, but Lives; and in the most illustrious deeds there is often not a manifestation of virtue or vice, nay, a slight thing like a phrase or a jest often makes a greater revelation of character than battles when thousands fall, or the greatest armaments, or sieges of cities.' So as much can be learned about Alexander the Great when he is resting in his tent as when he is winning a victory. The sixteenth-century French essayist Michel de Montaigne, a great admirer of Plutarch, summed it up well. 'The Lives linger more over motives than events, over what comes from inside more than what happens outside.' It might even be said that Plutarch invented the psychological biography well before the twentieth century made it commonplace.

Sadly the first of the *Lives*, that of the Theban general and statesman, Epaminondas, who destroyed the Spartan armies at Leuctra in 371 BC and liberated the Peloponnese from Spartan hegemony, is missing. Contemporary sources saw him as one of the greatest men of the classical world and Plutarch, as a fellow Boeotian, would surely have done him proud.* In the biographies that have survived Plutarch writes with relish, recording atmosphere and anecdotes as well as providing a wealth of detail not available anywhere else. He has a standard format: birth, education, then public life and the manner of death. The latter often tells Plutarch a great deal about his subject: his constancy, in the case of the orator Demosthenes; the hesitations typical of Cicero when he becomes aware of his impending assassination. Everywhere there is telling detail. Many of his lives ended centuries before he was writing but, as always with Plutarch, he works from sources that have long since been lost. In some comparisons, such as Theseus, the legendary founder of Athens, and Romulus, the equally legendary founder of Rome, Plutarch relies heavily on myths but evaluates the authenticity of each.

Plutarch does not rush, he is often not overtly moralistic, so his life of Alexander the Great shows the gradual way in which growing wealth and military success corrupts Alexander and his generals as the Asian campaign continues. The reader is not surprised when a drinking session spills over into violence and Alexander's murder of his commander Cleitus. Whoever was directly to blame, the wider context has been established and Alexander has passed from being fundamentally rational to allowing irrationality to dominate. Perhaps the abiding sin here, and elsewhere in the *Lives*, is overbearing ambition. For Cato the Elder, his disdain for Greek learning, and even Greek doctors, is set out without immediate censure but Plutarch provides the telling detail of the loss of his wife and son, as if providence had caught up with him, and when he brings in a young girl to the household (presumably for his own sexual pleasure) it marks his final dishonour. Plutarch quietly makes his

---

* It is all the more frustrating as the historian Appian seems have known of the text in the AD 160s.

disapproval of Cato's hostility obvious. 'Time shows that he was wrong. For Rome's greatest achievements came at the time when it was most welcoming to Greek studies and Greek culture.' In contrast, Plutarch admires the Athenian statesman Pericles for his moderation and refusal to make permanent enemies when so many opposed him. He did not react viciously when challenged. His caution in war was especially commendable – he did not risk everything by putting his own citizens in peril of death. Plutarch makes the point that a leader who knows he is acting virtuously has the right to impose his policies on a recalcitrant populace. It was only when Pericles was dead that those who had criticised him for exploiting his monopoly of power realised how easily his less honourable successors corrupted the state. Similarly Plutarch applauds the orator Demosthenes for his consistency and refusal to compromise with the Macedonians. Plutarch recounts how in recognition of this he is honoured after his death by his fellow Athenians.

Plutarch is sensitive to the balance between good leadership and tyranny. The Athenian statesman Alcibiades is shown using his wealth through victories in war and the games to boost his reputation in Athens. Plutarch tells how Alcibiades had the characteristics of a chameleon, able to change his personality to suit the context of whichever city he was visiting or which gave him refuge. 'At Sparta [where he defected to avoid trial in Athens], he was devoted to athletic exercise, was frugal and reserved; in Ionia, luxurious, gay and indolent; in Thrace, always drinking; in Thessaly, always on horseback...' He was all things to all men (and many women) and he won over even those who had avoided him because of his reputation. Plutarch balances his impressive skills in leadership with his total lack of scruple. But while he undoubtedly condemns Alcibiades' morality, he does not let this overshadow his achievements – Alcibiades' victories are described in detail.

In his life of Caesar, Plutarch relates the ambiguity of Caesar's dictatorship. Caesar still has the ambition to get things done but he is constrained by the republican traditions of Rome. While he can carry out reforms that are not contentious, such as recalibrating the calendar, it is really only by leading an army overseas that he can satisfy his energies. Perhaps when he remained in Rome after his return in 45 BC his assassination was inevitable. Plutarch is particularly good at death scenes. Those of Cato of Utica, Antony and Cleopatra, Cicero and Caesar are gripping. The scene is often set with the gathering of omens: crows caw around the litter of Cicero, Caesar's wife experiences troubling dreams and the auspices revealed in the bodies of sacrificial victims all warn against Caesar conducting public office on the Ides of March.

Many of the stories from the *Parallel Lives* have resonated through the ages. The barge scene in which Cleopatra stages her meeting with Mark Antony was later exploited by Shakespeare. The image of the boy Alexander taming the unruly horse Bucephalus is consistently reproduced in films. In a typical anecdote, Plutarch tells how the general Pompey, returning to Rome after a victory, insists on a triumph but then is made ridiculous by expecting his chariot to be drawn by elephants which cannot fit through the city gate. Plutarch provides a compelling account of the determination and discipline through which the stuttering Demosthenes learned to speak well, even practising with pebbles in his mouth. Much of what is known of the Athenian lawgiver Solon's reforms of the 590s BC is taken from Plutarch, who claims to have seen the relics of the wooden tablets on which the laws were displayed in Athens. In her acclaimed novel *The Bull from the Sea* (1962), Mary Renault draws heavily on Plutarch's account of Theseus.

Despite several biographies from the great years of classical Greece, the *Lives* can also be read as a commentary on the sequence of events through which Roman rule extended over Greece. So Plutarch warms to Flamininus who 'liberated' Greece and sees Aemilius Paullus, the victor over Perseus of Macedon, in a similar light. He presents Paullus as a man of culture who showed a genuine interest in the philosophical schools of Athens. The Athenians responded by offering him a statue of Athena that he took back with him to Rome. Yet by the first century BC the Roman republic is disintegrating, and Plutarch is highly critical of the brutalities of Sulla. Things get better with the emperors and by the time Plutarch is writing the *Lives*, probably in the benign reign of Trajan, 'there is, in fact, profound peace and tranquillity; war has ceased, there are no wanderings of peoples, no civil strife, no despotisms, nor other maladies and ills in Greece requiring many unusual remedial forces'. When Plutarch went to Rome, probably on embassies from Chaeronea, he may have lectured there and certainly mixed easily with the Roman elite. Trajan granted him the *ornamenta consularia*, a recognition of his distinction, and there is a late story that in his old age, he met Hadrian, who made him the (honorary) procurator of Achaia. He had earlier been made a Roman citizen (Lucius Mestrius Plutarchus) so, while he valued Greek culture over Roman, he was sympathetic to what Rome had achieved.

After the troublesome reigns of Nero and Domitian, there was now the possibility of peace. In the lives explored later in this book we will see how the leading Greek intellectuals would exploit these conditions to richly productive effect. Meanwhile Plutarch must remain as a superb example of how the most profound and searching scholarship can be linked to a humane mind. 'He is a chief example of the illumination of the intellect by the force of morals', was the view of the American philosopher Ralph Waldo Emerson. 'Feast your souls on Plutarch', wrote Friedrich Nietzsche in his *Untimely Meditations*, 'and dare to believe in yourselves when you believe in his heroes. A hundred such men educated against the fashion of to-day, made familiar with the heroic, and come to maturity, are enough to give an eternal quietus to the noisy sham education of this time.'

Interlude Two

Hadrian and the Patronage of Greek Culture

The emperor Hadrian (r. AD 117–38) lived in the glare of public life and made conscious efforts to present himself as accessible. Yet if we are to believe the words of one of his contemporaries, he was clearly not an easy man to deal with. This unnamed source records him as 'changeable, manifold, fickle, born as if to be a judge of vice and virtue… Controlling his passionate spirit by some kind of artifice, he expertly concealed his envious, unhappy and wanton character, immoderate in his urge for display, feigning self-restraint, affability and mildness and disguising his desire for glory.' In short, Hadrian was a restless figure who spent more than half his reign travelling from province to province, from northern Britain (as attested by Hadrian's Wall) to the far eastern borders of the empire and along the Nile in Egypt where his companion and lover Antinous was drowned. There was virtually no province of the empire that he did not visit.

Hadrian benefitted from being the nephew of Trajan (r. 98–117), probably the most respected of the emperors. Like Trajan he was of Spanish origin. In AD 117 he was serving in Syria with the emperor during the latter's Parthian campaign when Trajan fell ill and set sail for Rome. However, the emperor made it only as far as Cilicia (south-eastern Turkey) where he died. Hadrian's succession is attended by some controversy. It appears that he was able to produce a document, signed by Trajan's wife, which attested to the late emperor adopting him as his son and successor. This aroused suspicion among the senators in Rome, which may explain why Hadrian avoided the city for much of his reign.

Hadrian was passionate about the culture of Greece. By 111, having already held the largely honorary position of consul in Rome, he was at a loose end and decided to set out for Athens to view for himself its great monuments – the Parthenon and other buildings on the Acropolis, and a vast uncompleted temple to Olympian Zeus. He was well received in the city and, as a prominent Roman senator and former consul, was given the post of *archon*, the presiding magistrate, for the year of 112–13. Little else is known of this first visit but before he reached Athens he may have stopped at Nicopolis in Epirus (north-western Greece) to listen to the Stoic philosopher Epictetus (Chapter 9).

Hadrian's most memorable visits to Athens came later, when he was emperor. In early 124, he arrived from Rhodes in time to be fully initiated into the Eleusinian mysteries: the Lesser Mysteries in spring and the Greater Mysteries in late summer. The shrine at Eleusis, within walkable distance of Athens, was devoted to Demeter, the goddess of food and vegetation, and her daughter Persephone who, according to myth, was to be temporarily released each year from her abduction in the underworld by her husband (and uncle) Hades. The rituals, which probably went back as far as the fifteenth century BC, celebrated the birth of spring and then the return of Persephone to the underworld as winter arrived, and involved bathing in the seas, sacrifices to the goddesses and then a procession from Athens to the shrine where the initiates were introduced to the mysteries by night.

Athens had now acquiesced in Roman sovereignty and Hadrian was asked whether he would reform the government of the city. Having ordered research into ancient laws as far back as Solon, a reformer of the sixth century BC, Hadrian created a more efficient city council and 'dispensed many favours to the Athenians' including support for the city's traders. The emperor, accompanied by his wife Sabina, then spent the autumn and much of the winter of 124 touring the Peloponnese. The travel writer Pausanias, from Magnesia in western Anatolia, recording his own tour of Greece in the middle of the century, notes many of the cities Hadrian visited. Inscriptions have since been found recording his benefactions to these various places.

The first city on his route was Megara, an old adversary of Athens. Hadrian encouraged the citizens to have better relations with their neighbour. Passing across the isthmus of Corinth into the Peloponnese, Hadrian travelled to the great healing centre of Epidaurus, then as now revered for its magnificent theatre. Among the more ancient sites he visited were Nemea, where he revived games in honour of Heracles' mythical killing of the Nemean lion, Mycenae and Tiryns. At Mantinea he paid homage to the tomb of the great Theban general Epaminondas, who had brought about the final defeat of Sparta at Leuctra in 371 and liberated the local population that the city had dominated. Epaminondas had died on the battlefield of Mantinea after his troops had again defeated the Spartans in 362 BC. Hadrian dedicated an inscription that he composed himself for the monument. He was always ready to honour the heroes of the Greek past, especially those who had preserved the freedom of Greece.

Hadrian then moved south to Sparta itself and was received by the ruling family, the Euryclids. Again he was ready to revere the memory of a once great city whose unflinching warriors had defended the freedom of Greece against the Persian invasion of 480 BC. By now the city was more of a tourist centre where voyeuristic Roman visitors watched rituals in which the city's youths were whipped to improve their hardiness. Hadrian was able to grant Sparta the port of Corone in Messenia in the south-western Peloponnese and that quintessential Roman gift to a favoured city, an aqueduct. A series of altars honoured Hadrian as 'saviour, founder and benefactor of the city'.[*]

Hadrian must have moved across to the west coast of the Peloponnese early in the new year as an inscription in the sanctuary at Olympia records a sacrifice to Hadrian dedicated by the city of Argos on his birthday. He would have been forty-nine on 26 January 125. Another visit he made was to the city of Skillous, near Olympia, where the Greek general Xenophon, leader of the Ten Thousand,[†] had lived for many years in exile and where, according to the locals, he had been buried. Hadrian thus had the chance to visit the supposed resting place of a famed Greek military leader but also, in a region rich in wild boar and deer, probably to indulge in a little hunting there. On his way back to Athens, Hadrian is also recorded by Pausanias as visiting Corinth, the capital of the Roman senatorial province of Achaia. By now the city, refounded by the Romans after its total destruction in 146 BC, was thoroughly Hellenised and Hadrian donated an aqueduct and baths. He was back in Athens by March where he was asked to preside at the Dionysia, the festival of drama held in honour of the god Dionysus. He dressed as an Athenian for the occasion. An inscription found in the city records his meeting with philosophers. Hadrian particularly enjoyed such encounters, revelling in the opportunity to share his own views on intellectual issues.

However, the main business of Hadrian's months in Athens was to set in train an enormous building programme. No one could miss the vast unfinished temple to Olympian Zeus that the Athenian tyrant Pisistratus had begun nearly seven hundred

---

[*] 'Founder' (Greek *oikistes*) was the term used of a patron who had initiated a new era for a city, in this case Sparta.

[†] In 401–399 BC Xenophon unsuccessfully led a contingent of 10,000 Greek mercenaries into Persia to overthrow the ruling 'king of kings' in favour of his brother. It was recorded in Xenophon's *Anabasis*, a masterpiece of Greek literature; see further, p. 147.

years earlier. The project had been periodically revived over the years – the Seleucids had promised to finish it and after the conquest of Greece client kings loyal to Rome had proposed completing it in honour of the emperor Augustus – but little had actually been done. Hadrian was determined finally to complete the building by erecting an extensive enclosure around the temple. He also began work on a new aqueduct, the first to be constructed in Athens for many hundreds of years, which would allow mountain water to flow into a fountain house at the top of the agora. Excavating tunnels through the mountains would prove a formidable challenge and the aqueduct would take fifteen years to complete. Another initiative was a large stoa, 'the library', which was to be based on models in the imperial forums in Rome.

With these projects in hand Hadrian returned to Rome via Boeotia and Delphi. The oracle was long past its most fruitful years but was still a major cultural centre made famous by one of its priests, the philosopher and biographer Plutarch, who must have died just a few years before Hadrian's visit. (They had probably met when Hadrian was archon in 112.)* The oracle had been run by a council, the Amphictyony, since the seventh century BC. By Hadrian's time its membership was dominated by Thessalians and the emperor now insisted that 'the council may be a council common to all Greeks'. As a result the representation on the council of Athens, Sparta and other major Greek cities was enlarged. Hadrian also instituted a new class of citizens who would be given plots of the land owned by the sanctuary in the hope that a ruling class of landowners might emerge that would run the shrine. An inscription found on the wall of the shrine's major temple to Apollo records Hadrian's wish that the ancient traditions of the oracle be preserved.

---

* Hadrian had a question for the oracle. Where did Homer come from and who were his parents? The answers given were Ithaca, and Telemachus and Polycaste.

Another inscription records that Hadrian left soldiers at Delphi to carry out works. Columns of blueish marble alongside the running track within the gymnasium appear to date from this time. His visit and patronage was commemorated by the Delphians with two statues, one in the main sanctuary and one in the sanctuary of Athena below the shrine. Coins dating from Hadrian's reign depict the sanctuary on the reverse and the head of the emperor on the obverse. A remarkable Hadrianic legacy was the adoption (across the empire) of the cult of Antinous, Hadrian's lover, who had drowned in the Nile in mysterious circumstances in AD 130. A statue of the youth has been found in the sanctuary of Athena at Delphi.* There is evidence that Hadrian took a special interest in the affairs of Delphi until his death in 138.

Yet it was Athens that was to be the most favoured by Hadrian among the cities of Greece. The emperor arrived back in 131 in the late summer to take part in the Eleusinian mysteries and then wintered in the city. He may have presided again at the Dionysia the following March. He granted the Athenians money handouts and the largest grain dole outside Rome. Members of the Athenian *boule* or council were given privileges that made them equal to the senators of Rome. Yet the most important festivities involved the dedication of the now finished temple of Olympian Zeus. Four statues of Hadrian graced the entrance, two of them in porphyry, the purple marble from Egypt that symbolised the power and status of the emperor. Statues and columns of Phrygian marble surrounded the sanctuary. Prominent Greek cities donated portraits of Hadrian. The most impressive, from Athens itself, was a colossal statue of the emperor placed behind the temple. Close to the entrance of the temple was a triumphal gateway which still stands. Inscriptions mark the boundary between the ancient city of the hero Theseus, the legendary founder of Athens, and the new city

---

* It is now in the museum at Delphi.

of Hadrian. Other buildings included a Pantheon – a temple to all the gods of Greece that recorded Hadrian's donations to Greek cities – a shrine to Zeus, and then, most magnificent of all, a vast colonnade, again of Phrygian marble, that fronted a series of buildings including a library.

It is probable that the ceremony of the dedication of the temple of Olympian Zeus took place at the same time as the inauguration of the Panhellenion, also founded by Hadrian. The Panhellenion was an organisation of Greek cities from mainland Greece and across Asia that had 'a noble past', which usually meant that they had been founded by Athens or Sparta. Loyalty to Rome on the part of these cities was taken for granted.* The representatives of the cities were to meet in the sanctuary of the temple every four years with a presiding chairman. The festivities at each meeting would include competitions of athletes, poets, musicians and orators. The opening speech at the inauguration of the Panhellenion was given by a leading orator of his day, Polemon, a renowned sophist and close friend of Hadrian (see also p. 234). Polemon's voice was said to echo like the trumpet at the Olympic Games and he was well known for rising from his chair when he wanted to make a forceful point or even stamping his foot at a crucial moment in his argument. He stood on the steps of the finished temple to enthuse the gathered crowds. As fine oratory was believed to be the result of close association with the gods, Polemon was said to be divinely inspired.

In the years between the meetings of the Panhellenion, there was a revival of the ancient Panathenaic Games, held in honour of Zeus Olympias and, after the emperor's death, a new festival known as the Hadriana. Now boasting one major new festival every year, in addition to the traditional festivals such as the Dionysia, Athens found itself reinvigorated as a major cultural centre. And it had splendid new buildings to proclaim

---

* Records suggest that half of the council members were Greeks who were also Roman citizens.

its recovered glory. A minting of coinage celebrated Hadrian's patronage of the province of Achaia. On the coins the emperor is shown as the *restitutor*, the 'restorer' of Greece. A personification of the province itself kneels before the emperor and between them is a Panathenaic vase, of the kind awarded to victors in the games and, as finds of the vases in their tombs attest, treasured beyond their deaths. While he could not create an orator or philosopher (such individuals could only be authenticated through the respect of their peers), Hadrian was seen as 'the readiest of all past emperors to promote merit'. He represented a new phase in the relationship between Greece and Rome, the cultural integration of the two elites.

9

The Stoic Philosopher: Epictetus (c.AD 50–c.135)

We owe our knowledge of the teachings of the Stoic philosopher Epictetus to the diligence of his student Arrian, himself a philosopher – one of many other intellectual interests – whom we will encounter in the next chapter. Arrian studied with Epictetus when he was in his twenties and his teacher must have been in his fifties or sixties. By a stroke of good fortune, Arrian's transcription of Epictectus' *Discourses*, which provide an overview of his teachings, has survived. It is assumed to be an authentic transcription as Arrian normally wrote in a Greek which contained Attic elements while Epictetus taught in *koine*, which is the form of Greek used by the *Discourses*. They appear to provide a record of Epictetus talking in a relaxed way to young men who had already followed a course in philosophy. It does not seem that they were formally presented lessons and the title *Discourses* therefore seems particularly apt. The philologist Geoffrey Horrocks, in his meticulous analysis of the Greek language over time, claims that 'the language of these homely presentations of aspects of Stoic philosophy is probably the closest thing we have… to a representation of the educated spoken language of the second century AD'.

It may be that Epictetus revised the text of the *Discourses* from Arrian's notes. Whatever their exact provenance, the result is punchy and direct, even forceful at times, especially in Epictetus' denunciations of the followers of Epicurus. Although about half of the *Discourses* is lost, there is enough remaining to give a clear picture of Epictetus' beliefs. The *Discourses* proved enormously popular in elucidating Stoicism for a new era of adherents – the emperor Marcus Aurelius' *Meditations* were influenced by them while Herodes Atticus argued that Epictetus was the finest Stoic of them all. Even the Christian theologian Origen noted that 'Epictetus is admired even by common folk who have an inclination to receive benefits because they perceive the improvement which his words effect in their lives'.

Remarkably, in contrast to most of my subjects, Epictetus was born a slave, in about AD 50. His native town was Hierapolis (modern Pamukkale), a city about a hundred miles east of Ephesus, and he was brought up speaking *koine*, the Greek of the streets. At some point he was moved to Rome as a slave to one Epaphroditus, who was himself a freedman (a freed slave) and an important figure in the administrations of the emperors Nero and Domitian.* Slaves were, of course, vulnerable to the whims of their masters. Quite how rigid attitudes could be was exposed in AD 61 when a city prefect was murdered by one of his slaves. Under such circumstances, it was the custom that all the slaves in the household were executed and in this instance the rule was upheld by the Senate and some 400 slaves were despatched, despite protests from the Roman crowds. There are many records of slaves being treated brutally within households or used as sexual playthings by their owners.† A later account by the second-century Greek philosopher Celsus of Epictetus' experience suggests that his leg was callously broken by Epaphroditus and his restrained 'stoical' response was simply to

---

* Epaphroditus was secretary to Nero. He was executed by Domitian in AD 95 for failing to prevent Nero committing suicide.
† The first-century AD novel *Satyricon* by Petronius portrays the outrageous figure of Trimalchio who personifies these vices.

say that he had warned Epaphroditus that his leg would break if Epaphroditus went on mistreating him. In his *Discourses*, Epictetus tells us that he was lame in one leg but does not tell us why, although there is a sixth-century report by a Neoplatonist philosopher, Simplicius, that Epictetus had been born disabled.

But it may be that Epaphroditus' conduct was not always reprehensible. It was an unexpected feature of Roman slavery that a slave could be given his freedom and his children could achieve full Roman citizenship.* Many freedmen grasped the opportunities to do business and trade and could grow very wealthy. Manumission, as it was called, was available for slaves at the will of their masters and was often given to those that were particularly trusted and respected for their skills. When Epictetus was freed in about AD 89 he was already studying Stoicism with a leading tutor, Musonius Rufus, 'the Roman Socrates'. So perhaps Epaphroditus, having been a slave himself, recognised his talents and was generous enough to sponsor his education.

And his hours of study with Musonius were certainly fruitful. Epictetus' gratitude towards Musonius increased when he realised how many potential students Musonius had rejected as not being worthy of his teaching. He absorbed the works of the founders of Stoicism, notably Zeno and Chrysippus, as well as the dialogues of Plato. His confidence was such that, when Domitian banned the teaching of philosophy in Rome in 89, Epictetus was ready to start in his own school in Nicopolis in Epirus, in north-western Greece. Despite its distance from the traditional centres of learning (such as Athens, where Stoicism had been founded), the school became famous and attracted many leading Greeks and Romans – even Hadrian, before he became emperor. Arrian probably attended the school between 104 and 107. Epictetus was self-effacing, never putting himself

* This seems the most likely way that the apostle Paul achieved his Roman citizenship, as the descendant of a freedman.

before his philosophy and expecting a philosopher such as himself (although he called himself 'a trainer') to maintain high standards of cleanliness, with a neat beard and respectable attire. He ridiculed the more flamboyant of his contemporaries who would stoop to any 'tricks' to attract an audience and he even turned away students who flaunted themselves. Like Plato, Epictetus never married but he adopted a boy who was not otherwise cared for. He died about AD 135.

Epictetus praises the Stoic Chrysippus in particular. We know from Diogenes Laertius' biographies of philosophers that at least 700 scrolls of Chrysippus' writings still survived by the time Diogenes was writing in the third century but now only a few fragments remain. The evidence from these fragments suggest that Epictetus followed in Chrysippus' and Zeno's footsteps so far as traditional Stoic philosophy was concerned but that he created an original and distinctive method of teaching. He must have been charismatic to earn himself his reputation but he also had a positive and inspiring message, that the ultimate aim in life was to be a flourishing virtuous person – and to achieve what he called *arete*, excellence. The search for *arete* made practical ethics the central concern of Epictetus' philosophy, although his teaching was as much a course in self-improvement as in philosophy. Epictetus expected his students to be active learners. He claimed that texts were only useful if they inspired a change in the personality of the reader. There was no place in his classes for rote-learners. In fact, he contrasted the easy and friendly atmosphere of the school with the reality of the harsh life outside. It was easy to behave as a Stoic in class, not so easy in the real world.

Epictetus' world picture provides the context in which the search for *arete* could take place. Like most Greek philosophers, certainly Stoic and Platonic ones, he believes in a divine force which he describes as Zeus, 'God' or even 'the gods' in general. This 'God' is benevolent and stands by our side when we search for *arete*. The existence of 'God' for Epictetus is proved by the overall harmony of the universe. 'God' works continually to bring order. 'He has appointed summer and winter, and abundance and scarcity, and virtue and vice, and all such opposites for the harmony of the whole.' 'He' brings rationality into the world and a fragment of this rationality presides in each human being. The seeds of the divine have been given 'to all things that are born and grow upon the earth and, above all, to the reasoning beings [i.e. humans] since according to nature, they alone are in communion with the society of the divine and are implicated in him through reason.' The fact that 'God' has given humankind this rationality enables each individual to have the freedom to be in charge of his or her search for virtue and thus the possibility of excellence. This is the permanent and abiding gift that 'God' has given to humans. All else – possessions, family, status – can easily be taken away by the workings of the cosmos and so one must learn to disdain them or not be agitated when they are lost.

Epictetus goes on to elaborate. We all absorb 'impressions', the everyday events and feelings that are a natural part of life. So long as virtue remains the overriding ambition, we must use our rationality to sort out logically the best way to deal with 'impressions'. We must not rely on 'God' to do it for us. In a striking passage in the *Discourses* Epictetus berates those who sit idly by hoping that God will somehow intervene in their lives. 'What, has God given you nothing to help you in this predicament [fear and anxiety when too dependent on possessions]? Hasn't he given you endurance? Hasn't he given you courage? And yet, being equipped with the hands that you have, do you still look for someone else to wipe your nose?'

We have two tasks. The first is to assess what we can control and what we cannot. As Epictetus says in the introduction to his so-called *Handbook*, a summary of his views also recorded by Arrian: 'Some things are within our power, while others are not. Within our power are opinion, motivation, desire, aversion and, in a word, whatever is of our own doing; not within our power are our body, our property, reputation, office, and, in a word, whatever is not of our doing.' The body is not under our control, it ages, it picks up illnesses. It is the mind that is important. Once this has been appreciated, it is vital to live a life of the mind which is not constrained by external pressures. One must train oneself to concentrate only on what is within one's control. Here psychology takes over in the sense that Epictetus says that we must learn not to be angry or agitated over events that we cannot avoid. This requires discipline, reflection and meditation. There must be no rush. 'Impression, wait for me a little. Let me see what you are, and what you represent.' Repetition is needed to embed the evolving consciousness of what is required in one's behaviour. Epictetus counsels regular self-examination. By cancelling out unhealthy desires, one can release new energies.

The next task is to decide on action. While Plutarch, a contemporary of Epictetus, complained of the passivity of the Stoics, Epictetus focused rather on the importance of activity so long as it was directed towards achieving excellence. Crucially this involved living with nature rather than against it. As all Stoics believed in an unfolding cosmos, it was rational to accept that one should not oppose the rhythms of the natural world. Epictetus regarded the order of the universe as supportive of the ideal of the rational mind. Today he would have condemned the destructive use of resources in modern times as this would be in conflict with the god-given harmony of the cosmos. This is one reason why Epictetus has found a new popularity. Yet one also had to live among other human beings, who might not share one's achieved tranquillity of spirit. 'Endure abuse: bear with an unreasonable brother, bear with a father, a son, a neighbour, a travel-companion,' counselled Epictetus. Yet concern for others is a natural response. Epictetus talks of the critical importance of love of humanity (the Greek word, still used in English, is *philanthropia*), and of the predominant duty of the individual to help others achieve their rationality. In a moving passage he berates the Epicureans for claiming that human beings have no natural affection for their children. How, he argues in another

passage, were the Spartans able to fight together at Thermopylae*
if they did not feel a common bond of brotherhood? One must
keep a wider perspective, however, and realise that, for instance,
all human beings are mortal and therefore one should not be
overwhelmed by the deaths of others. The emotional attachment
is characteristic of the mature Stoic philosophy of Epictetus,
who cites Socrates and Diogenes the Cynic as his models in the
activities he undertakes. He borrows from Socrates the idea that
one should make oneself aware of the contradictions in everyday
thought – and work to resolve them.

Epictetus also places an emphasis on performing well in the
activities he undertakes. He gives the example of a ball game.
If the ball is lost, one should not get agitated, since the ball is
merely a possession. The key element is how one acquits oneself
as a ball-player. 'That is how we should act, with the close
attention of the cleverest of ball-players, while showing the
same indifference to what we are playing with, as being no more
than a ball... In the same way a weaver does not make wool
but employs his skill on whatever wool he may receive.' What
matters is that one has played the game to the best of one's ability,
without, of course, losing one's self-control. Epictetus also cites
the example of a spectator at the Olympic Games. Screaming
for one competitor or another is not worthy behaviour; praising
the skill of the winner, whatever their identity, certainly is. The
ideal follower of Epictetus, he or she, is a rational being, living
in harmony with nature, receptive to fellow human beings,
fulfilling whatever role they have chosen but above all a person
who is at peace with him or herself. With his emphasis on free
will, Epictetus may well have influenced Christian thinking on
the subject. Christian theologians such as Origen found little to
object to in his philosophy.

---

* This was the celebrated stand of the 300 Spartans against the Persians at
the pass of Thermopylae in 480 BC.

The Politician, Historian and Philosopher: Arrian of Nicomedia (c.AD 85 – after 161)

'There is no need to say who I am, though my name is not obscure; there is no need for me to speak of my country, or my family, or the public offices I have held. It is enough to say that this book, now and since my earliest years, has, for me, taken the place of all these things.' Arrian, or Lucius Flavius Arrianus to give him his Roman name, is referring to the work by which he is best known, his *Anabasis*, a vivid account of the conquests of Alexander the Great. Arrian is also worthy of our attention as he represents a talented Greek who is fully integrated into the Roman administration but who is also an intellectual, a student of Stoic philosophy (as described in the last chapter) and a prolific writer.

Arrian was born in Nicomedia, the capital of Bithynia, between AD 85 and 90, and lived a long life, well into the reign of Marcus Aurelius (r. 161–180). His family had acquired Roman citizenship sometime before his birth. Despite his travels and other postings, he remained close to his 'fatherland', and even wrote an eight-volume history of Bithynia (now lost), which took the story up to the Roman conquest in the 70s BC. In AD 120 Nicomedia was hit by a devastating earthquake and it seems that Arrian, by now a wealthy man, was able to provide funds for its rebuilding. Within his writings there is a record that, probably later in life, he was a priest in the most important cult in Nicomedia, that of the harvest goddess Demeter and her daughter Kore (Persephone). There is no reason to doubt that Arrian saw himself as Greek but he was actually aware that he lived in a world in which Roman administration had become deeply embedded and an active opportunist such as himself did not hesitate to seek ways of advancing within it.

It was the emperor Hadrian who gave him his chance. They may have met each other in Nicopolis when Arrian was studying with Epictetus. Hadrian is known to have visited the philosopher and Hadrian's biographer, Anthony Birley, has suggested possible references to Hadrian attending Epictetus' lectures in the *Discourses* recorded by Arrian.* The two men shared a passion for hunting and it may have been in the field, as much as in philosophical debate, that they bonded. There are hints in the sources, and from his writings, that Arrian served in Dacia where Hadrian was tied up with pacifying the region during the emperor Trajan's campaign and also as a cavalry leader in Noricum (modern Bavaria). Arrian's history of Parthia, now lost, contained such a detailed account of the campaigns of the armies of Trajan against the Parthian empire (115–117) that modern scholars assume that he fought there. While he was in Parthia he may have taken the opportunity to visit some of the sites of Alexander's early battles. Military history was to become his passion.

When Hadrian became emperor in 117, Arrian's career was assured. He was made a senator and was probably governor of Andalusia in 125. In 129 he was awarded one of the suffect consulships,† which would have meant he spent time in Rome.

---

* It is difficult to reconcile the dates when they might have been there together, however.

† Consulships survived as honorary positions under the emperors. The suffect consul was appointed later in the year after the first consul for the year had vacated the post.

Soon afterwards he was appointed by Hadrian to the governor-ship of Cappadocia with two legions under his command. This was a rare achievement for a Greek; the vast majority of the governors came from the Latin west.

By now Arrian was at home with his writings and one of these, the *Periplus*, is a travelogue of a journey around the Black Sea, part of whose coastline lay within his province. It is addressed to Hadrian and, significantly, Arrian identifies himself as belonging among 'us Romans'. Hadrian had visited Trapezous, the modern Trabzon (often anglicised as Trebizond), some years earlier and, in the *Periplus*, Arrian reports on the progress of the building of a temple to Hadrian which the emperor had commissioned. He orders a replacement for a defective statue of Hadrian and criticises the quality of the inscriptions. In his circuit of the Black Sea, Arrian provides advice on which ports can be used for military purposes or for shelter in a storm. He was always a practical man.

Soon afterwards Arrian faced a major challenge. The Alani were a nomadic pastoral tribe who had settled north of the Black Sea. In 135, they raided down through Armenia and threatened Cappadocia. Arrian beat them back and wrote up the tactics he used as 'The order of battle against the Alani' which survives only in fragments. To celebrate twenty years of Hadrian as emperor, Arrian presented him with a text on military tactics. Only the part dealing with cavalry survives but Arrian praises the Romans for adopting tactics from the many peoples they had encountered. When Hadrian died in 138, Arrian's governorship came to an end and he spent much of his remaining life either in Nicomedia or in Athens. He was appointed archon of Athens, a largely honorary but prestigious* position as chief magistrate which Hadrian had held before him, in 145.

---

* The archon was honoured by having the year of his office named after him.

Arrian took Xenophon (c.430–354 BC), the historian, philosopher and military commander of the fourth century BC, as his mentor. There was a remarkable overlap between the two in terms of interests and experience. Both were linked to philosophers – Xenophon to Socrates, Arrian to Epictetus. As with Hadrian, Arrian shared with Xenophon an enthusiasm for hunting and Xenophon had written a similar work, whose title *Cynegeticus* ('related to hunting') Arrian also used in his own survey of the subject. Xenophon's most famous work, still read today, is the story of his advance and retreat from Babylon in 401 BC as the leader of a Greek mercenary army fighting in the cause of Cyrus the Younger as a claimant to the Persian throne. The most memorable scene comes as the soldiers catch their first sight of the sea at Trapezous and know that the rigours of their march are over. As Arrian stood overlooking the sea at Trapezous, he wrote to Hadrian: 'It was from the very same spot as did Xenophon – and you – that we looked down with pleasure on the sea.' Xenophon had chosen the title *Anabasis* – meaning 'up-country' – for his account and Arrian was to choose the same title for his masterwork, although Alexander's campaigns were to cover a much vaster area than Xenophon's.

The most popular life of Alexander, written soon after his campaigns in Asia, was by the historian Cleitarchus who was based in Alexandria, the city founded by Alexander in 331 BC. Only fragments of Cleitarchus' *History of Alexander* have survived, but in its complete form it provided a full account of Alexander's reign which was to prove influential with Roman historians. However, Cleitarchus had not himself served with Alexander and he may have depended on Alexander's court historian Callisthenes of Olynthos as his source. Arrian wanted to use direct eye-witness accounts and he relied on Alexander's general Ptolemy, who later founded the Ptolemaic dynasty in Egypt, and Aristobulus, an engineer in Alexander's retinue whose account is considered reliable. Both men tended to eulogise Alexander, although Ptolemy noted his increasing instability after the death of the Persian king of kings, Darius. Another source used by Arrian was Alexander's naval commander Nearchus, who left a vivid account of his voyage along the south Asian desert coastline from the Indus river back to the Tigris.*

Arrian's view is that Alexander, in comparison with other, lesser, commanders, has never been given the credit he is due for his achievements. 'There has never been another man in all the world, of Greek or any other blood, who by his own hand succeeded in so many brilliant enterprises... that is the reason why I have embarked on the project of writing this history.' It is instructive to compare Arrian's *Anabasis* with the earlier and shorter life of Alexander by Plutarch. The focus of Plutarch's *Life* is a moralistic narrative in which the ambition of Alexander gradually corrupts him. While Arrian talks of Alexander's 'insatiable desire for glory', as an experienced soldier he is more concerned with military tactics and how Alexander used them to achieve his conquests.

Arrian, as a true Greek, supports the idea of spreading Greek civilisation and this enables him to look favourably on Alexander's initial conquests and destruction of the Persian empire. The first three books of his *Anabasis* are a straightforward narrative of Alexander's victories and the accounts of the battles have enough detail to inspire confidence that they are accurate. In Book Two, for instance, there is a dramatic and detailed description of the Battle of Issus (333 BC). Alexander, having advanced across Anatolia, confronts the much larger Persian army under the personal command of Darius. Unaware of the imminence of Alexander's arrival, Darius throws away the advantage of making a full deployment of his troops on the plain. Alexander, in the spirit of Herodotus, emphasises the superiority of his men. 'Our enemies are Medes and Persians, men who for centuries have lived soft and luxurious lives; we

---

* Nearchus was from Crete and had been a boyhood friend of Alexander.

of Macedon for generations past have been trained in the hard school of danger and war.' Once the armies are deployed (and the Macedonians have moved onto the open plain), Alexander launches a shock cavalry attack with himself at its head.* As the Persian cavalry breaks and Darius takes flight, his army disintegrates. Arrian recounts the story of Darius' mother, wife and children abandoned in the Persian camp and Alexander's generous treatment of them. His clemency was to become a common theme in European art.

Having praised the achievement of Alexander, Arrian shifts his narrative in Book Four. Darius is now dead. After recounting the brutal storming of resisting cities in Bactria, the eastern province of the Persian empire, and the ensuing massacres, Arrian describes how Bessus, the local governor (satrap), claimed the throne of the empire, and was captured and mutilated by Alexander before being sent off for execution. It is here that Arrian pauses to reflect on Alexander's actions. He describes the mutilation as 'a barbarous custom' and goes on to decry the way that Alexander adopted the extravagance and arrogance, even the dress, of the Persian court and its humiliating treatment of its subjects. However great the victories of Alexander, notes Arrian, presumably under the influence of Epictetus, the only way to achieve happiness is through victory over oneself. A further digression dwells on Alexander's killing of his friend and general Cleitus, which Plutarch had seen as a turning point in the development of his character. Arrian also views it as a critical moment in the campaigns and describes how Alexander spent three days overcome with guilt.

It is only in the final Book Seven, after the death of Alexander, that Arrian provides a more positive overview. 'In the course of this book I have, admittedly, found fault with some of the things which Alexander did, but of the man himself I am not ashamed

---

* A later (*c.*100 BC) mosaicist recorded the moment on a famous pavement found in a house in Pompeii.

to express ungrudging admiration... He had great personal beauty, invincible power of endurance, and a keen intellect; he was brave and adventurous, strict in the observance of religious duty, and hungry for fame.' Arrian goes on to praise Alexander's acute perception of the opportunities that confronted him, how he was able 'to seize the moment for a swift blow before his enemy had any suspicion of what was happening', his readiness to take risks and to inspire his men. As for his character, Arrian states that Alexander was the only monarch he knew of who showed remorse for his mistakes, not least because this taught him not to repeat them. He is prepared to forgive Alexander's claim to be of divine birth – even the sober Arrian has to admit that 'some power more than human was concerned in his birth'. He excuses Alexander's adoption of Persian dress on the grounds that Alexander's aim was to bring the Persians within a wider community and dilute the arrogance of the Macedonians. Even Alexander's heavy drinking, recorded as destructive in most biographies, is seen as no more than rooted in his enjoyment of companionship. Arrian's account is still regarded as largely accurate and full of detail not recorded elsewhere, although modern scholarship is more critical of Alexander's achievements.

There is one further work of Arrian's that deserves mention. In his *Indica*, which is mainly an account of Nearchus' voyage of retreat from the Indus river back to the Persian Gulf, Arrian embellishes his narrative with digressions on the geography, culture and peoples of India.* By Arrian's time trade between Rome and India was flourishing and there was a great deal of interest in Indian culture. Ultimately, however, *Indica* is a pastiche. Although Arrian claims authority as the knowledgeable author, it is obvious he has never travelled there and is heavily reliant on Nearchus and other sources. Among these is Megasthenes (360–290 BC) – the expert on India already

---

* *Indica*'s concentration on Nearchus' epic voyage is such that it is often included as Book Eight of the *Anabasis*.

known from Plutarch's *On the Apparent Face in the Orb of the Moon* – and Eratosthenes (276–194 BC) whose *Geography* Strabo made much of. Both works were now hundreds of years old, but they were at least written close to the time of Alexander. In his attempts to delineate the culture of India, Arrian relates a tradition that many of the fruits of Indian civilisation, its cities and even its agriculture, were brought to the subcontinent by the god Dionysus, and even suggests that Heracles (the Roman Hercules) was born in India and that his daughter became the country's queen. He makes observations on religious rituals and describes methods of hunting elephants and a caste of 'wise men' who dispense wisdom naked. Clearly *Indica* does not provide much accurate information about Indian society but it illustrates the ways in which the Greeks conceived of a civilisation that lay far beyond their borders. And again, it shows the sheer breadth of the Greek intellectual tradition and its enduring spirit of curiosity.

II

The Geographer and Astronomer: Claudius Ptolemy (c.AD 100–c.170)

In the preface to his great work of mathematical astronomy, best known as the *Almagest*, Claudius Ptolemy compares the various sources of knowledge. He claims to follow Aristotle in dividing them between the theological, the physical and the mathematical. While one might agree, argues Ptolemy, that there is some first cause of the universe, one can only guess its identity 'because of its completely invisible and ungraspable nature'. On the other hand, one can observe physical phenomena but here again it is difficult to find certainty because of 'the unstable and unclear nature of the matter'. 'Only the mathematical, if approached enquiringly, would give its practitioners certain and trustworthy knowledge with demonstration both arithmetic and geometric resulting from indisputable procedures.' Ptolemy envisages a combination of observation of the universe with the use of mathematical logic to achieve the truth about the movements of the heavens. He then goes on to provide one of the most formidable texts in the history of science, one that would remain authoritative until Copernicus in the sixteenth century.

Very little is known of Claudius Ptolemy. A name deriving from the Egyptian dynasty of Greek kings, 'Ptolemy' had been widely adopted within the Greek population. It is assumed, therefore, that he was of Greek birth, although it is just possible that he was a Hellenised Egyptian. 'Claudius' suggests Roman citizenship, possibly from a grant to his family during the reign of the emperor of that name. In none of his works does Ptolemy record travelling beyond Alexandria and he used the city as a meridian* for his works on astronomy. The observations made in his *Almagest* are taken from Alexandria between AD 127 and 141. A later reference records his death as taking place during the reign of the emperor Marcus Aurelius (161–80). All his works are dedicated to an individual named Syrus of whom nothing is known. It is assumed that Ptolemy exploited the resources of the library and Mouseion of Alexandria which were still flourishing during Ptolemy's time, but it is only through reading his works, which cover an impressive range, that one can assess his remarkable influence.

The breakthrough in Greek astronomy had come in the third century BC with the use of geometric proofs to create models of the patterns of the stars, Sun, Moon and the planets. Crucially, other than a claim by Aristarchus of Samos that the Earth moved round the Sun, all these models depended on a spherical and motionless Earth. There was nothing to suggest that the Earth was moving. After all, arrows fired straight up in the air landed at the same spot rather than further on. However, an Earth-centred universe required ingenious models to explain the movements of the Sun and Moon and the five 'wandering' planets (Greek *planetes*) known at that time whose names, Mercury, Venus, Mars, Jupiter and Saturn, were already established. It was particularly difficult to explain how the planets appeared to go backwards at times during their supposed circuits of the Earth. Having accepted that any planet

---

* The meridian is a line of longitude extending round the Earth and taking in each pole.

could only move in simple circles* one way for the observations to make sense was to assume that the planets moved on their own circles (epicycles) whose centres ran alongside the edge of other circles (the deferent circles). If one posited a relationship between the two circles and defined the speed at which the encirclings took place, then one could explain the irregularities of the observed movements of a planet.

The high point of Greek astronomy had been reached in the work of Hipparchus (190–120 BC) who had gained access to a vast body of Babylonian observations stretching back 600 years. The Babylonian inheritance brought with it the sexagesimal system (with 60 as its base, still used in minutes in an hour and seconds in a minute today) and a stock of elaborate arithmetical calculations built up over past centuries which allowed astronomers to predict eclipses and other celestial events and patterns. An alternative approach by Greek astronomers was to create models which could tell where a planet was situated at any one time. The two systems could be combined so that the position of a planet on its circular passage could be determined. This Hipparchus was able to do with such sophistication (he invented trigonometry along the way) that he was even able to record the way the Earth shifted as a viewing platform (via the change in orientation of its rotational axis known as the precession of the equinoxes). Now that the position of the stars and planets could be calculated as they would have been at an earlier date, astrologers, who were able to offer assessments of the character and fortune of individuals on the basis of the movements of heavenly bodies, found their expertise was much in demand. In some ways astrology became the senior partner to astronomy.

The years after Hipparchus present a lacuna in the history of

---

* It was not until the early seventeenth century that the elliptical movement of the planets was discovered by the German astronomer Johannes Kepler (1571–1630).

astronomy. There are fragments of Greek texts but these exist only in Indian sources. The paucity of texts may be explained by the fact that Ptolemy either ignored his immediate predecessors or, once he had produced the *Almagest*, it was seen as so authoritative that no one bothered with copying out the earlier texts.

The word *Almagest* is the corruption of the Arabic title of the original Greek *Megale syntaxis*, meaning 'a compilation of astronomical phenomena'. It comes in thirteen books. There is scholarly dispute concerning the extent to which Ptolemy adopted the catalogue of stars devised by Hipparchus, a catalogue which has not survived. But Ptolemy's ambition went far beyond this. He aimed to provide such sophisticated models that the future positions of the Sun, Moon and the five known planets could be predicted for eternity. In order to achieve this accuracy, Ptolemy, working within the confines of his Earth-centred universe, felt impelled to add an extra point, the so-called equant, to his models of planetary movement. The equant was imagined as the centre of a circle outside the Earth and if it were assumed that a planet circled around this point, perhaps on an epicycle, then a further array of observations made sense. (Later astronomers would criticise Ptolemy for inventing the equant simply to make his observations fit!*) Ptolemy's system had the advantage of accounting for a wider range of astronomical observations and brought mathematical models into the Western tradition. This was probably Ptolemy's most influential contribution to science.

In addition to the refining of earlier models, Ptolemy also compiled a catalogue of over a thousand stars, arranged in forty-eight constellations, including the longitudes and latitudes of each and its brightness. It was an astonishing achievement. Geoffrey Lloyd, a historian of Greek science, has described the *Almagest*

---

* These concerns stimulated the creation of alternative models of the planetary movements by the Arab astronomers and then, comprehensively, by Copernicus.

as 'extraordinary for the rigour of its mathematical arguments, for the range of ideas encompassed and the comprehensiveness of the results proposed'.

Ptolemy composed the so-called *Handy Tables* which could be used to plot the past and future positions of the planets, including eclipses. They were essentially the findings of his calculations without the theoretical backing that had been laid out in the *Almagest*. In subsequent works, such as his *Planetary Hypothesis*, Ptolemy elaborated his view that the planets circled round the Earth without their orbits overlapping. Ptolemy's order of the planetary circles was, from those closest to the Earth, the Moon, Mercury, Venus, the Sun, Mars, Jupiter and Saturn.* Ptolemy calculated that the radius of the universe would be 19,865 times the radius of the Earth – so 7.5 million miles. While this is infinitesimally small compared to the reality, it was the first time that the universe had been calculated as being so immense. Human beings were at the core of a vast creation and this idea permeated Islamic and medieval astronomy.

It has already been noted that once one could plot the positions of the planets at any earlier point in time, it opened up the possibilities of astrology. The Sun clearly had a significant influence on every aspect of human life. Similarly, if the Moon affected the tides, then the movement of the planets might influence other physical objects on Earth, even human beings. Ptolemy wrote a companion volume to the *Almagest* on the subject of astrology, the *Apotelesmatika* ('influences'), better known as the *Tetrabiblos*, reflecting the 'four books' into which it is divided. The resulting text supported astrology as a rational activity. While the *Tetrabiblos* is in no way as mathematically sophisticated as the *Almagest*, it presented a systematic overview of earlier material in which Ptolemy rigorously weeded out those prognostications that were not backed by actual observations.

* The correct order is Sun (at the centre), Mercury, Venus, the Earth and the Moon, Mars, Jupiter and Saturn.

He accepted the possibility that the conjunction of planets at the time of an individual's conception and birth might affect their temperament and considered that as life progressed different planets might exert their influence, the fieriness of Venus producing the burgeoning sexuality of years fourteen to twenty-one, Saturn bringing about the coldness and weakness of old age. Eclipses would have differing effects on individuals depending on their temperaments and depending on their length and the position of the eclipse in the sky. However, Ptolemy cautioned that the complexities of astrology are many, that fraudsters are ever-present and only the most skilled astrologer can assess the influences of the stars. Ptolemy's authority has ensured that the *Tetrabiblos* is still read to this day, but the work has been criticised by some as unscientific in comparison to the *Almagest*.

It remains extraordinary that Ptolemy was able to create an influential masterwork in a different discipline. This was his *Geographike* (Greek, 'writing about the Earth'). Ptolemy was heavily dependent on the work of a Syrian Greek, Marinus of Tyre (*c*.AD 70–130), who, having complained that merchants were so busy calculating profits that they exaggerated the distances they had travelled, understood that there needed to be an accurate way of setting out a map. While Hipparchus had initiated the use of longitude and latitude, it was Marinus who assigned the concept to place any location and relate it to any other. Marinus' maps stretched from the Canary Islands (where he placed the meridian) to China. Realising that there must be a pole in the south, equivalent to the one in the north, he coined the term Antarctic as an opposite to the Arctic (the Greek *anti-*, 'opposite to').

Ptolemy began the *Geographike* by mathematically establishing a way in which a flat map could be created to represent a part of a globe. This was the subject of the first of eight volumes. The next seven presented no fewer than 8,000 locations, each with their position marked by longitude and latitude. Of course, there was no way that he could have visited and plotted each location himself, but it was possible to use what information he had to create actual maps. None of the originals exist today but later Islamic and European cartographers were able to work from the text and even incorporate new regions that had not been discovered in Ptolemy's day. Marinus had estimated the circumference of the Earth to be 20,700 miles, some 17 per cent less than the real figure. Ptolemy followed him but with the smaller circumference his largely accurate land masses stretched further round the world than was actually the case. It seemed that at the 'back' of the globe it would just be a short hop from western Europe to India. This would lead to much geographical confusion when the Americas were discovered in the fifteenth and sixteenth centuries.

Ptolemy is also known to have written several minor works, including one on music, which influenced the sixth-century scholar Boethius' text on music which became popular in the medieval universities. Perhaps the most important of these texts was a treatise on optics, hardly known today as it survives only in a poor and incomplete Latin translation. However, David Lindberg, in his *The Beginnings of Western Science*, describes it as 'the greatest Hellenistic text on geometrical optics' and as 'one of the most important works on optics written before Newton'. Ptolemy suggested that rays were emitted through the eyes to capture the essence of perceived objects, which were then interpreted by the brain. His achievement lay in mapping this out geometrically, especially in establishing the principles of refraction (the bending of light when it transfers from one environment to another). Ptolemy tested the different angles of refraction in air, water and glass. The *Optics* was to prove a fundamental source for the work in this field of the great Arab scientist Ibn Al-Haythem (965–1040) which then influenced European work on the subject.

It is sad that we know so little of Ptolemy as a person. He clearly had an outstanding brain, not only in its grasp of mathematical principles but in its imaginative solutions to a variety of issues in different disciplines. He had the capacity to back up his proposed solutions with extraordinarily comprehensive theoretical explanations. But his achievements extend beyond the theoretical, as his listing of some 8,000 locations in the *Geographike* reveals. One personal statement of Ptolemy's has come down to us, which might be said to combine an awareness of the transitory nature of human existence with a statement of the thrilling possibilities of astronomical investigation:

Well do I know that I am mortal, a creature of one day,
But if my mind follows the winding paths of the stars
Then my feet no longer rest on earth, but by standing by
Zeus himself I take my fill of ambrosia, the divine dish.

12

The Satirist: Lucian of Samosata
(AD 125 – after 180)

Lucian was born about AD 125 in Samosata (modern Samsat in south-eastern Turkey), a city on the banks of the Euphrates and thus far inland from the traditional centres of Greek culture. Samosata was absorbed into the Roman empire in 72 BC and its strategic position on the river had made it the base for a frontier legion. The native language was probably Syriac, a variant of Aramaic, but Lucian learned Greek and he used it to embark on a career as an orator. His speciality was sophisticated ridicule of everything he saw around him. Lucian was a rhetorician who mocked the speeches of others, a philosopher who laughed at the pretensions of other philosophers. In a world of diverse spiritual movements and cults, including the first communities of Christians, he is particularly caustic about the superstitions and religious practices of his day. He is acutely aware of being a Syrian and thus an outsider, a role he plays with aplomb. As his satires show, it is possible for even a Syrian to achieve *paideia*, but most outsiders who set out to do so failed to attain it.

Most lives of Lucian begin with his account of his early search for a career.* As a boy he had enjoyed making wax models. Since

---

* From his text *The Vision of Lucian*.

his mother's brother was a sculptor, his father thought this would suit him as a career and arranged for him to take lessons with his brother-in-law. On his first day, his uncle gave him a piece of marble which he asked him to strike gently. Impulsive by nature, Lucian delivered a blow that shattered the marble into many pieces. He was beaten by his outraged uncle and went home in tears. So ended his career as a sculptor.

That same night he describes how he had a vision of two women fighting over him. One was dishevelled, her hair unkempt and her clothes full of dust, the other had a beautiful face and was neatly dressed. They agreed that each woman would try to persuade him to accompany her.

So 'Sculpture' stressed that this had been Lucian's family business, that hard work would make him fit and strong and that there were great names to emulate: the reputations of Pheidias, Polycleitus and Praxiteles echoed down the ages.* Next, 'Eloquence' began speaking. She derided the life of a labourer, always dependent on the patronage of others and limited to endless drudgery and dust. If, on the other hand, Lucian chose her: 'I will show you the wonderful works of antiquity, illustrate and explain to you the maxims of the sages and adorn your mind, the best and noblest part of you, with modesty, justice, piety, gentleness, prudence, fortitude and the love of virtue.' A good speaker is always honoured and respected wherever he goes, she continues. In the vision, Lucian, to the fury of 'Sculpture' (who then turns into a statue herself), climbs into the chariot of Eloquence and flies across the world as if he is a deity. Eloquence has won out.

Lucian has such a tendency to exaggerate and satirise that most of what he writes must be treated with caution. There are no sources for his life outside his own writings so his career as a rhetorician is obscure. He seems first to have moved to the

---

* These were the major sculptors of the fifth and fourth centuries BC and are seen as the supreme exponents of classical art.

wealthy Greek cities of the Ionian coast; Ephesus and Smyrna (modern Izmir) were known for their rhetoricians. Here, as an outsider to Greek culture, he must have studied the Attic texts intensively. As a result he accumulated a wide knowledge of the myths and personalities of classical Greece, nuggets of which he scattered liberally throughout his satires. He used Attic expressions extensively in order to attract the intellectual elite. His own works suggest that he was eventually able to take on pupils of his own and to give public displays of oratory. He then moved westwards to mainland Greece, then to Italy and Rome and finally to Gaul where, according to his own assessment, he became a successful professional rhetorician able to earn good money. Yet he claimed that the achievement of riches as an objective in itself offers a false happiness. In his work *The Ship or the Wishes*, Lucian presents a character, Adimantus, who lusts after wealth. Adimantus imagines wearing fine clothes and owning a house in Athens near the Painted Stoa with slaves, clothes, carriages and horses.* He will also have a ship of his own which will bring him in vast trading profits. Every kind of delicacy will be imported to his home from Italy, Spain, Numidia and even India. He will eat off gold plates and even his slaves off silver ones. The harbour at Piraeus will be extended inland so that everyone can see his fine ship. Yet he is misguided if he thinks that these treasures bring him happiness.†

It is unlikely, of course, that Lucian made anything like this kind of money himself, but he must have been wealthy enough to be accepted in elite circles. By the age of thirty-five, he was ready to return homewards. In another work, describing a stay in Antioch, the capital of Syria, he praises the mistress of the emperor Lucius Verus, who is on his way to campaign against

---

* Horses were a comparative rarity in Athens as there was insufficient pasture for them in the hot summers and so they would prove a mark of wealth.
† The list of treasures in the Book of Revelation 18:12–14 (written *c.*AD 95) echoes Lucian's belief that riches are illusory.

the Parthians. It may be that Lucian was part of the court circle and was awarded Roman citizenship as a result. From Antioch he migrates, with his father, who is still alive, to Athens. Some sources suggest that he worked in the civil service in Egypt, probably towards the end of his long life in the 170s. The last historical event mentioned in his writings is the death of Marcus Aurelius (AD 180) so it is assumed he died during the reign of Marcus Aurelius' successor, Commodus.

At some point in his forties, Lucian became dissatisfied with rhetoric. He appears to have been convinced by Socrates' assessment, notably in the Platonic dialogue *Gorgias*, that rhetoric demands the emotional manipulation of its audiences at the expense of truth. So he was drawn to philosophy. One of his works, *Nigrinus*, named after the philosopher who recounts it, compares the peace of Athens with the clamour of Rome. Nigrinus

> commended the Athenian liberty, and unpretentious style of living; the peace and learned leisure which they so abundantly enjoy. To dwell among such men, he declared, is to dwell with philosophy. A single-hearted man, who has been taught to despise wealth, may here preserve a pure morality. No life could be more in harmony with the determined pursuit of all that is truly beautiful.

This idealistic portrayal of Athens leads on to a diatribe against Rome and the Romans, who are said to be so corrupted by wealth that they cannot be described as living as true philosophers. In another tract, *On the Dependent Servants*, Lucian revels in outlining the life of a Greek intellectual with a position in a wealthy Roman household. He is continually humiliated, forced to stand about while his master is getting on with other business, and treated as little more than a cultural ornament. One telling passage reveals him to be hopelessly confused by Roman dining customs. The family dog plays with his beard and further humiliates him by giving birth to its puppies on his cloak. Given Lucian's habit of describing his own personal experiences, this text is usually seen as reflecting his own sensitivities as an outsider and his distaste for clumsy displays of Roman superiority.

Intellectually speaking, Lucian is forever restless. He concludes that philosophy can never find absolute truth (as Plato had assumed it could) and he gradually becomes more and more dismissive of the discipline and philosophers in general. He has become a Sceptic but a particularly sarcastic one. At times his imagination runs riot. In *A True Story*, for instance, he and his companions travel through the Pillars of Hercules, into the Atlantic, and head west to discover the limits of the ocean. On the way their ship is whisked up in a waterspout to the Moon where a battle is raging between the King of the Moon and the King of the Stars over who should rule over the stars. After further adventures their ship is deposited back on Earth and enters a vast whale. *A True Story* has been described as the founding text of science fiction. Lucian's last years in Athens were devoted to writing and with some eighty of his works still extant he is one of best represented writers of the classical world. It is assumed that he travelled around Greece and declaimed his works. If the style and verve of his writing are anything to go by, he must have been a star act.

Among Lucian's most light-hearted texts is his *Philosophies for Sale*. The background is a slave auction, a reminder that the Greek and Roman elites relied heavily on a slave economy, both in their households and in the workshops and mines that generated their wealth. Zeus and his messenger god Hermes are the auctioneers and each philosophy could be interrogated by potential purchasers. The Pythagoreans, who are revealed as subsisting on a diet of beans, offer a course that begins with five years of silent contemplation, while the Stoics are presented as arrogant know-alls. ('Here', says Hermes, satirically introducing Chrysippus, 'is monopoly of wisdom, monopoly of beauty, monopoly of courage, monopoly of justice. Sole king, sole orator, sole legislator, sole millionaire.') Also up for auction is a Cynic who, when asked how he will provide help for a new owner, replies, 'I shall give you a course of hard labour. You will sleep on the ground, drink water, and fill your belly as best you can. Have you money? Take my advice and throw it into the sea. With wife and children and country you will not concern yourself; there will be no more of that nonsense. You will exchange your present home for a sepulchre, a ruin, or a tub.' When it comes to the Peripatetic philosopher, Hermes goes for the hard sell. He tells the hoped-for purchaser:

> Snap him up before it is too late. Why, from him you will find out in no time how long a gnat lives, to how many fathoms' depth the sunlight penetrates the sea, and what an oyster's soul is like... But these are trifles. You should hear some of his more abstruse speculations, concerning generation and birth and the development of the embryo... and his distinction between man, the laughing creature, and the ass, which is neither a laughing nor a carpentering nor a shipping creature.

Lucian has great fun with the Sceptics, for whom Socrates speaks.

> Prospective purchaser: 'Tell me first, though, what do you know?'
> Socrates: 'Nothing.'
> Prospective purchaser: 'But how's that?'
> Socrates: 'There does not appear to me to be anything.'
> Prospective purchaser: 'Are not we something?'
> Socrates: 'How do I know that?'
> Prospective purchaser: 'And you yourself?'
> Socrates: 'Of that I am still more doubtful.'
> Prospective purchaser: 'Well, you are in a fix! And what have you got those scales for?'
> Socrates: 'I use them to weigh arguments in and get them evenly balanced. They must be absolutely equal – not a featherweight to choose between them; then, and not till then, can I make uncertain which is right.'

One of Lucian's most thorough and perceptive analyses of the problems of philosophy comes in his *Hermotimus*, a dialogue between Lucian, under the pseudonym of Lycinus, and a would-be philosopher, Hermotimus. Lycinus asks Hermotimus how he is getting on:

> For twenty years now, I should say, I have watched you perpetually going to your professors, generally bent over a book taking notes of past lectures, pale with thought and emaciated in body. I suspect you find no release even in your dreams, you are so wrapped up in the thing. With all this you must surely get hold of Happiness soon, if indeed you have not found it long ago without telling us.

Hermotimus replies: 'Alas, Lycinus, I am only just beginning to get an inkling of the right way. Very far-off dwells Virtue and long and steep and rough is the way thither, and travellers must bedew it with sweat.' He believes that he is only half-way there and he will need another twenty years to complete the journey. 'So, what will be the final result?' asks Lycinus. 'Wisdom, courage, true beauty, justice, full and firm knowledge of all things as they are; but wealth and glory and pleasure and all bodily things – these a man strips off and abandons before he mounts up.' Even a single day of absolute happiness will be enough, says Hermotimus. Naturally Lycinus is sceptical. How does Hermotimus know that he will attain his desired end point, and what happens if he dies before he has reached it? 'There is one thing I should like to know: are they [those who have reached the summits of truth] allowed to come down from their elevation sometimes, and have a taste of what they left behind them or when they have once got up, must they stay there, conversing with Virtue, and smiling at wealth and glory and pleasure?' Hermotimus replies that once one has reached the summit, wealth and fame will never matter again.

The dialogue continues with Lycinus probing how one chooses the best among all the philosophies on offer. Eventually, after much tortuous debate, Hermotimus sums up Lycinus' (Lucian's) argument:

> What you say amounts to that: philosophy is impossible and inaccessible to a mere mortal; for you expect the aspirant first to choose the best philosophy; and you considered that the only guarantee of such choices being correct was to go through all philosophy before choosing the truest. Then in reckoning the number of years required by each you spurned all limits, extended the thing to several generations, and made out the quest of truth too long for the individual life; and now you crown all by proving success doubtful even apart from all that; you say it is uncertain whether the philosophers have ever found truth at all.

Hermotimus decides, therefore, to turn his back on philosophy. 'And now I will be off to metamorphose myself. When we next meet, there will be no long, shaggy beard, no artificial composure; I shall be natural, as a gentleman should. I may go as far as a fashionable coat, by way of publishing my renunciation of nonsense.'

One of Lucian's works that has aroused particular interest, as the subject-matter includes early Christianity, is *The Death of Peregrinus*. Peregrinus actually existed, although how much Lucian distorts his life is unclear. According to Lucian, he is a charlatan, already an outlaw in his native Armenia where he has killed his own father. Lucian gives him many of the attributes of a Cynic, a philosophy he delights in deriding, notably by arguing that Cynics are primarily exhibitionists.

The text describes how, among his other 'exploits', Peregrinus infiltrated a Christian community in Palestine – 'he pretty soon convinced them of his superiority; prophet, elder, ruler of the place of prayer – he was everything at once; expounded their books, commented on them, wrote books himself...' He made such a nuisance of himself that the authorities threw him into prison. The reaction from the Christian community was immediate – they poured in money and food and did everything they could to release him. In fact, the governor, presumably unaware of Peregrinus' misdeeds in Armenia, assumed he was under some form of illusion and let him go.

Lucian then offers his opinion on the Christians as he saw them. These are very early days for Christianity and it is hard to believe that Lucian knew much about the religion other than what he had heard from its critics, which he then spiced up to serve his own purposes. His prime aim was to expose Peregrinus as a con man. But he also understands that Christian communities were vulnerable to self-proclaimed preachers.

> You see, these misguided creatures start with the general conviction that they are immortal for all time, which explains the contempt of death and voluntary self-devotion which are so common among them; and then it was impressed on them by their original lawgiver that they are all brothers from the moment that they are converted. They deny the gods of Greece, and worship the crucified sage, and live after his laws. All this they take quite on trust, with the result that they despise all worldly goods alike, regarding them merely as common property. Now an adroit, unscrupulous fellow, who has seen the world, has only to get among these simple souls, and his fortune is pretty soon made; he plays with them.

Lucian goes on to say that the Christians found Peregrinus out and would have nothing more to do with him.

It is clear from Peregrinus' wanderings, first in Rome and then back to Greece and Olympia, that he had the Cynics' habit of deliberately outraging public opinion, to the extent of ridiculing the philanthropist Herodes Atticus, who had arranged a much-needed water supply for the Olympic Games (see p. 239). He even urged the Greeks to throw off the yoke of Rome. At first he was a figure of amusement, who drew in the crowds, but after four years in and around Olympia, everyone was fed up with him. Peregrinus then conceived the most extreme way of earning celebrity status – he would sacrifice himself on a funeral pyre after the games of that year had ended. The crowds gathered and – rather than clamouring for him not to sacrifice himself, as Peregrinus hoped they would – urged him on (the prospect of such a spectacle being too tempting to forego). So he was consumed in flames. Lucian witnessed his suicide, which is dated to AD 165.*

Among Lucian's targets is religious credulity. In his satire *On Sacrifice*, for instance, he ridicules the idea that one can buy gifts from the gods by sacrificing animals to them. 'Is he to call them devout worshippers or very outcasts, who think so meanly of God as to suppose that he can require anything at the hand of man, can take pleasure in their flattery, or be wounded by their neglect?' The gods have no need for sacrifices, so he wonders why they are so avid for smoke and blood when in heaven they have ambrosia and nectar. He asks how is it that the best meat from a sacrifice is kept to be consumed on Earth and queries the measurement of the efficacy of a sacrifice when a rich man can offer so much more, an ox, for instance, than a poor man who can only provide a chicken. In his *The Lover of Lies*, Lucian takes on those who create foundation myths for their communities.

> A Cretan will look you in the face and tell you that yonder is Zeus's tomb. In Athens, you are informed that Erichthonius sprang out of the Earth, and that the first Athenians grew up from the soil like so many cabbages; and this story assumes quite a sober aspect when compared with that of the Sparti, for whom the Thebans claim descent from a dragon's teeth. If you presume to doubt these stories… you are a fool and a blasphemer, for questioning such palpable truths.

Lucian's world was one of intense intellectual activity that drew on sophisticated and well-established traditions of philosophical thought. Yet the rich variety of ideas and the

* Other sources who mention Peregrinus in passing suggest that he may have been a more respected philosopher than Lucian makes him out to have been.

hunger to absorb them also allowed those with the ability to speak well both to educate and inspire but also to deceive their audiences. Here Lucian comes into his own. He is quick to expose charlatans but he also probes the difficulties of finding truths. Some of his texts are more sober. Much of what he says in *How to Write History* would be useful advice for the aspiring young historian today. ('Let him bring a mind like a mirror, clear, gleaming bright, accurately centred, displaying the shape of things just as he receives them, free from distortion, false colouring and misrepresentation.'*) He praises Thucydides above Herodotus, whom he sees as too dependent on myths. If a treatise *On the Syrian Goddess* is Lucian's, as traditionally believed, then he has, as an Assyrian, provided an accurate account of indigenous Syrian religion during the Roman period. Yet one of Lucian's most valuable legacies is to tell his readers how difficult it was for an outsider to gain entry to the Greek cultural elite. However much he mastered the texts, it was virtually impossible for a Syrian such as himself to acquire the manner of dress, the way of using language – which harked back to earlier Attic dialects – and even the way of walking required to pass as a member of the Greek elite. Similar barriers exist in many cultures today.

---

* It would be useful to compare Lucian's advice with what Polybius was writing about the purposes of history (pp. 65–9).

13

The Medical Man: Galen (AD 129–216)

Galen of Pergamum was, after Hippocrates, the most influential physician of the classical world, his reputation extending well into the nineteenth century. He led an extraordinary life, not least as a prodigious writer of texts, many of which survive.[*] He was exceptional in linking philosophy to practical medical skills, an ability that – despite bitter rivalries with his fellow physicians in Rome – led to him being chosen by the emperor Marcus Aurelius to look after himself and the imperial family. Galen was typical of his class and time in that he revelled in public performance – in his case showing off his medical skills to an audience.

Galen was born to an aristocratic family in Pergamum in AD 129. Pergamum had enjoyed a distinguished and honourable history as a cultural centre under the Attalid dynasty before coming under Roman rule from 133 BC. Galen's father was a successful architect and wealthy landowner. There is some evidence that he was given Roman citizenship by the emperor Hadrian when the emperor visited Pergamum in AD 123. Such grants, binding the recipients in loyalty to the empire, were

---

[*] One estimate is that he authored about 370 texts, a third of which are still extant.

becoming increasingly common among the Greek elite of the more opulent Greek cities. On his visit Hadrian had given funds for the rebuilding of the temple of Asclepius, the god of medicine, which was a major feature of the Roman extension of the city in the plain below the citadel. Such temples functioned as hospitals as well as shrines, with patients coming to stay overnight in the hope of obtaining a cure from the god himself through a dream. The Asclepium at Pergamum soon became a meeting place for the sickly members of the Greek and Roman elite. Medical instruments uncovered by excavations on these sites reveal how 'scientific' medicine, such as it was in the second century AD, was practised. As was the case with many Greek philosophers, Galen's speculations incorporated a spiritual component. He paid special homage to Asclepius, at times allowing him to overrule 'science' with dreams that Galen claimed the god had given him. His contemporary the orator Aelius Aristides felt the same (see Chapter 16).

Galen appears to have been an only child and his father gave him a fine education. 'In my fifteenth year he [my father] steered me towards dialectic, with a view to my concentrating entirely on philosophy.' As was typical for members of his class, he studied a wide range of different schools: Platonism, Aristotelianism, Stoicism and Epicureanism. He was unusual, however, in not choosing one above the others – he seems to have studied each of them throughout his life. The historian of Greek science Geoffrey Lloyd notes that 'Galen is probably unique among practising physicians in any age or culture for his professionalism as a logician... conversely he is also remarkable among practising logicians for his ability in, and experience of, medical practice.' Here he was following Aristotle. In the *Nicomachean Ethics*, Aristotle had counselled against merely reading textbooks and using them only within the context of practical experience. Galen extolled geometry, and hence logic, as the basis of secure knowledge. In his surviving works on logic, he was obsessed with the lack of precision in language, especially as it was used by the Stoics. He was close to Aristotle in that he extolled the close observation of subjects even though he often criticised the philosopher for inaccurate observations. It is unfortunate that Galen's major work on logic, *On Demonstration*, which he recommended as reading for any aspiring doctor, has not survived. Nevertheless, two of his surviving treatises, *A Good Doctor Must Also Be a Philosopher* and the autobiographical *On My Own Opinions*, contain valuable advice for the medical profession, emphasising the importance of detachment and placing healing above monetary gain. In his text *On the Doctrines of Hippocrates and Plato*, he argues that the two intellectuals of the title were in harmony.

Despite his father's insistence on an early concentration on philosophy, Galen's choice of a career in medicine also seems to have been his father's idea. Galen pursued it with determination, seeking out the best practitioners in Smyrna, Corinth and finally Alexandria (where he may have spent four years) before returning home to Pergamum in his late twenties. The dissection of human bodies is known to have been practised in Alexandria but it is not known whether this was still done during Galen's time there. (Galen is not known ever to have dissected a human body.) Galen is another example of a Greek who believed that through studying the works of earlier practitioners he was carrying on a great tradition – in this case that of Hippocrates and the texts later generations attributed to this pioneer in Greek medicine. One meticulous scholar has counted over 2,500 references to the Hippocratic Corpus in Galen's works. In his discussion of the Hippocratic text known as *Epidemics III*, Galen names eight commentators on the original text. Among the most important of these texts for Galen was Hippocrates' *The Nature of Man*, which contained an overview of the doctrine of the four humours. As previously noted, the doctrine held that there were four relevant bodily fluids, blood, phlegm, black bile and yellow bile, which needed to be kept in balance for good health. So a surplus of one would need to be treated by reducing it. The most common treatment, which continued to be practised for centuries after Galen, was bloodletting. Other 'surpluses' could be removed by diet, exercise (Galen was a champion of the gymnasium), sweating or purging. Galen developed the tradition of humoural medicine further by extending it to temperaments. An individual's temperament was dependent on their inherited balance of fluids and this needed to be taken into account when they were treated. Galen believed that the human body was created in such a way that, through providence, each part was designed to function well and contribute to a healthy whole. This perspective was set out at length in Galen's *On the Usefulness of Parts of the Body*, which many scholars have seen as his masterpiece.

Yet having an overriding theory was not enough; medical practice also required an empirical basis. Galen always made precise notes from observations of his patients before deciding on the appropriate treatment. His training in logical reasoning was a fundamental part of his diagnoses. For instance, Stoics such as Chrysippus believed that the soul was situated in the heart, which controlled respiration and rational discussion. From close observation and the distasteful practice of cutting specific nerves of live animals, Galen showed that respiration is controlled by nerves that emanate from the brain. In so doing he confirmed Plato's belief that the higher part of the soul and reason itself was controlled from the brain. He accorded the heart a secondary position as the supplier of blood which infused the *pneuma*, the vital spirit of a human being, that is located in the brain. He understood the functioning of nerves. Confronted by a patient with paralysed fingers, which other practitioners had manipulated in the hope of bringing about a cure, Galen traced the problem back to nerves in the patient's spine and succeeded in restoring feeling to the affected digits. But some of his observations were misguided. As we will see below, he did not recognise the circulation of the blood. His dissections of Barbary apes, which he believed were close enough to human beings to provide definitive evidence of human anatomy, also led him to make erroneous assumptions. Even so, for the care he took in the use of reason in his diagnoses, he was well ahead of any of his contemporaries.

Galen began his career as the physician to the gladiators of Pergamum. Patching up a wide variety of injuries provided him with excellent experience but there is also early evidence of Galen's arrogance: he boasts that, compared to his fellow doctors, he hardly ever lost a life.* In many of his later texts he describes battles with other physicians in which he would overrule their diagnoses and be proved right. He records the joy and amazement of the household when he triumphs and the patient makes a full recovery from serious illness. In one case of a young man with a fever, Galen questioned him on his activities over the previous days. He had been travelling, but when he received some bad news, he had to hurry back to the city under a hot sun. He then had an argument in a gymnasium which turned violent, causing him further exhaustion. When he drank, he vomited. The doctors who had seen him counselled further fasting, but Galen realised that he was dehydrated (the stomach rejects water when it is severely dehydrated) and that he had to take liquids. To the consternation of his rivals, Galen was proved right. The episode showed the value of a full physical examination and interrogation, which was part of the secret of Galen's success.

Such ambition and confidence could not be contained in a provincial town, even one as prosperous as Pergamum, and, after four years, Galen set out for Rome where he would practise medicine for most of his life. On his way there, he journeyed round the coast of Anatolia, visiting Cyprus and travelling into Syria in search of minerals he could grind up for his treatments.

---

* He must have lost some, in fact, as he 'proved' that the heart was not the seat of reason when he noticed that dying gladiators wounded in the heart were able to keep on talking.

He even encountered a camel train from India carrying *lycium barbarum* (goji berries), then, as now, used widely in Chinese medicine, which he acquired. He was typical of his time in searching out remedies of every kind, braving the roads and seas to find any recommended medicine. On the Aegean island of Lemnos, for instance, there was a type of earth that was said by Homer to cure snakebites and heal abscesses. Galen bought 20,000 medallions of it to add to his stores.* A substance was only useful in so far as it effected cures and Galen was even ready to burn his own skin to try out a remedy. He rejected as 'vile and shameful' any which he found dangerous. On his travels he talked to peasants he met, and was an eloquent witness to the poverty and degradation of agricultural life. He noted how in times of famine the cities seized any surplus food, leaving only roots for those in rural areas. Galen was always ready to treat cases he came across in the countryside, substituting local plants for those he did not have with him. He became famous throughout the eastern Mediterranean for his recommended cures even though we now know many of these to have been misguided.

Galen arrived in Rome probably in AD 161 or 162. Like many of the Greek elite, he was ambivalent about the Romans. They provided the security in which professional life could thrive but, as Lucian had shown in his satire *On Dependent Servants*, they could be hopelessly unsophisticated and condescending to the Greek visitor. Galen says little about them as a group and there is no strong evidence that he even bothered to learn Latin. The wealthy clients he sought would have been able to speak Greek and were accustomed to using Greek doctors. Rome appears in Galen's writings only as a stage set. Yet conditions in the city were appalling: there was no proper sanitation, the

---

* The 'medallions' appear to have been coin-size pellets of clay which were dug out by a priestess. Archaeologists have conducted surveys of Lemnos to ascertain where the extraction of the clay took place.

air was polluted by carbon emissions and malaria was common in the Tiber valley. Disease would have spread quickly through fleas, mosquitoes or simply, in an overcrowded city, by personal contact. The city benefitted from millions of gallons of fresh water flowing in each day by aqueduct but once it had left the fountains it quickly became contaminated. Analysis of skeletons from Rome suggests that even the upper classes may have had an average life expectancy of only twenty-five years at birth.* Marriages lasted perhaps fourteen or so years before one partner died. Remarriage was common, with children from different parents mingling together in the same household. 'Fevers', most of them probably malarial, were the most common illnesses in Rome, but Galen would be confronted by ailments of every kind.

Among all this misery, there were extraordinary buildings in the ceremonial centre of Rome: the great temple of Jupiter on the Capitoline Hill, the imperial forums around it, the Colosseum, the Circus Maximus for the chariot races and by now the palaces of the emperors on the Palatine Hill. Yet Galen does not seem to have been awed by the splendour of his surroundings or by the established doctors of the day, who bitterly resented newcomers. Early on he became involved in a case where he advocated bleeding against the advice of those who were treating the patient. His advice was not listened to, however, and the patient died coughing up blood. In the public debate that followed, Galen eloquently defended his position (as he would have been trained to do) and started to acquire clients of his own. He also benefitted from a relationship with an individual named Eudemus, a friend of his father who included Galen among his entourage. Eudemus, of course, knew some well-known doctors whom he could consult but Galen outdid

---

* Compare my previous subjects who often lived into their eighties! The archaeology from burial sites shows that the inhabitants of outlying provinces such as Britannia lived longer, often into their forties and fifties if they survived childhood.

them by successfully predicting the outbreak and course of the fevers Eudemus was suffering. The other doctors pronounced Eudemus' case beyond help but he survived – as Galen said he would – and Galen's reputation was further enhanced. He placed special emphasis on his ability to forecast the course of a fever by feeling the patient's pulse and comparing it to the normal rate.*

Eudemus' support led to an introduction to Flavius Boethus, a senator and philosopher from Palestine. Boethus provided the setting, probably in the courtyard of his opulent home, for Galen's surgical skills, which involved severing the nerves of live animals, usually pigs or goats.† He had pinpointed tiny nerves, the nerves of the larynx for instance, which he could cut and re-attach, temporarily depriving a pig of its squeal but then restoring it. This was a form of spectacle that gave specialists such as Galen the chance to show off their skills and knowledge in a manner similar to that of an orator flaunting their rhetorical prowess. The essence of the presentation was to amaze an audience. Sometimes Galen would challenge a rival physician to carry out a surgical procedure without killing an animal, relying on his superior knowledge of anatomy to avoid vital organs which his opponent would not. In a world in which crowds were used to seeing human beings ripped apart in the arena, his spectators would have been inured to the pain inflicted on the animals, but it remains horrifying to a modern audience.

Galen believed that the liver was responsible for receiving food from the stomach and turning it into blood which was then distributed through the veins. The blood then received *pneuma*, breath, or the spirit infusing human life, from the lungs and passed through the heart into the arteries. The primary purpose of the lungs was to ventilate the heart. While he could see blood

---

* Galen was obsessed with taking his patients' pulses and he wrote no fewer than seventeen texts on the phenomenon.
† This is another example of the semi-public spaces available for those displaying their skills, whether medical or rhetorical.

travelling through the heart and between veins and arteries, Galen never discovered the circulation of the blood. He made the error of assuming that blood could pass through tissue. He did, however, make important advances in understanding the importance of the brain as the control system of sensation and vision. He also noted the contractions of the stomach and the alimentary canal. These achievements have earned Galen the title of 'father of experimental physiology'.

Although he stopped his public presentations as his reputation grew, Galen continued to dissect both living and dead animals throughout his life. The dissection of human bodies was taboo in Roman culture and, as noted above, Galen chose Barbary apes as the most suitable models. He believed them to be closest to the anatomy of human beings. (Given the respect awarded to Galen as an authoritative source, confusion would arise in later centuries when the dissection of human bodies was resumed and revealed very different results from those recorded by Galen.) He describes many other animals he dissected, including elephants (their trunks he considered to be of special interest), horses, dolphins, seals and weasels. He later brought together his findings in his *On Anatomical Procedures* which would prove especially popular when it was rediscovered in the sixteenth century.

Like most Greek philosophers, Galen refused to be swayed by the lure of profit. He lambasted those doctors who came to Rome simply to make their fortunes. In such a large city they could get away with bad practice. Of course, Galen could afford not to worry about money. He would always have land in Pergamum, a house in Rome and a country villa in Campania. In his texts he posits a creative intelligence that lies behind the workings of the human body. Every part of the body has its reason for being there even if that purpose is not always apparent.* This

---

* This was the theme of a major text, *On the Usefulness of Parts*. In a later text, *On My Own Opinions*, he confesses himself agnostic on the nature of the 'intelligence'.

tied in with his emphasis on the use of logic as fundamental for understanding disease and he was typical of his time in fearing that emotions could overrule reason. While Galen accepted that sex was a pleasure to its participants – otherwise how would the human race procreate? – he was mistrustful of the intensity of the feelings it could arouse. In Galen's view, the release that sex provided should never be allowed to distort rational thought. The small number of references he makes to Christians suggest that he admired them for their emphasis on restraint and their readiness to endure death.

Galen's talent for publicity, allied to his profound knowledge of anatomy and reputation as an effective physician, soon made him famous in Rome. Yet his works show that he was always up against unscrupulous competitors. He tells of one of the best doctors in Rome who was forced to leave the city after his rivals cooked up a trumped-up case of murder. It was possibly as a result of such professional jealousies that Galen left Rome hurriedly in about 166, some five years after he had first arrived, and returned to Pergamum. It was also a time when plague had broken out in Pergamum. It had been brought back by the armies serving on the eastern frontier, and it may be that Galen felt that his priority was to minister to the afflicted in the city.*

In 168, Galen's stay in Pergamum was interrupted by a command he could not ignore. The emperor Marcus Aurelius was setting out for the northern frontiers to lead the legions stationed on the Danube against barbarian invaders. It says much for Marcus Aurelius that, while he was not a soldier, as a practising Stoic he felt it was his duty to lead by example. Once he was on campaign, he would write, significantly in Greek, his famous *Meditations*, one of the most thoughtful, if largely unoriginal, expositions of Stoic philosophy. But he was not in good health and he needed an entourage of doctors among

---

* It is thought from the records that this may have been the first global epidemic of smallpox.

whom he picked Galen. Looking after the emperor's health was an awesome responsibility. If any physical misfortune befell Marcus Aurelius, the physician in charge would be ruined.

Galen met Marcus Aurelius in the city of Aquileia, at the northern end of the Adriatic, where the emperor was planning his campaign. He persuaded Marcus not to take him further north but to allow him to remain in Aquileia to treat plague victims. Galen returned to Rome in 169 where he cared for Marcus' unstable son Commodus.* The emperor would spend the year 176 in Rome where he celebrated his triumph over the Marcomanni, Quadi and Sarmatian tribes. Galen was among his doctors at this time and appears to have cured a stomach complaint. Marcus took daily doses of theriac, an expensive concoction of over sixty ingredients, including both plants and animal flesh, originally developed to deal with snakebites but which became a cure-all for those rich enough to be able to afford it. Galen describes in detail the provenance and the exact mix of ingredients, an essential guide to the concoction that went on being used even as late as the nineteenth century. While narrative accounts of Galen's life are missing after the 170s, he seems to have had continuing contact with the families of the later emperors. He lived on into the first or second decade of the third century and there is some evidence that he may have died in Egypt, where a tomb to him is recorded. The most devastating event of Galen's later years was a fire which spread through the centre of Rome in 192 and destroyed the sole copies of a number of his texts that he had stored for safe keeping in the Temple of Peace (see earlier, p. 20).

Galen's success came largely from his careful examination of a patient's condition and from intensive interviewing of not only the patient but also his or her friends and household staff. He took into account the temperament of the individual and

---

* It was said that the only mistake that Marcus Aurelius made in his life was to allow his son to succeed him as emperor.

any event which might be a cause of anger or anxiety, including recent bereavements. He would attribute depression to an excess of black bile. He seems to have been very sensitive to the patient's mood and many of his cures were the result of his supportive bedside manner. Although he favoured certain treatments and remedies, Galen was imaginative and flexible enough to vary them when he felt the need to do so. His immense experience probably gave him an intuitive feeling of how an illness would progress. He also seems to have known – with some cancers, for instance – when it was too late to intervene. There is plausible evidence that he treated women (including – successfully – Boethus' wife) and also slaves; but his texts concentrate on his treatment of male patients. As Galen's biographer, Susan Mattern, puts it: 'The sickroom in Galen's stories is a crowded, competitive, masculine social scene.'

The legacy of Galen rested too heavily on his expertise and his surviving texts, which became canonical. About AD 500 his works were collected, and his belief in a supreme intelligence was enough for him to be accepted by both the Christian and Muslim worlds. Because of their range and critical sensitivity to earlier medical traditions, his works provide much important knowledge about Greek medicine that otherwise would have been lost.

14

The Travel Guide: Pausanias (c.AD 117–c.180)

The ancient city of Messene is one of my favourite sites in the Peloponnese. It is often deserted – there was not even a ticket kiosk the first time I visited – and from the terrace of the restaurant above the site there is a fine view of its ruins. The city was founded on an earlier, abandoned, site in 370 BC. In 371, the Theban general Epaminondas had smashed the army of the Spartans at the Battle of Leuctra, in southern Boeotia. The liberation of the people of Messenia, a distinct and fertile region of the Peloponnese, from Spartan rule had followed. Many Messenians had migrated and they now flocked back. Epaminondas exhorted them to build a strongly defended city and the Messenians constructed an impressive 9 kilometres of walls, much of which still stands. One of the road entrances to the site is through one of the original gates and other segments of walls can be spotted dotted along the ridges surrounding the city.

The fate of the Messenians was the preoccupation of Pausanias, a geographer and traveller of the second century AD. In Book IV of his *Periegesis Hellados*, or *Guide to Greece*, Pausanias provides an extensive narrative of the wars in which the Spartans subdued the Messenians. These wars took place as early as the eighth century BC and major revolts against the Spartans followed in the seventh and fifth centuries. Messenian heroes who led the fightback included King Aristodemus in the eighth century and, greatest of all, Aristomenes in the seventh who held out against the Spartans for eleven years. The Athenians naturally supported Messenian independence during the Peloponnesian War with Sparta, but it was not until the Battle of Leuctra that this was achieved. Pausanias notes that the statue of Epaminondas in his capital Thebes, in Boeotia, had an inscription that ended with the words 'Greece is free' and that the captured shields of the Spartan officers killed at Leuctra were still displayed in a sanctuary to the goddess Demeter in Thebes more than 500 years after the battle. The freedom of the Greeks – even those escaping the tyranny of other Greeks – is perhaps the most pronounced historical theme of the *Guide to Greece*.

Pausanias' hometown was the Lydian city of Magnesia ad Sipylum, at the time of his birth, *c*.AD 117, a flourishing trading centre in the Roman province of Asia in western Anatolia. He was clearly a wealthy man. While his guide confines itself to mainland Greece, he appears to have travelled more widely, across Asia, into Syria, Judaea and Egypt, where he saw the pyramids, and in Italy, where he visited Rome and the cities of Campania. It is assumed that the first book of the *Guide* was compiled by AD 160 and the complete work by 176. It is divided into ten books, each covering a specific region of central Greece or the Peloponnese. It is the most comprehensive travel guide to survive from the ancient world but was long dismissed as a pastiche composed of irrelevant material. Modern archaeologists, however, have discovered that Pausanias is usually accurate and he has proved an important aid in identifying sites and their dedications. Many of his informants appear to be local antiquarians and to be trustworthy. He mentions some 200 inscriptions and those that have been rediscovered conform to his descriptions. Scholars have become aware of the sophistication with which Pausanias planned the *Guide* as a coherent whole. He is treated with increasing respect.

As a writer, Pausanias comes across as a scholarly, conscientious, at times pedantic, guide attuned to the complex past, victories and defeats, prosperity and decay, of the sites he visited. He uses a literary *koine* with some concession to Atticisms but in many ways seems to stand apart from the other intellectuals of his day. His digressions and anecdotes and the stories he recounts remind one of Herodotus, although he has none of the clarity of narrative and style of the 'father of history'. He sometimes records monuments, as he does with the statue of Zeus at Olympia, in detail, but he never enthuses about the impression they make on him. He is an antiquarian rather than an aesthete.

While he is not primarily a historian, Pausanias is well aware of the Mycenaean foundations of the Greek past. He describes Mycenae itself, 'which led the Greeks in the Trojan war', as deserted, but he refers to 'underground chambers and the graves of Atreus, king of Mycenae, his son Agamemnon, and those who came back with Agamemnon from the Trojan war'. He briefly mentions the Lion Gate which still greets visitors when they enter the citadel. He also alludes to the surviving 'fortress wall' of the Mycenaean site of Tiryns and its enormous stones, still visible today. They were, he says, rumoured to have been erected by the Cyclops, mythical one-eyed giants of enormous strength.

Pausanias' references to Greek history peter out in the second century BC and there are few mentions of monuments later than the third century BC. The *nymphaeum* (a fountain, often monumental, dedicated to the nymphs) that Herodes Atticus had recently donated to Olympia (see p. 239) must have been imposing, but Pausanias makes no mention of it. The striking funerary monument to Philopappas of Commagene, a senator, Athenian citizen and intimate of emperors, erected on the Museum Hill in Athens c.AD 115, is referred to only as the tomb 'of a Syrian' while Hadrian's majestic library building (p. 133), completed just thirty years earlier, is dealt with in three lines. While he concentrates on the major centres of Greek civilisation,

Athens (Book I), Olympia (Books V and VI) and Delphi (Book X), Pausanias is also fascinated by obscure cults and out-of-the-way sanctuaries. The sheer variety of religious sites he describes creates an image of a Greece that is whispering with spiritual presences. At Marathon, north-east of Athens, site of the famous battle in which the Athenians threw back the invading Persian army in 490 BC, he describes how every night one can hear the whinnying of horses and the clash of arms. Tradition had it that those who come to Marathon deliberately to hear the din of battle will not prosper, but those who hear it by chance will not be harmed by the experience.

Pausanias is a man of his time in that he recognises the importance of the spiritual life: 'In matters of divinity... I shall adopt the received tradition.' He always records those gods or heroes who have founded a shrine or city he has described. For Pausanias the gods have their impact on human life. In an aside to his description of Olympia, Pausanias refers to a shipwreck from which none were likely to survive but did; he believes that 'the favour of the gods can bring relief in any conditions'. He hints that setbacks are often the result of divine displeasure – that the Spartan domination of the Peloponnese was offensive to the gods and its collapse therefore inevitable. Perhaps, he argues, the squabbling Greeks deserved to fall under Roman domination. Nor was divine displeasure visited only on Greeks. Sulla was afflicted with 'the most foul of diseases' after his brutal treatment of the Greek cities. Discussing the possibility of cutting a canal through the isthmus connecting the Peloponnese with mainland Greece, a project imagined by Herodes Atticus (and before him by Nero), he suggests that it would do 'violence to the works of God', much as Herodotus describes a similar insolence on the part of Xerxes when the Achaemenid king of kings was planning the invasion of Greece in 480. In a digression in Book VIII Pausanias admits that, originally, he had considered many of the myths to be 'rather silly', but on reflection he realises that they are often repositories of wisdom. While he is too shrewd to be taken in by many of the myths he is told – he recognises that 'those who like to listen to the miraculous are themselves apt to add to the marvel, and so they ruin the truth by mixing it with falsehood' – he appreciates the importance of spiritual tradition.

So Pausanias values sacred monuments above secular ones. His veneration of traditional religion acknowledges what he perhaps considers is the most valuable characteristic of the great age of Greece. When assessing a local cult, he respects longevity and the vitality of worship. His piety is shown in his reverence for ancient cults such as the Eleusinian mysteries and on occasions he makes his own sacrifices at shrines he visits. His accounts of the processions of citizens to outlying rural sanctuaries suggest that they remain vital to the identity of the community. And yet the leaders of such processions may have been using the role as one way of enhancing their civic status. He notes that if one city decayed and abandoned a shrine, neighbouring cities took it over, marking an expansion of their territory. He is acutely sensitive to the losses suffered by shrines when the Romans loot their sacred objects. He gives little place to imported cults such as that of Isis and Osiris and completely ignores the cult of the emperors. He complains that the 'Roman' Corinthians no longer follow the traditional cult honouring the children of Medea.*

Theban domination of Greece did not last long. Epaminondas himself was killed in battle in 362 (during another victory over Sparta and their allies at Mantinea in the Peloponnese). The defeat of the Greeks, predominantly Athenians and Thebans, by Philip of Macedon at the Battle of Chaeronea in 338 BC was, in the words of Pausanias, 'the beginning of catastrophe for the whole of Greece'. Nevertheless, there were moments of revival. In Book X Pausanias dramatises the Celtic attack on the shrine of Delphi in 279 BC. (The contrast is made with 480 BC when the oracle had vacillated in the face of the Persian invasion.) The

---

* A renewed academic interest in the spiritual landscape of Greece has been one reason why Pausanias has come into scholarly favour.

Celtic forces, whose chaotic progress across Greece saw them ravage cities as well as suffering heavy losses, eventually reached Delphi itself. Pausanias tells us that the gods of the sanctuary showed their power, reacting with thunder, snow, earthquakes and rockslides. Ancient heroes from earlier campaigns appeared to inspire the defending forces. Pausanias singles out the Aetolians as playing a key role as defenders of Greece and inscriptions tell us that they did indeed take control of the sanctuary at Delphi after the assault.

The last of the Greeks that Pausanias presents as a champion for Greek values is Philopoemen. Born in 252 BC, Philopoemen was a native of Megalopolis and held the post of *strategos*, general, of the forces of the Achaean League eight times. He was trained in philosophy and took Epaminondas as the hero on which he modelled himself. In a varied military life, he upheld the integrity of the League against rival Greek despots and so earned himself a reputation as a defender of Greek freedom. Polybius, who was said to have carried the urn of his ashes at his funeral in 182, wrote a life of Philopoemen, now lost, and Plutarch also provided one, which has survived. Pausanias must have read it as he follows Plutarch in telling the story of how Philopoemen was present at the Nemean Games when one Pylades – 'the most famous instrumental singer of his generation' – was singing an oratorio which contained the words 'Creator of freedom, the glorious ornament of Greece', at which the entire audience turned back to face Philopoemen and applauded him.

Having consolidated the Achaean League, Philopoemen faced a revolt from Messene where he was captured and died after being poisoned. 'From that time onwards Greece ceased to produce courageous men,' wrote Pausanias. He goes on to describe the Roman crushing of the Achaean League in the war of 146 BC and the end of a free Greece. Once the Greek heroes had communed with the gods and could even become gods themselves. But now, laments Pausanias, that link is broken: 'The most impious of sins, betraying one's ancestral city and its inhabitants for personal profit, was fated to begin the misfortunes of the Achaeans.' As Pausanias concludes pessimistically: 'In my day – since evil has grown to a great extent and visits every land and all the cities – not a single god arises from the ranks of mankind, except in name only and in the flattery addressed to the powerful, and for the wicked the wrath of the gods comes slowly.'

Pausanias sees the Greeks as responsible for their own downfall in that the Romans took advantage of their weakness. But he condemns the destruction of Greek cities by Roman generals: Corinth in 146 BC by Lucius Mummius, and Athens by Sulla in the 80s BC. The latter's treatment of the Athenians in 86 BC (see p. 11) was described by Pausanias as 'so brutal as to be unworthy of a Roman'. Nero desecrates Delphi by robbing it of 'five hundred different bronze images of gods and men'. Later, however, Pausanias acknowledges that the Roman rule of Greece in his day was not harsh. 'Hadrian took very good care to honour the gods and contributed very much to the happiness of each of his subjects.' The emperor Antoninus Pius, like Hadrian, was reluctant to go to war except against 'barbarians', while both emperors donated buildings to favoured cities. So while Pausanias may have reconciled himself to Roman rule (or at least the rule of 'good' emperors), he was Greek enough to define himself against 'barbarians'. He never suggests, however, that a new Aristomenes or Epaminondas will arise to restore Greece to its ancient glory and he does not extol the close relationship between Greek and Roman in the way that many of his contemporaries do.

Back in Messene, it is instructive to observe how Pausanias describes a site that is still recognisable today. He probably visited it in the 160s. The returning Messenians refused to restore their original cities as they saw them as a reminder of their defeats. The site of Messene was chosen when a dream told of a hidden chamber on Mount Ithome, where an ancient scroll hidden by Aristomenes, one of the heroes of Messenian history, was to be found. It contained a sacred text dedicated to 'the mysteries of the great gods', a cult deeply rooted in Messenian religious identity. Once the Messenians were confident that ancient curses on them had been lifted and that other good omens were present, the site was confirmed and construction began, 500 years before Pausanias' visit.

His exploration of the city itself starts with its formidable walls, which he says are comparable to those of Byzantium or Rhodes. He describes the agora, where there is a statue of Zeus and a fountain fed by waters flowing down from a spring on the neighbouring Mount Ithome. The spring still flows and the ruined fountain house, rebuilt over successive generations, is still there. Pausanias then moves on to sanctuaries dedicated to Poseidon and Aphrodite. He highlights works by a native sculptor, Damophon, who, scholars believe, was active in about 190 BC. Pausanias tells us that Damophon's reputation was such that he was called to restore the statue of Zeus by Pheidias at Olympia after it was damaged in an earthquake. His respect for Damophon is supported by inscriptions recently excavated in Messene in which other cities that have accorded him citizenship praise him for his skills and piety.

It appears that Damophon specialised in statues of gods and heroes and Pausanias records that the finest of his statues are in the Asclepium of the city of Messene. In addition to a representation of the god Asclepius himself, he tells us that the sanctuary held statues of Apollo, Heracles and a personification of the city of Thebes. A statue of Epaminondas is, unusually, made in iron. Most of these are by Damophon, except, Pausanias tells us, the statue of the Theban hero.*

The two heroes of the city are, of course, the fourth-century BC liberator Epaminondas and Aristomenes, who led the resistance

---

* In the nineteenth century excavations recovered some parts of those statues attributed by Pausanias to Damophon which are preserved in a small museum on the site.

against the Spartans in the seventh century BC. Pausanias records two statues of Epaminondas, the one in the Asclepium and another in bronze in front of an 'Altar of Sacrifices'. The bones of Aristomenes had come to rest in Rhodes, but the priestess at Delphi ordered the Messenians to repatriate them to their city, where they were enshrined in a monument surmounted by a pillar. Pausanias describes a bronze statue of the hero in the stadium, which has been partially excavated. He also hears the legend that Aristomenes appeared at the Battle of Leuctra to urge on the Theban forces. However, at Thebes itself he had heard an alternative story, according to which the oracles instructed the Thebans to place a shield of Aristomenes facing the Spartans at Leuctra and this display led to the victory. It is a good example of how Pausanias recognises that legends vary from one informant to the next.

As with many Greek cities of the period, the public spaces of Messene are characterised by an extraordinary mix of deities and local heroes. Although Pausanias does not mention them, the city was embellished in the Roman period with stoas surrounding the fountain and the Asclepium. Typically, Pausanias also highlights the myths of the region. Mount Ithome is, Pausanias tells us, named after the deity Ithome who, by tradition, washed the child Zeus in the gushing waters of the mountainside. Musical contests, the Ithomia, were once held here in honour of the god. In Pausanias' day, water was still taken up every day to the sanctuary of Zeus Ithome on the summit of the mountain. In the sanctuary, there was a statue of Zeus by the late fifth-century BC sculptor Ageladas, again brought to the city by exiled Messenians. Pausanias' accuracy in this regard is confirmed by the fact that this statue is represented on coins.

The most sustained description, stretching over two books, is Pausanias' account of Olympia. He remains the primary source for the details of the mass of temples, altars and statuary on the site and for many of the rituals of the games. At the time Pausanias was writing, the games were already more than 900

years old – the traditional date of their foundation is 776 BC
– but the lush valley was occupied well before this. Pausanias
talks of the sanctuary being open to visitors between games; its
mass of minor altars must have made it the scene of continuous
religious activity. As a sanctuary Olympia was much more than
a sporting venue and in this sense the pious Pausanias was right
to give it so much prominence in his guide. He accords Olympia
equal status with Eleusis, the scene of the ancient mysteries, as
a religious site.

Pausanias begins his description with the Alpheios river
which ran beside the sanctuary. This was the boundary which
no woman could cross during the games. Pausanias provides a
sacred foundation for the games, by Zeus. One legend records
that Zeus may have wrestled with his father Kronos here and
inaugurated the games to celebrate his victory. Heracles, son of
Zeus, was involved in the administration of the first games while
Apollo was said to have won every event that he competed in.
Passing into historical times, Pausanias accurately records the
takeover of the games by the city of Elis (471 BC) after their
victory over the neighbouring city of Pisa and their building
of the great temple to Zeus from the spoils. This was where
Pheidias later placed his famous statue of the god (see Dio
Chrysostom's speech, pp. 213–4). The vast temple dominated the
site and it was only brought down by a later earthquake which
left the columns concertina-ed around the base. Pausanias'
account of the figures and myths adorning the pediments and
the temple (the metopes on the latter contain depictions of
the labours of Heracles) bear witness to his accuracy as can be
seen by observing these sculptures in the site museum where
they are displayed. The statue of Zeus has vanished (it was said
to have been transported to Constantinople and perished in a
fire in the fifth century AD) so it is particularly valuable to have
Pausanias' description of it. The statue is embellished with gold
and ivory and every kind of precious metal. Zeus' cloak, also in
gold, is inlaid with 'animals and flowering lilies'. The throne is

particularly richly decorated and the whole so magnificent that Pausanias records that the god himself signalled his approval by a flash of lightning. He also talks of a circle of oil surrounding the statue to keep the ivory moist in the marshy atmosphere of the valley. He describes a workshop of the celebrated sculptor Pheidias that was triumphantly identified when a cup with Pheidias' name on it was found by excavators.

Olympia is crammed with monuments, altars and statues. There is also a banqueting hall where the victors were dined. One especially sacred site that Pausanias describes is the vast altar in front of the temple of Zeus, whose summit was built from the thigh bones of bulls from the sacrifices. The ashes from the sacrifices were mixed with the sacred waters of the Alpheios before being pasted on the mound. The nearby temple to Hera, the wife of Zeus, is the focus of the women's games. Every four years the women weave a cloak for the goddess' statue. In a rare moment, departing from his normal disdain for Roman monuments, Pausanias mentions Roman statues at Olympia, of the emperors Augustus, Trajan and Hadrian, and the twenty-one shields, fruits of his victory over the Achaean League, that Lucius Mummius placed on the frieze of the temple of Zeus. The reference to these 'good' emperors is understandable, but it is perhaps only for reasons of accuracy that Pausanias records the feats of a man who had destroyed the city of Corinth in 146 BC. A precinct close by these temples is dedicated to Pelops, the hero after whom the 'island of Pelops', the Peloponnese, was named.

There are many statues of Zeus in the sanctuary. Often the god is shown in a specific role, as god of war or of thunder, although a Zeus whose task it is to drive off flies from the sanctuary is not known from any other site! These statues were erected as private or public donations. As so often at these Panhellenic shrines, cities commemorate their victories, and Pausanias describes a statue of Zeus erected to celebrate the Greek victories over the Persians in 480 and 479, with a list of all the cities that took part. One particularly interesting set of statues is to be found at the entrance to the athletic stadium. These are the Zanes, statues commemorating those who have cheated at the games, placed there as a warning to competitors. Pausanias describes them as bronze statues of Zeus, each one paid for by the fines imposed for bribery or fraud and name-shaming the offender and his crime on an inscription on the base.* Without Pausanias' description it is unlikely that we would know what the bases still in place today represented. Among the forest of monuments, Pausanias describes one full-size bronze of a mare that had such an aura that stallions went wild for it and broke into the sanctuary to mount it. The attendants had to fight them off with whips.

Next Pausanias describes many of the statues erected to celebrate the victors of the games. Remarkable was one dedicated to an all-in fighter, Sostratus of Sikyon. Nicknamed 'Fingertips' for his ability to bend back the fingertips of his opponents until they surrendered, he had achieved twelve victories at the Isthmian and Nemean Games, two at the Pythian Games at Delphi and three at Olympia, the first of these at the 104th Olympiad (in 364 BC). He must have been a superstar as a similar inscription of his victories has been found by excavators at Delphi. Another victor in the all-in wrestling in the games of 408 BC, Poulydamas, was so strong that there were reports of him killing wild lions, in emulation of Heracles killing the Nemean lion. In another story he approached a herd of cattle, caught the biggest beast by the hoof and hung on until the hoof came off in his hand. Then he prevented a chariot moving despite its driver urging on its horses. His statue at Olympia listed all these feats.

There are two other descriptions that have continuing relevance today. Pausanias gives a prominent position to a cedarwood chest in which, according to legend, the future dictator of Corinth, one Kypselos, was concealed by his mother as a baby after he had been pursued by members of rival families. Following his survival, the chest was dedicated by

---

* 'Zanes' was the plural of Zeus in the local dialect.

his descendants to the shrine at Olympia. Pausanias provides a detailed description of the richly decorated reliefs on each side of the chest.* They represent a plethora of myths and inscriptions. Scholarly analysis of the depicted myths finds echoes of both Olympian and Corinthian legends which suggest that the reliefs were added when the dedication was made. Textual evidence dates the chest to the second half of the seventh century BC. Judith Barringer in her meticulous survey of Olympia argues that a Corinthian-style bronze relief of that date, depicting a griffin mother protecting her young, might have originally come from the chest.

Pausanias also mentions 'a stone statue of Hermes carrying the baby Dionysus' which he claims is by the celebrated sculptor Praxiteles (395–330 BC).† He describes it as being situated in the *cella*, the interior of the temple to Hera, where it was indeed discovered, though in a damaged state. Now displayed as an original work by Praxiteles in the Olympia Museum, the statue is of Parian marble, which has led many scholars, among them the authoritative Judith Barringer, to believe that it is the original version and dates from the late fourth century BC. Other scholars disagree, claiming that it is Greek but of a later date or even a Roman copy of the original.

Pausanias concludes his exhaustive survey of the monuments by describing some of the venues for specific competitions – including the stadium at whose far end is the starting point for races and a platform for the judges. The only woman allowed to see the games was the priestess of Demeter whose altar overlooked the stadium. It may well be that the altar that Pausanias saw was one erected for Regilla, wife of the great Athenian benefactor Herodes Atticus (see p. 235) who took on

---

* This was clearly a celebrated treasure as Dio of Prusa also mentions it.
† Dionysus was a favourite god of the Eleans who controlled the shrine at Olympia. The most celebrated sculpture by Praxiteles was the Aphrodite of Cnidus, the earliest life-size nude representation of the goddess.

the role of priestess. The stadium was fully excavated between 1958 and 1962 when the starting and finishing lines were uncovered. It has been estimated that 40,000 spectators would have crammed in to watch the athletics. Pausanias describes climbing over the mound which encloses the track to reach the arena where the chariot races took place. He mentions the ingenious device at the starting gates which prevented any of the charioteers having an advantage over their rival competitors. No trace of the track remains and it may well be that it was a temporary structure reassembled every four years.

Recently scholars have referred to Pausanias' travels as a form of pilgrimage. In so far as he was seeking out sacred sites from the Greek past there is some truth in this. However, his determination to provide a complete survey of what was, in effect, the Roman province of Achaia, suggests something more about his personality. It is important to remember that he was a member of the Greek diaspora returning to his original homeland. It may be that nostalgia for the past greatness of Greece was a significant driving force behind his narrative. It is a pity that his personality is so elusive. One wonders what local antiquarians would have felt when he wandered onto their patch and started quizzing them. Would they and his eventual readers have understood the ambition of his enterprise in a way that is now lost to us?

Interlude Three

City Life in Second-century Asia Minor: Sagalassos

In Book X of his *Guide* Pausanias stops at the city of Panopeus, located on the border of Phocis and Boeotia and not far from Chaeronea where Plutarch had his estates. Though ancient (and even mentioned in Homer), it had had an unsettled past, having been sacked several times by Greeks, Macedonians and Romans. By the time Pausanias visited he tells us that there were little more than huts remaining but Panopeus still insisted on calling itself a *polis*. Pausanias was dismissive that anyone could call a community a *polis* which had 'neither government buildings [*archeia*] nor a gymnasium, neither theatre nor agora, who do not even have a water supply feeding a fountain and who live in shelters like mountain cabins right on a ravine'.

Writing in the second century AD, Pausanias would have been used to seeing prosperous cities which possessed such buildings, even if he did not describe the most recently built ones in his *Description*. The eastern (Greek) part of the Roman empire had a much longer tradition of urbanised communities than the west, though there were reports that many, like Panopeus, had decayed considerably from their former prosperity. Even so, archaeological surveys suggest that Achaia, in the north-western Peloponnese, was one of the most urbanised regions of the empire. Well-placed positions on the now peaceful trade routes, local resources of stone, marble or clay, water and a fertile hinterland helped sustain the larger cities. The manipulation of a classical past by those seeking to attract patronage or enhance their status – 'the political uses of nostalgia' in the words of the scholar Susan Alcock – was particularly common in the second century AD.

Sagalassos, in the region of Pisidia in the province of Galatia (now south-western Turkey), offers an excellent example of a well-excavated and recorded city. The city has been expertly explored by the university of Leuven in Belgium whose archaeologists have also plotted changing patterns of land use in the surrounding countryside.* Reconstructions have even got the fountains flowing.

Sagalassos had been sacked by Alexander as he passed through in 333 BC (the battle for possession of the city is described by Arrian), but it quickly recovered. An inscription in correct Greek from the early third century BC defines Sagalassos as a *polis* with elected magistrates.† Set on rugged ground 1,500 metres above sea level, the city overlooked a fertile plain which produced surpluses of grain, olives and fruit, far more than was needed for its population, which reached 5,000 inhabitants at its peak. It also had good supplies of fresh water from the neighbouring hills. While Aphrodisias had a source of marble close by, Sagalassos had access to quarries of stone (although these were limestone rather than marble) and clay. It could embellish its monuments and created a ceramics industry. These ceramics, fine red slip tableware, were favoured by Roman veterans settled in the area

---

* One of the recent developments in archaeological studies is to include rural surveys alongside those of the civic centre in order to link the two. See the two items by Susan Alcock in the general section of the Bibliography.

† Interestingly the names recorded in funerary inscriptions of the region are native to Pisidia but they are written in Greek letters. This goes to show how Greek had become adopted by native populations in areas conquered by Alexander.

by Augustus (an estimated 60,000 of them largely from Italy and Gaul). A 'Potters' Quarter' at Sagalassos has been excavated.

Sagalassos' greatest days came after 6 BC when a new road, the Via Sebaste, built originally by Augustus to allow the legions access to unsettled mountain peoples, gave the city a direct route to the sea. Exploitation of these military roads was common. Sagalassos assumed direct control of 42 miles of the Via Sebaste and forests were cut down to create pastureland along its length. Its leading citizens soon realised the advantages that the links to the Mediterranean could bring them, not least in providing contacts with the well-established trading networks. The economy flourished: examples of the red slip tableware have been found as far afield as Carthage and Ostia, the port of Rome. And the rural population grew: sarcophagi have been found that mark where wealthy landowners were buried alongside their estates. The more successful entrepreneurs, whether landowners, merchants or patrons of building projects, became Roman citizens. Their city homes were fitted with private bathhouses and a complex system of water courses was fed by two aqueducts.

The city now began to glorify itself on its spectacular site. A promontory overlooking the plain was separated from the high ground by a crevice which was soon filled in and a colonnaded street constructed across it. The grand processional ways of Rome and Athens may have provided the model. Entry along this street and through the city gate would bring the visitor to a temple of Apollo (the god associated with Augustus) on one side and a bathhouse on the other and then into a lower agora. By the time of Trajan this was backed by a beautiful *nymphaeum*. The *nymphaeum* masked the remains of an earlier *odeion*, a smaller theatre, that may have been used for political meetings or entertainment. It is estimated that two or even three thousand spectators could have been accommodated in it. It would have been here that the art of rhetoric would have been practised either through the declamation of poetry or in the cut-throat arena of local politics. It must have been in a similar setting that Dio Chrysostom, covered in the next chapter, learned his rhetoric. A few star orators would be chosen to represent the city in disputes with neighbours or embark on a freelance career as a teacher or lawyer.

These cities distinguished those who were citizens from those who were not. In many cases citizenship was restricted to those who spoke Greek or were otherwise regarded as 'Hellenised'. It is not always clear where the division lay but orators often distinguished those who were socially privileged in some way from those who were not. The term *proteuontes* was used to describe this elite. The *proteuontes* appear to have been accorded public roles – as leaders in religious processions, for instance – even if they did not hold a formal office in the city. Since a certain level of wealth was required for the membership of the ruling councils of cities, positions on the latter were usually reserved for the *proteuontes*. A minimum of fifty councillors was needed to ensure that a city was accorded the status of a *polis* but larger cities, such as Ephesus, would have had between 400 and 500. The larger the number the greater the prestige for the city in question. From this body of councillors, officials would be elected: an *archon*, or presiding magistrate; treasurers; the *strategoi*,* responsible for keeping good order; holders of the city priesthoods; managers of grain supplies; supervisors of the gymnasium and overseers of the supply of clean water. Citizenship could be granted to outsiders, as we shall see in the case of Dio Chrysostom (see Chapter 15), on a number of different grounds: because they would give the city – or had given it – financial support; because they were distinguished, as a poet, for example; or because they would be a useful ally in negotiations with other cities or with the Roman governors.[†]

* Originally, 'generals', as in Athens, but during more peaceful times, the *strategoi* formed the local police force.
† As we have seen (p. 190), the Messenian sculptor Damophon was granted citizenship of other cities as a result of his fame and expertise.

Passing the *odeion* and the city's food market, the visitor would find themselves in the ceremonial centre of the city, the sumptuous upper agora, filled with statues of prominent citizens and benefactors. A number of columns were topped by bronze statues of those favoured, including the two citizens who had first been awarded Roman citizenship. They must have provided an incentive for future citizens to emulate their generosity. There was another opulent *nymphaeum* (whose water flow has been restored by Belgian archaeologists). One particularly striking monument, still largely intact, is a memorial building with an exquisite frieze of dancing girls. The frieze suggests that its unknown honorand, probably an aristocrat, may have introduced, or have been a patron of, a festival of Dionysus.

Roman taxation was light – one estimate is that the rate was about 10 per cent of produce – although there are accounts of richer citizens exerting pressure on the tax collectors (the *publicani*) and shifting the burden onto the poor.* Officials were normally required to contribute payments to their communities known as *leiturgia* (literally 'work for the people') and it is extraordinary how successful the requirement proved.† Plutarch noted how in the old days, before Roman rule, cities were often at war with other cities, which provided opportunities for young men to excel in war, diplomacy or the overthrow of tyrants. During the *pax Romana* there had to be alternative ambitions and the requirement of offering gifts to one's city provided one of them. Surviving epigraphs suggest that the most common donations were of public buildings, followed by the financing of festivities and then grain handouts or communal meals for the inhabitants. The wealthy Opramoas of Rhodiapolis (a city in Lycia, in what is now south-western Turkey) made a series of extraordinary philanthropic commitments. A citizen of several Lycian cities, he is recorded as having donated baths and

---

* Note the unpopularity of the tax collectors in the gospels.
† *Leiturgia* is the root of our word 'liturgy'.

theatres, funded the repair of buildings after a major earthquake in Lycia in AD 141, made distributions of food to children, and even supplied dowries for the daughters of poor families. Not surprisingly he was given special accolades, a place of honour at festivals where, decked out in a purple gown and a wreath, his benefactions were read out before the proceedings began. Damianus, an Ephesian orator of the second century AD who inherited considerable wealth from his wife, donated to the city a covered stoa, built entirely of marble, running from the centre of Ephesus to the temple of Artemis so that pilgrims could avoid the rain! He also paid for a large banqueting hall close to the temple. The memorial monument at Sagalassos must have been erected for such a benefactor.

The major patron of the early second century in Sagalassos was Titus Flavius Severianus Neon, founder of a library whose ruins have now been located and restored. Hadrian was also a patron. His reign saw the foundation of a vast temple to the emperor on the promontory, where it would have advertised the grandeur of the city to any visitor approaching it. It was finished in the reign of Hadrian's successor, Antoninus Pius, and dedicated to both men.* Hadrian accorded the city the title 'first city of Pisidia, friend and ally of the Romans' – a status Sagalassos declared proudly on its coins – and granted it an imperial cult with games and festivals. Recent excavations have uncovered a massive statue of the emperor in a new bathhouse built over the foundations of the old one.

Such public buildings and an expanding residential quarter for the new rich† in Sagalassos required new aqueducts to bring water in from the surrounding mountains. By the second

---

* One of the most prestigious magistracies in any city with a cult to the emperor was 'custodian of the temple'.
† Fine Romano-Greek examples, with mosaics and painted walls intact, have been found in Ephesus. The so-called Terrace Houses are a delight to visit and show off the opulence of the era.

century there were five of them. However, the theatre and new bathhouse were far bigger than was needed for the citizens, which suggests that the city festivals attracted large crowds. Like most prosperous Greek cities of the empire, Sagalassos possessed a stadium, though this is now in ruins. A gymnasium, with what appears a school attached to it, has also been uncovered. Only in the third century AD did the building boom peter out, but by this time every space had been filled and Sagalassos had all the attributes of any wealthy Greco-Roman city.

Visiting Sagalassos today, with its spectacular position, is an absorbing experience – its greatest days would be when a festival was being celebrated. Such occasions included the visit of a Roman governor to a city where assizes were held. Dio Chrysostom, the subject of my next chapter, described a governor's visit as 'bringing together a huge throng of people, litigants, jurors, orators, governors, attendants, slaves, pimps, muleteers, tinkers, prostitutes and craftsmen'. It was on such days that the processional ways would come into their own. Often a statue of the god to be honoured was carried through the streets, a custom adopted by Christians in the Catholic Mediterranean and still observed today. Participants would dress in white, the temples would be decorated with garlands and bands with wind instruments and drums would add to the merriment. As the dancing girls depicted on the memorial to a patron of Sagalassos suggest, dancing played a prominent part in the festivities, as did games, theatre and declamation contests. Cities competed fiercely to put on the best show. Robin Lane Fox in his survey of religious life in this period, *Pagans and Christians*, notes: 'There were prizes for every kind of virtuosity, for acrobatics, conjuring, spoken panegyrics, announcing, blowing the trumpet and "Homerism", the valiant miming of scenes from Homeric epics.' A writer named Anacharsis recorded 'the great multitude of people gathering at such festivals, theatres filling up with tens of thousands, the competitors praised, and the winner regarded as equal to the gods'. The culmination of a procession would be a sacrifice, followed by communal feasting on the meat in halls specially built for that purpose.

Orators visiting the city would exploit any public space. The most obvious arena was the city's theatre. Sophisticated methods were used to improve the acoustics of such buildings.* Today's visitors to the fourth-century BC theatre at Epidaurus in the Argolid peninsula will know how a voice can be easily projected to its highest steps. Sometimes embellishments were introduced on the stage (such as a wooden awning extending from the stage building, as at Aspendos, in southern Turkey) and within the *cavea*, the seating area, to allow greater resonance. The *odeions* were equipped with roofs to enhance the transmission of sound, although this appears to have benefitted musical performances more than it did the human voice. Herodes Atticus' *odeion* at Athens (see pp. 238–9) used expensive and exotic cedarwood (now known to absorb sound and enhance the voice) for its roof. Council chambers or *odeions* provided smaller, more intimate performance spaces, but gymnasiums were also used and grew in size during this period. Colonnades for philosophical discussion and auditoriums were often added to gymnasiums so that, while keeping their original function as exercise spaces, they would become important social centres. An example was the extravagant rebuilding of the original gymnasium at Pergamum in the first half of the second century AD. Hadrian's library in Athens appears to have had rooms for lectures.

Unlike many of its rivals (see Interlude Four, pp. 241–5), Sagalassos' prosperity survived into late antiquity. With the coming of the debilitating Persian Wars in the third and fourth centuries AD, its surplus of grain was diverted to the legions. Even an earthquake in AD 500 did not threaten its splendour

---

* The English word 'acoustics' is derived from the Greek original *akoustos*, 'audible'.

– the city was soon rebuilt and it was only the plague of the
540s* which sapped its vigour. A symbolic moment came with
the collapse of the waste collecting system. Fountains and the
stage of the *odeion* were filled with refuse, which must have made
the city unpleasant to live in. Even then the countryside was still
intensively farmed – surveys have shown that some of the valleys
had a greater population than ever before. Only after a more
destructive earthquake in about AD 620, which created a fissure
that split the theatre's auditorium, was the city abandoned.

Christianity came to Sagalassos in the fourth century; its
bishop was ranked third within the province of Pisidia. The
bishop of Sagalassos was recorded as attending the Council
of Constantinople in 381 but there is also evidence of tensions
existing between Christian and pagan communities. The defacing
of the pagan mosaic on the central floor of the Neon library and
the sacking of the library was probably – the excavators believe
– the work of Christians. The temples of the city appear to have
been gradually abandoned as new basilicas and a large building,
possibly a bishop's palace, was constructed. Sagalassos remained
the seat of a bishopric long after it had decayed as an urban
centre.

For the Greeks, the life of the *polis* had been the peak of civilised
living for generations. It is haunting to visit the abandoned cities
of south-western Turkey where the glorification of the setting is
enhanced by the prestigious buildings, fountains and colonnades
that embellished the monumental centres. I have powerful
memories of excavating one such, Knidos, during the summer
of 1968. Its great treasure was a statue, the Aphrodite of Knidos,
a life-size nude by Praxiteles, considered scandalous when it
was set up in the fourth century BC, but, inevitably, a tourist

---

* This plague, known as 'the plague of Justinian', may have started in Lower
Egypt and then, carried in grain ships, spread with devastating effect
across the Mediterranean. Constantinople was especially hard hit, with an
estimated 10,000 dying each day for four months.

attraction for centuries.* It was this sense of past glories that gave vibrancy to city life in the early centuries AD and this was treasured by its orators who dwelt on their inheritance. One of the most important is the subject of the next chapter.

* Even Hadrian had a copy of the shrine in his villa at Tivoli. The famed statue was, according to records, taken to Constantinople where it perished in a fire. However, the base of what appears to be the original shrine has been uncovered.

15

The Politician and Orator:
Dio Chrysostom (AD 40–120)

It is fitting that you should show yourselves gentle and
magnanimous toward men who are so close to you, virtually
housemates, not harsh and arrogant neighbours, since they are
men with whom you have common ties of wedlock, offspring,
civic institutions, sacrifices to the gods, festive assemblies, and
spectacles; moreover, you are educated together with them
individually, you feast with them, you entertain each other, you
spend the greater portion of your time together, you are almost
one community, one city only slightly divided. Besides, several
citizens of Prusa you have even made citizens of Apameia, you
have made them members of the Council, you have deemed
them not unworthy of becoming magistrates among you, and
you admitted them to partnership in these august privileges
which pertain to Roman citizenship.

The orator who spoke these words is Dio, a native of the
small city of Prusa (modern Bursa, in north-western Turkey),
speaking at the beginning of the second century AD. Dio was
first and foremost a public speaker, and steeped as he was in both
Platonism and Stoicism, dedicated to providing a philosophical
underpinning to the politics of the Greek cities around him.
He was not as well read or as intellectually sophisticated as his
contemporary Plutarch, but he became more involved in the

political wranglings of the cities than ever Plutarch did. His speeches, couched in a literary *koine* – this was before a return to Attic Greek became popular – are infused with the belief that mortals must act with the gods for the harmonious good of all. In this he was influenced by Stoicism. He persuaded through gentle eloquence as if, his biographer Philostratus (*c.*170–*c.*247) notes in his *Lives of the Sophists*, he was guiding an unruly horse by the bridle rather than by the whip. It is the variety of his surviving orations that impresses but scholars have difficulty in finding an underlying coherence in his beliefs. What is true is that, like many orators of his generation, he was able to shift his identity to suit the occasion. Dio is especially valued for providing a mass of background information about life in the Greek east in the early years of the second century.

In the speech quoted above, Dio was using his oratory to advocate a common community of his native Prusa with the Roman colony of Apameia on the coast.* The two cities had already had links: Prusa used Apameia as a port; the Apameians bought their timber from Prusa. There were obvious advantages for Prusa in the coming together of the two cities: consolidating access to the Mediterranean and using the status of Apameia as a colony (populated by Roman settlers) to create a more effective link to the Roman provincial governors. Yet there was little in it for Apameia, which revelled in its higher status as a colony. At the same time the conservative councillors of Prusa were hardly likely to entertain such a radical move since the change would have meant an enlargement of the city council and a threat to their prominence. Dio was imagining a broader and more ambitious status for Prusa than his fellow citizens could conceive of and, as we shall see, his position in his native city

---

* A Roman colony was established with Roman citizen settlers, often veterans discharged from the legions, and, as such, had a high status within the hierarchy of cities.

was not secure. Thus the initiative came to nothing. In a later oration Dio berates the councillors for their lack of vision and gives examples of prominent intellectuals, Pythagoras, Homer, Aristotle and the leading Stoics, who had abandoned their native cities after similar frustrations.

Dio was born in Prusa, in Bithynia, in AD 40. His mother had inherited Roman citizenship from her father, who appears to have been 'a friend of the emperor', probably Claudius, but she had married 'below' herself, wedding a native of the city who was a financier, probably a moneylender. This background left Dio in an ambiguous position: he may not have inherited his mother's Roman citizenship, for instance, and his father's modest background excluded him from the landowning social elite of the city. However, he was clearly an optimist – sociable, charismatic and ambitious – a man of boundless self-confidence. As a young man he took on several magistracies in the city after the death of his father and considered that he had been accepted by the social elite. Whether through inheritance or through his own efforts he became wealthy. In his forties, he decided to seek his fortune in Rome where, like Epictetus, he is known to have studied Stoicism with Musonius Rufus, the 'Roman Socrates', and mixed with powerful families, among them that of Nerva, a senator.

This was a troubled time for Rome. Nero had committed suicide in AD 68 after an increasingly unstable reign and his successor Vespasian (emperor 69–79) distrusted philosophers. He insisted that the heads of the four philosophical schools in Athens should be Roman citizens and that they provide a testament in Latin as to their worthiness for the post.* Vespasian's son and successor Domitian (emperor 81–96) became increasingly tyrannical and Dio found himself in trouble when one of his patrons fell out of imperial favour and

---

* These posts were for the schools of Plato, Aristotle, Stoicism and Epicureanism.

THE CHILDREN OF ATHENA

was executed. Dio was among those who were believed to have conspired with the emperor's relatives to overthrow him and he was exiled from Rome and also banned from returning to his native Bithynia. Dio remarked that Greece had now entered a 'wretched age', in the cycle of rise and decline in which the Stoics believed. In short, Dio is more ambivalent about the benefits of Roman rule than those who came after him. In a speech to the citizens of Rhodes he warns them not to be servile to their Roman rulers. Replacing the original names of their statues with those in power in Rome suggests, says Dio, that they have debased themselves. In a later oration, he casts doubt on how new emperors are chosen.*

Undeterred by his ban, Dio took the chance to travel widely, relying on his amiability and energy to survive. He tells us that he visited the oracle at Delphi for advice (which was to travel to the ends of the Earth) and he only carried two scrolls, the *Phaedo* of Plato (for Dio an inspirational text) and a speech by Demosthenes. He also sported a beard: at this time, before Hadrian popularised facial hair for Romans of an intellectual bent, it was a mark of a Greek itinerant philosopher, a recognised species which needed no other occupation.† Dio presents himself as a Cynic, a rejecter of every convention, but his accounts of his exile suggest that he was often welcomed and respected in the cities he visited. 'The men whom I met, on catching sight of me, would sometimes call me a tramp and sometimes a beggar, though some did call me a philosopher... Many would approach me and ask what my opinion was about good and evil.' He tells us that he considered such matters deeply in order to give his questioners effective answers.

Dio's most famous oration of this period, later delivered to

---

* Dio's orations were preserved as a collection later and not in chronological order. There is scholarly dispute as to the dating of individual orations.
† One way in which Domitian expressed his distaste for philosophers was to humiliate them by ordering their beards to be shaved off.

his fellow citizens in Prusa after he had returned from exile, describes a visit to the city of Borysthenes. Also known as Olbia, Borysthenes had been a trading entrepôt at the mouth of what is now the Dnieper river, running through Ukraine to the Black Sea. In the middle of the first century BC it had been destroyed by the Getae, a tribe from what is now the borderlands between Bulgaria and Romania. As a result, there was only a small remaining Greek population and even their command of Greek had deteriorated. When Dio visited the city, it was still in ruins. The Greek population was not strong enough to initiate trade and the Scythians, the 'barbarian' majority of the population, had no experience as seafarers.

Dio was met outside the city by a Greek, Callistratus, who, while dressed 'as a barbarian', told him that the local Greeks paid homage to Homer so enthusiastically that most of them knew the *Iliad* by heart. They worshipped the Homeric hero Achilles as if he was a god. So here Dio is probing the nature of 'Greekness' and he suggests that adulation of Homer seems to provide the key. Speaking to the assembled citizenry of Prusa, Dio told them his 'doctrine', which 'aims to harmonise the human race with the divine, and to embrace in a single term everything endowed with reason, finding in reason the only sure and indissoluble foundation for fellowship and justice'. He assumes that this end can only be achieved through a ruling elite, perhaps even a single ruler. The Prusan audience would have been forced to consider where they fitted within this spectrum.

Dio's attitude to Homer has been much discussed. He refers to him so often in a variety of his speeches that he clearly has detailed knowledge of the epics. There is an extraordinary story, recorded by his biographer Philostratus. Dio had been near a military camp when he heard of the assassination of Domitian in AD 96. The soldiers were restless and Dio had the confidence to confront them. He stripped off his clothes, climbed up on an altar and proceeded to declaim lines from the *Odyssey* stark naked. Using Homer he spoke so eloquently about the tyranny of the emperor, which, of course, he had suffered from, that the soldiers calmed down. However, Dio also challenges Homer. In his Oration 11, Dio even claims that the Trojan War never took place, that the Greeks never captured the city and that Homer knew this and fabricated the story of the conflict. This was a period in which other versions of the Trojan myths were being narrated – was Helen ever swept off her feet by Paris, for instance? – and Dio seems to play around with these alternatives. Did he seriously believe in any of them or was he just showing off the breadth of his knowledge, as was typical of these performance orators?

While it is not clear when precisely they were written, Dio composed several Stoic treatises. His theme is that philosophers should be independent in their views and careful not to trust even their friends; they should regard public opinion as shifting as the shadow of a man does, long at sunrise and sunset but diminished at midday. The Stoics always had difficulties in talking about wealth: most of them came from opulent backgrounds and were dependent on slaves in their households but they always denied that possessions meant anything to them. (The Roman Stoic Seneca was ridiculed by Nero for his hypocrisy in deriding wealth while being enormously wealthy.) In his Oration 7, probably composed later in his life, Dio confronts the issue. An unnamed narrator tells how he was shipwrecked on the notorious northern coast of the island of Euboea and ended up alone on the rugged shore. Here he was rescued by a hunter. Though the hunter had few goods, he had self-respect and was prepared to share his possessions with those he had rescued from shipwreck. Dio compares his life to that of someone wealthy. 'When will you find a rich man who will give the victim of a shipwreck his wife's or his daughter's purple gown or any article of clothing far cheaper than that: a mantle, for example, or a tunic, though he has thousands of them, or even a cloak from one of his slaves?' While Dio had certainly spent years 'on the road', with no apparent possessions, this oration is idealistic and its purpose disputed. Was it a veiled attack on the selfishness of the Romans? There can have been few poor hunters who genuinely lived a life as healthy and generous as the one described!

One of Dio's most telling orations concerns Charidemus, a young man whom Dio has known and admired since he was a child. In return Charidemus saw Dio as a father figure and mentor. Now Charidemus has died but Dio records his last thoughts on the nature of mortal life (presumably in Dio's words, taking the model of Socrates' dying words in Plato's *Phaedo*). There are some, Charidemus says, who see life on Earth as a prison, which the gods have designed specifically as a place of suffering. Others believe that the gods created the world as if it were a colony – allowing mortals to live in it but for the gods to take responsibility for their welfare. The third possibility is to see mortals as coming from the gods themselves and having the potential to see the best in their creation

as a gentleman who has been invited by some superior, such as a king or a prince, neglects the food and drink and pays attention to what is in the palace and enjoys this; so the reasoning visitors neglect the drinking and draughts and dice and look at the state of things within, admire the banqueting-hall in which they are reclining, try to learn how it was made, and observe everything that is in it, just as they would some fair and beautiful paintings; and they notice the management also and its orderly system, and the seasons too, observing how well and intelligently they do everything; they observe attentively all these things and alone perceive their beauty.

So Dio's advice as a philosopher is to think positively and see everything at its best.

The assassination of Domitian in AD 96 saw Dio's exile rescinded. It had lasted fourteen years. It may be now that Dio made his famous speech at the Olympic Games of that year. He relates how he has just come to Olympia from the Danube and is standing before the celebrated statue of Zeus, the patron of

THE CHILDREN OF ATHENA

the games, carved by Pheidias some five hundred years earlier.*
There are, he says, several reasons for believing in the gods. The
most basic is an innate sense that they exist, but this is reinforced
by the words of the poets and the prescriptions of the lawgivers.
To these Dio adds a fourth reason, the impact of the arts, and
he cites as an example the famous statue of Pheidias, 'that wise
and divinely-inspired creator of this awe-inspiring masterpiece
of surpassing beauty'.† Its impact is such that even the bulls on
the way to sacrifice would happily consent to their deaths. Dio
then imagines that Pheidias is present and able to talk about his
creation. 'Pheidias' takes up the theme that belief in the gods is
innate, 'yet on account of our belief in the divine all men have
a strong yearning to honour and worship the deity from close
at hand, approaching and laying hold of him with persuasion
by offering sacrifice and crowning him with garlands'. 'Pheidias'
continues to explore the nature of art. Unlike a poet who has
complete freedom to imagine a figure, the artist is constrained
not only by his subject but by the difficulty in finding materials
that are strong enough to endure but easy enough to mould.
In the case of Zeus, the god has many titles and attributes and
the statue has to give a sense of them all. 'But the most difficult
thing of all is that the sculptor must keep the very same image
in his mind continuously until he finishes his work, which often
takes many years.'

Dio was warmly received back in Prusa. He was already well
into his fifties and now only the most senior magistracies would
have suited his status. However, he claimed that during his exile

* As my chapter on Pausanias has reminded us, the Greeks were surrounded
by survivals from earlier periods of greatness.
† For Pausanias' description see above, p. 192. The geographer Strabo argued
that it was a description of Zeus in the *Iliad* which inspired Pheidias
(*Geography* 8.3.30).

what land he owned had deteriorated, and he did not have the substantial funds needed to seek public office. Nonetheless his rhetoric was appreciated – especially when he had made a speech to the city community expressing his pleasure in returning to his home. As a stop-gap in the political vacuum left by the sudden death of Domitian, Nerva, 'a philanthropic emperor who cherished me and was my long-time friend', had been made emperor and it made sense to appoint Dio as leader of a delegation to the new emperor. Dio was commissioned to plead for the enlargement of the city council, the grant of an assizes and even freedom from taxation. This last appeared hopelessly ambitious. Unlike the active support that the city of Aphrodisias had given to the Caesars, Prusa had no record of special allegiance to the emperors and was hardly powerful enough in its own right to expect such favours. Perhaps the community thought that Dio had enough prestige and rhetorical skills to succeed.

Certainly Dio's fame must have spread. On his way to Rome, he was offered an honorary citizenship of Nicomedia, the capital of his province Bithynia.* His speech of acceptance survives and tells of the rivalry between Nicomedia and nearby Nikaia (Nicaea). They had fallen out over which one of the two was 'first city' in the province. Dio laments the continuing tensions between the two cities and shows that he is a pragmatic settler of the inevitable disputes that arise when cities compete for imperial favour. This is a good example of Dio's spiritual side: he talks of the blessedness of the gods as similar to the healthy body of a mortal. Yet mortals, despite knowing how to keep healthy, neglect their bodies through the search for pleasure and they lapse into bad habits. Individuals have to conduct themselves with temperance so as to achieve unity with the gods. This is a theme to which Dio will return in his speeches on monarchy. The oration to the citizens of Nicomedia is considered Dio's most accomplished advocacy of harmonious relations.

* Dio describes the citizenship as an 'adoption', Greek *eispoietos*.

By the time Dio arrived in Rome, Nerva was dead and his adopted successor, the Spanish general Trajan, had become emperor. Trajan proved to be a model emperor, conscientious and fair, and ready to fulfil all the obligations of his office. So it was that he received the Prusan delegation (probably in Upper Germany, where Trajan was governor on his accession in AD 98) and here Dio showed his foresight. He had composed four orations on perfect kingship and it is known that Trajan listened to at least two of them.* They would become enduringly famous, so much so that they would be an inspiration to the Roman court orator, Themistius, 250 years later (see pp. 286–7).

The dominant theme of the orations is that monarchy is the best form of government but, again, the mortal earthly ruler must relate to the gods above him. Dio takes Zeus, as the father of the gods, the god of cities, of friends, of comrades and of families, as the model. Here, in the first of the orations, he introduces a Stoic view of the universe. '[The universe] journeys through infinite time continuously in infinite cycles guided by the good soul and by the justest and best rule and makes us like itself, for we are through our nature, which is common with it, marshalled by one ordinance and law and share in the same polity.' Here the heavenly and earthly worlds are locked together in a whole infused by divine providence.

Dio does not assume that Trajan is perfect, or indeed that any earthly government can be perfect. His own experience had shown him that emperors could be good or bad. The underlying assumption, however, is that it is the duty of the good ruler to act in harmony with the gods and so provide a stable government which is appropriate for the age. This is not a panegyric of the kind that would be common in later centuries when addressing

---

* Trajan's courtesy with which he listened to citizens' concerns resonated through the centuries, even to the extent that he was seen as an 'honorary' Christian by later generations. Dante, relying on a legend that Trajan had been reborn and converted to Christianity, even placed him in Paradise.

an emperor; Dio's orations are as much philosophical as political. In fact, in Dio's case it is hard to find a distinction between the two. Dio had meditated deeply on the challenges of harmonious co-existence between communities and cities, and he applied his principles to specific instances of tensions that he identified within and between cities. As an accomplished orator he was able to adapt these underlying principles of concord to the individual city or ruler he was addressing. As he was to show later in his dealings with his native Prusa and other cities, he was deeply concerned with the practical problems of politics. And Dio was prepared to act as a leading benefactor to his city – behaviour that one would be unlikely to encounter with some other-worldly philosophers.

Dio's orations seem to have paid off. Trajan clearly warmed to him (or so the self-confident Dio would claim). He achieved the grant of an extra hundred councillors (with the fees they would have to pay for admission) and the promotion of Prusa to an assize town, subject to biennial visits from the provincial governor who would hold his court there. This was the high point of Dio's political career. By AD 100 or early 101, he was back in Prusa but this time his welcome was not as warm as it had been before. Perhaps class had something to do with it, as the hostility towards him appeared to come from the landowning elite. Dio's success in enlarging the council risked undermining their status as individuals. He may also have made his fellow citizens jealous with his achievements – intimacy with an emperor was more than most provincials could boast and it may be that the ebullient Dio made too much of the connection. There are other hints in his orations that he felt his rhetorical skills demanded greater respect and this may well have alienated many. He seems to have argued that he had the status of a philosopher and therefore had the right to be listened to on account of his 'wisdom'. Many of his orations begin with a statement of self-justification with regard to his rivals, and he lays claim to divine inspiration. His comment that 'the business of the true philosopher is none other than rule over mankind' has already been noted (in Chapter 3) and at times he compares himself with Homer and Socrates. However, whatever the reason for the Prusan unease, it was put about that Dio was using his links with the emperor to mask his political ambitions and that his delegation was considered to have been a failure. Comparisons were made with rival cities, such as the much larger and more prosperous Smyrna, whose delegations had achieved more imperial favours. However much Dio argued that his welcome by Trajan had reflected great credit on the city and on himself personally as its representative, it was of no avail. His initiatives were spurned.

Much of the local opposition centred on a project to construct a colonnade along the main street of the city, an act of patronage which Dio had devised before he left for Rome. Colonnades or stoas were one of the embellishments that other leading cities of the region had added to their architecture (a wealthy city like Sagalassos added colonnades to its streets and agoras throughout the second century AD). Dio may well have been following the example of his maternal grandfather who had spent much of the family money on benefactions in Prusa. Dio had gained the approval from the local Roman governor for his colonnade but he now needed financial contributions from the citizens to complete it. His opponents tried to stop the project on the grounds that historic buildings would be destroyed. Dio reacted angrily to their opposition but his later orations suggest that the colonnade was eventually completed.

Dio presented himself as a man of wisdom with 'both the desire and ability to give advice on what is expedient for all'. He appears to have used his connections to the Roman emperors to boost his status. Among the most famous of Dio's orations were those addressed to the city of Tarsus, capital of the province of Cilicia and, to later generations, famous for being the native city of the Christian apostle Paul. The 'first' oration is relaxed and humorous. Dio goes through all the reasons why he might have been invited to address the city, whether he is more 'sweet-voiced and more pleasant of utterance than the rest', or has special powers of persuasion, or has been invited simply to shower praise on Tarsus. In fact, he tells the citizens, he has a more serious purpose, to offer them advice on how they may better conduct themselves with their neighbouring cities. Tarsus, says Dio, engages in far too many unnecessary conflicts with others, even squabbling – as he puts it – 'over an ass's shadow'. 'I ask that you behave mildly, considerately, with regard to your honour, and not in a spirit of hostility and hatred. For if you do, all men will follow your leadership willingly, with admiration and affection... whereas anyone seeing the disputes and occasions for hostility of the present time would blush for shame, for in reality they make one think of fellow-slaves quarrelling with one another over glory and pre-eminence.' On the other hand, Dio continues, they should not regard themselves as mere servants of their Roman rulers and should feel free to run their city as they wish.

There is evidence that political tensions increased in Prusa in the early second century AD to such an extent that the Roman provincial governor temporarily suspended the city assembly. The causes are unknown but there are hints that the integration of a further hundred councillors had caused difficulties. Dio's last years were unhappy ones. He continued to suffer for his reforming views and was criticised for reaching out to the local Roman governor who had alienated and exiled many prominent Bithynian Greeks. Following the death of his wife and one of his two sons, who had already started on a career on the city council, complaints were made that he had buried them too close to a statue of the emperor, so intruding on what was considered a sacred spot. He was also accused of financial irregularities. We know some details of the dispute since the local Roman governor, Pliny the Younger, was drawn into it and asked Trajan, who was still emperor, for advice. Dio reacted strongly to the accusations and his opponents failed to present evidence to the court. The case appears to have petered out. Pliny learned from this and other disputes that it was unwise for a Roman governor to become entangled in internal city politics.

As the second century progressed, cities would create the myth of *homonoia*, concord, as an ideal and even present it as a symbol on their coins. Often a public declaration of concord would be made to acknowledge the achievement of peaceful relations between two hitherto bickering cities. Since Dio, despite his failure to achieve as much as he wanted for his home city, was the most eloquent advocate of this ideal, his speeches were preserved. He is usually seen as one of the founders of the so-called Second Sophistic and is the star of the philosopher Philostratus' *Lives of the Sophists*: 'In him is compounded the noblest of all that has been most nobly expressed.' Here was an echo of the 'first' Sophistic of classical Athens which was now considered a cultural pinnacle. The Second Sophistic, a term created by Philostratus, was characterised by the high standards of rhetoric. So successful did its most prominent orators become that they felt themselves, in Philostratus' words, 'superior to entire cities, not subservient to emperors, and equal to the gods'. Their sense of their own pre-eminence rested partly on their meticulous knowledge of the Greek past. But ambiguities remained. Did these members of the Second Sophistic resemble the 'first' sophists, who were criticised by Plato as manipulating audiences for gain? The question remains open, but the undoubted emphasis of the Second Sophistic on public performance might well have blurred the boundaries between sincerity and the desire to impress with esoteric knowledge. The subjects of the next two chapters, Aelius Aristides and Herodes Atticus, present the same challenges.

16

The Rhetorician: Aelius Aristides (AD 117–81)

You have made the word 'Roman' apply not just to a city but to a universal people... no envy sets foot in your empire. You have set an example in being free from envy yourselves, by throwing open all doors and offering to qualified men the opportunity to play in turn a ruler's part no less than a subject's... The whole civilised world prays all together for the eternal duration of this empire emitting like an aulos [a double flute] one note with more perfect precision than a chorus; so beautifully is it harmonised by the leader in command... Cities glisten with radiance and charm, and the entire earth has been made beautiful like a garden... You, better than anyone else, have proved the truth of the proverb: 'The earth is everyone's mother and our common fatherland'... You constantly care for the Greeks as if they were your foster-fathers, holding your hand over them[*] and raising them up when they are down, giving freedom and self-rule to the best of them who were leaders of old, guiding the others moderately and with great consideration and care... Let us pray that all the gods and their children grant that this empire and this city flourish forever and never cease until stones float on water and trees cease to put forth shoots in spring, and that the emperor and his sons be preserved and obtain blessings for all.

[*] Cf. Plutarch's more realistic: 'The boots of the Roman soldiers are just above your head.'

So spoke Aelius Aristides in his most famous speech, an oration in praise of Rome, delivered in the city itself, probably in AD 155 after he had established his reputation as one of the finest speakers of his time.* Its words are, of course, hopelessly idealistic, but the oration is seen as the ultimate expression of Greek tolerance of Roman hegemony. Aristides stresses in particular the benefits of peace, the acceptance of all peoples within the wide boundaries of the empire, and competition between its many cities to be considered the most beautiful. In a limited way his speech expresses the Stoic ideal of a common humanity.

Aristides prided himself on his rhetoric. He was one of the first among the intellectual elite to adopt Attic Greek in his orations (see earlier, pp. 16–7) and became perhaps its finest exponent. In one oration he even imagined himself as Demosthenes: 'For me, oratory means everything, signifies everything. For I have made it my children, parents… This is my play, this is my work. In this I rejoice, this I admire, its doors I haunt.' In the same oration he describes a dream in which he shared a tomb with Alexander the Great. 'I conjectured that both of us had reached the top, he in the power of arms, I in the power of words.' Aristides saw his skills as having an ethical dimension. He believed that 'Only the best, the noblest, and those with the strongest natures' were worthy of assuming the role of orator. And their aim, he said, should be to 'save themselves and others'. The occasion of a visit by the emperor Marcus Aurelius to Smyrna, the city Aristides had adopted as his home, says much about his high opinion of himself. So deep was he in consideration of a particular problem that he could not break off his train of thought to attend his distinguished visitor.

Indeed, Aristides appears to have had a gift for avoidance, skilfully side-stepping the political demands that were inevitably made of someone of his wealth and status. He seems to have

* Some scholars prefer AD 144, the year of his first visit to Rome.

been plagued by illness, and sought the assistance of Asclepius, god of medicine, visiting his shrines regularly.* Philostratus, who greatly admired Aristides, makes clear that he could appear arrogant and remote: 'He did not discourse with the aim of pleasing the crowd and he could not control his anger against those who did not applaud his lectures.' In Aristides' own words: 'I understand oratory better than the critic and those like him and I am more capable of judging what deserves praise than a member of the audience.' In contrast to many orators whose 'party tricks' included making an impromptu speech on whatever subject was presented to them, Aristides was known for refusing to speak publicly without careful consideration in advance of exactly what he would say, an attitude which receives the support of Philostratus.

Aristides was born in Mysia, to the north-east of Pergamum, in AD 117. Hadrian is known to have visited the region in 131 or 132, and founded a city known as Hadriani. The emperor may have conferred Roman citizenship on Aristides' father, Eudaemon, a leading landowner in the area. Aristides, who would have inherited the citizenship (and so formally became Publius Aelius Aristides Theodorus), had a good education; his tutor, Alexander of Cotiaeum, also taught the young Marcus Aurelius and his adoptive brother (and co-emperor-to-be) Lucius Verus. Herodes Atticus, who we will meet in the next chapter, was also one of his tutors. Aristides' *Embassy Speech to Achilles* confirmed that he had, like most of the educated Greek elite, studied Homer in depth. His speeches reveal a considerable understanding of the Greek past. He is also seen as a master of Attic Greek. His hymn of praise to Athens, the *Panathenaicus*, delivered at the

---

* No wonder another such, the fourth-century rhetor Libanius (Chapter 22), was attracted to Aristides – they shared a passion for describing their ailments in minute detail.

city's ancient Panathenaic festival,* is infused with his profound knowledge of the city's buildings and history. As a young man he seems to have undertaken the equivalent of a Grand Tour, sailing up the Nile as far as the cataracts and returning via Rhodes, then still renowned for its teachers of rhetoric. He travelled to Rome on two occasions, an ill-fated visit in AD 144 and a more successful one in 155. At some point, while retaining his contacts in Pergamum, Aristides moved to Smyrna (modern Izmir) and grew to love the city and the estate he acquired nearby. The city assembly made several attempts to make the wealthy Aristides assume public office but he successfully resisted them. In his later years, apart from the visit to Athens to deliver his panegyric to the city, he seems to have travelled little.

The famous oration to Rome was delivered in front of the imperial family of Antoninus Pius in 155. Given the audience he was addressing, it cannot be trusted as revealing Aristides' true feelings about his overlords. Attempts have been made to find traces of ambivalence towards Rome in his other orations and in the dreams he recorded. However, he often makes the point that concord between Greek cities was achieved *as a result* of Roman hegemony. In his oration *To the Cities, On Concord*, Aristides describes the leading cities of the province of Asia, Pergamum, Smyrna and Ephesus, as equally praiseworthy. He goes back to earlier Greek history to describe the hostility between Athens and Sparta and the subsequent strife between the Greek cities which allowed Philip of Macedon to defeat them at the Battle of Chaeronea in 338 BC. In the old days, he argues, cities had distinct identities which they were anxious to defend. Now they all have temples and festivities and much else in common but have transferred their energies to quarrel over which of these is the finest. Aristides ends the oration by stressing that concord

* It is not known at which Panathenaic festival this oration, later famous as a model of Greek oratory among Byzantine intellectuals, was delivered, possibly around AD 160.

between cities is pleasing to Rome and is likely to ensure a benevolent response. Inter-city harmony will also attract the support of the gods. 'For the sake of the gods themselves and for the divine emperors let it be our wish to strive against each other in the single issue of which city is the first to initiate concord.' In his panegyric of Athens, Aristides idealises the city as a model of rectitude. Even when it has been an imperial power it has acted wisely.* The many challenges to its supremacy have not affected it. The Athenians may 'have followed the imperative of empire' but in 'generosity [they] have voluntarily dispensed with the fear of empire... For not only they thought that they must save the Greeks from their enemies, but also that they must reconcile them when they were sick with factions at home.' Athens, he concludes, provided in its era of greatness a model for the Roman empire.

Among the most compelling of Aristides' orations to cities are those to Rhodes and Smyrna. Both sets of speeches concentrate on devastating earthquakes the cities had suffered, Rhodes in AD 142 and Smyrna in AD 178. It was common in such cases for orators to describe the beauty of the original city and contrast it with its present ruined state. Two hundred years later, the rhetor Libanius would deliver a similar oration, probably modelled on Aristides' on Smyrna, after a major earthquake in Nicomedia in 358. In the second century AD the emperors were the most likely source of help so orations would be directed towards them. The orator would also gain in status from any successful appeal.

The first of Aristides' two speeches to the citizens of Rhodes, the *Rhodiakos*, was delivered soon after the earthquake. It includes an account of the previous beauty of the city ('there were avenues uninterrupted from beginning to end... and the

---

* Aristides is referring to the Athenian empire of the fifth century BC which was ostensibly created to resist any new invasion from Persia. It incorporated many of the islands of the Aegean but the contemporary historian Thucydides relates many acts of brutality in its administration.

whole city, glorious and gloriously extending in every direction'), a description of the effects of the earthquake, expressions of consolation for those affected and a promise that the ancient traditions of the city would inspire its reconstruction. Aristides highlights the extensive high walls of the citadel of Rhodes and describes the triremes and bronze beaks of ships captured in wars against the Etruscans centuries before. This was a city that lived on its military past yet an analysis of coinage from these decades suggests economic decline. Five years after the earthquake there was little sign of the successful regeneration of the city.

Aristides was not well enough to deliver his second speech, *To The Rhodians on Concord*, in person. The occasion was an approach by citizens of Rhodes who were in distress from factional fighting within the city. The *stasis*, strife, appears to have had social and economic roots as the speech alludes to the greed of the wealthy and the poverty of the masses. Aristides shares with his listeners the example of Solon, the sixth-century lawgiver of Athens who had introduced laws to relieve the suffering of those oppressed by a rich aristocratic elite. Yet Aristides was no radical. He talks of 'a natural law', promulgated by the gods themselves, 'that the inferior obey the superior'. Much of the speech offers a traditional condemnation of discord, using stories from Greek history to illustrate how civic strife has brought great cities down. Aristides then turns to the Rhodians' past achievements: the unity they displayed as their navy took on the Etruscans; their success in building a magnificent city; their deserved pride in their history. He stresses the depth of their ancestry. 'Since you are originally Dorians from the Peloponnese,' he says, 'alone to this day [you] have remained purely Greek and have had as your founders and kings the sons of Hercules and Asclepius.' Next he talks about their democratic constitution, their maintenance of freedom within the Roman empire and the threat that this freedom could be lost through unrest. By this time, in the second century AD, the democracy of Rhodes, well known in the days of Posidonius (see pp. 77–8), had atrophied in the hands of local aristocratic landowners. Even so it remained a symbol of the city's identity and, if the Romans attempted to intervene, the memory of their ancient liberties could be exploited as a means of rallying the Rhodians. This oration has been interpreted as Aristides arguing for the maintenance of the status quo, and a situation in which elite orators such as himself could thrive within the complex relationship between the Greeks and their Roman overlords.

Aristides' orations relating to Smyrna are especially interesting. Several of them are straightforward panegyrics. In his *Political Speech in Smyrna*, Aristides supplies a full survey of the city – the centre is harmonious, 'compatible with the whole in the human body'. There are gymnasia, agoras, theatres, harbours, both natural and man-made, stretching down between the ceremonial centre and the sea. This oration – a hymn of praise in which a rhetor attempts to portray his city as more beautiful than its rivals – is typical of its period. In four subsequent orations, Aristides focused on the earthquake of AD 178. The first, a *Monody for Smyrna*, is a private lament for the destroyed city. A day later, in what appears to be a letter, Aristides pleads with the emperors, now Marcus Aurelius and his son Commodus, to favour the city with their patronage and aid the rebuilding of Smyrna. He argues that, since Smyrna had emerged the victor – by an overwhelming margin – in an earlier competition to erect a temple to the cult of the emperor Tiberius, it deserves to be the recipient of imperial benevolence. Here Aristides is exploiting rhetoric to use Roman rule to the advantage of a Greek city. Reports suggest that Marcus Aurelius was deeply moved by his eloquence and his ensuing patronage accorded Aristides the status of second founder (*oikistes*) of the city. The last two orations dedicated to Smyrna celebrate the help given by both emperors and other cities of Greece to rebuild the city. So the four orations describe a trajectory from destruction, followed by recovery, to renewed glorification of a fine city.

A significant feature of Aristides' career is his attempts to secure the official status of rhetor, which would remove the requirement to take on other forms of public office. In the larger cities there were often as many as five posts for rhetors but when Aristides moved to Smyrna he was told that he had been nominated to a high priesthood in the province and when he turned this down he was offered instead a priesthood of Asclepius, his favoured god. He cunningly refused, saying he had not received a direct communication from the god instructing him to accept the post! Nevertheless it took a great deal of eloquence on Aristides' part, much buttering up of the local governor Severus, and even the support of the emperor Antoninus Pius, for the city council of Smyrna to give up. At a final hearing, Aristides played on his array of prominent supporters so successfully that he reduced the city fathers to awed submission. If he had taken up the post Aristides would have been expected to provide financial backing for building projects and to represent the city in its public dealings. Whether Aristides was stingy and didn't like the idea of having to contribute funds or simply thought such posts were beneath him is not clear. Plutarch would certainly have thought him mean-spirited.

The nature of the ailments from which Aristides suffered remains a mystery – they included both mental and physical symptoms which he describes in excruciating detail. They include intestinal problems, difficulties in breathing and what appears to have been an epileptic seizure. His contemporary Galen reported that Aristides was physically weak (even to the extent of emaciation) and worked too hard. His breakdown in health appears to have been associated with his first visit to Rome in 144, a nerve-racking experience even for a well-educated Greek, but exacerbated by the cold and rain Aristides encountered on his journey. In the spring of the following year, back in Smyrna, he believed that he was especially favoured by Asclepius and soon became a frequent visitor to the Asclepium at Pergamum, known as a gathering place for elite Greeks and Romans.*

Aristides' *Hieroi Logoi* (*Sacred Tales*) are more than just jottings. Like all of Aristides' works, they are carefully composed pieces of prose which contain detailed accounts of his dreams at the Asclepium. Since they were published by their author, they must be seen as more than private reminiscences; he understood these to be direct communications from the god himself.†
Aristides may well have used his ailments to publicise the fact that he enjoyed the god's special favour. Not surprisingly there have been a mass of psychoanalytical interpretations by scholars of his motives. Some have seen him as hypochondriacal or narcissistic. Yet in his adulation of Asclepius he was not out of the ordinary. When Aristides met the emperors Antoninus Pius and Marcus Aurelius, and explained to them that Asclepius had forbidden him to offer them the traditional kiss, his words were accepted without question by both men.

The *Sacred Tales* shed interesting light on the functioning of an Asclepium in Aristides' day. In many ways, arrangements were similar to those described at Epidaurus in the fourth century BC, some 500 years earlier: suppliants slept in the Asclepium itself in the hope of receiving a dream directly from the god. Asclepian shrines remained popular places and there are signs that the treatments offered there had become more sophisticated. There were a number of doctors on site and, while a dream message from the god always overruled their diagnoses, they could present their own opinions both before and after the god had spoken and could offer their interpretation of the dreams Asclepius transmitted to the patient. In one of his orations Aristides describes some of the remedies prescribed by

---

* The Asclepiums served a similar function to the European spa towns of the eighteenth and nineteenth centuries.

† As we have seen, Galen allowed his own empirical observations to be overruled by communications from Asclepius received in dreams.

Asclepius at Pergamum. They include long walks and sea- and river-bathing to cure colds and catarrh; for Aristides' breathing problems, Asclepius ordered him to speak and write when he was experiencing these symptoms. This appears to have been a healing community which offered a route back to good health, especially for those suffering from emotional turmoil or depression. The doctors at Pergamum became intermediaries between patients and the god in a way that had not been the case in Epidaurus where they simply carried out the god's instructions.

Aristides was always ready to advertise his favoured relationship with Asclepius. He tells us how a swelling in his abdomen was assumed to be cancerous. The Asclepium doctors reacted to his condition in various ways; their suggestions included surgery and drug treatment – and even giving up and doing nothing at all. One prognosis predicted that an infection would finish Aristides off. However, Aristides was told by Asclepius in a dream that he should allow the swelling to grow, which it did. His friends pleaded with him to follow the advice he had been given by doctors but he refused. The swelling eventually subsided – it was probably a build-up of fluid (known as oedema). So Aristides could claim that he was a recipient of the god's favour. On another occasion, when Aristides was on the Aegean island of Delos and about to set sail with companions whom he was paying to accompany him, he received a premonition that there would be a violent storm and the group decided to stay on the island and not to embark. The storm duly occurred and Aristides' companions and the crew praised him for having a relationship with the gods that enabled him to receive such warnings. Aristides was adept at using these experiences to emphasise the power of Asclepius and the fruitful relations he enjoyed with him. It was an essential part of his self-presentation as superior to others.

It is hard to pin down Aristides. His Attic style and the quality of his speeches made him a favourite of the Byzantines, which ensured that his orations were preserved for posterity. He was an expert rhetor at a time when oratorical skills were especially venerated. He grasped that reaching an accommodation with Roman power gave him his best chance of maintaining his status. To meet Aristides in person would have been challenging. He comes across as impenetrable, obsessed with his status as a rhetor and gracelessly unwilling to join the ranks of the public servants of his city who shared his background. His loyalty was primarily to his god, and his many ailments, real or imagined, gave him an excuse to communicate with him and fend off intrusions from human audiences.

17

The Politician and Philanthropist:
Herodes Atticus (AD 101–77)

The Odeion of Herodes Atticus, an orator and philanthropist, is the finest surviving building of the second century AD in Athens. A steep-sided theatre built in commemoration of his wife Regilla after her death in 160, the *odeion* was destroyed in a raid by the Germanic Heruli people in 267 (for more of whom see p. 243). Restored in the 1950s, in the modern era the *odeion* has played host to musical performers from Callas to Karajan and Pavarotti to Vangelis. Today an online search for the Odeion of Herodes Atticus is as likely to turn up a programme of summer concerts as it is to provide archaeological evidence of its original construction. Another of Herodes' benefactions to Athens was a vast stadium, equal to that at Olympia, which was restored for the revival of the Olympic Games in Athens in 1896. The most important shrines in Greece, Delphi and Olympia, benefitted from his patronage as did the cities of Sparta and Corinth. Ruins of these buildings still survive, which means Herodes has left more material evidence of his presence than any other individual explored in this book. This appears to have been his intention. His most ambitious project, never begun let alone completed, was to cut a canal through the isthmus connecting the Peloponnese with the rest of the Greek mainland. As he told a friend, this would be 'an immortal deed, and incredible in nature', but probably only achievable through the help of Poseidon, the god of the sea.

The fullest contemporary life of Herodes is by Philostratus in his *Lives of the Sophists*, written some forty to fifty years after Herodes' death but based on documents and personal reminiscences that Philostratus, who sets himself up as an arbiter of who qualifies as a member of this scholarly elite, had accumulated. Originally the family wealth may have come from estates in the fertile countryside of Marathon, scene of the great Athenian victory over the Persians in 490 BC. For generations leading members of the family were involved in the politics of Athens. They obtained Roman citizenship in the first century AD (so adding Tiberius Claudius to their names), built up personal relationships with the emperors and participated as priests in the imperial cults. Yet there were often setbacks. Herodes' grandfather, Hipparchus, was accused of 'tyranny', probably by Domitian who targeted wealthy Roman citizens, and vanishes from the record – possibly he was executed for whatever 'crime' he had committed. Herodes' father, known as Atticus, was apparently impoverished until a vast treasure was found on one of his estates. (It may have been family money shrewdly concealed during the reign of Domitian.) Atticus married well, to his niece, Vibullia Alkia, who was also wealthy and had family connections with Sparta and Corinth. Herodes, born at Marathon in AD 101, was their only surviving son, so he enjoyed a rich inheritance.

Naturally Herodes was given the very best education, first in Athens, where he became absorbed in Platonic studies and rhetoric, and then in Rome, where he went to participate in imperial politics. His father had been the first known Greek to have been a consul suffect (see footnote on p. 145), probably in 108, so it was family tradition which enabled Herodes to gain several magistracies in the city. This proved a stepping-stone to membership of the Senate. He remained close to the imperial family – as has already been seen, Hadrian warmed to wealthy and sophisticated members of the Greek elite – and in 134 he was appointed a corrector of the free cities of Asia Minor by the emperor. This gave him oversight of the judicial and financial affairs of the coastal cities in Asia Minor. Herodes' preferment soon aroused jealousies. Rumours circulated that he had been involved in a scuffle with the proconsul of the province of Asia, Antoninus Pius, later to succeed Hadrian as emperor, when their entourages met in a narrow defile. Then, in his first act of patronage, he persuaded Hadrian to provide three million drachmas to build an aqueduct for the thriving port of Alexandria Troas. The project went over budget by four million drachmas, which Herodes' father Atticus generously agreed to pay, but other officials complained over the way that a single project in the province had consumed so many resources.

Meanwhile Herodes had been perfecting his rhetorical skills. In Rome he had built up a close friendship with the celebrated sophist and Sceptic Favorinus who became his mentor and left Herodes his house and library when he died. In Asia he attended the lectures of Polemon, an intimate of Hadrian and a major political figure in Smyrna, whom Herodes believed was the finest rhetor in the city (see p. 135). When his term of office as corrector was completed, he returned to Athens to teach rhetoric but also was made president of Hadrian's Panhellenion. However, his clumsy handling of his inheritance was soon to infuriate the Athenians. When Atticus died in 138, it was found that he had left a sum to every Athenian citizen, a legacy that would have diminished Herodes' capital. The story went that Atticus felt that Herodes had been cruel to his slaves and freedmen and this was some form of compensation. Herodes challenged the will and dug up records of debts that citizens owed to his family and insisted that they be paid. This behaviour of a man flaunting his wealth and abusing the generosity of a father would damage his reputation among the Athenians for ever. Herodes was also becoming known for emotional outbursts, unseemly behaviour for a Greek aristocrat.

Perhaps not surprisingly, Herodes soon left for Rome, where once again his relationship with the imperial family of the day prospered. He became a teacher of rhetoric to Marcus Aurelius and Lucius Verus, who were the adopted sons of Antoninus Pius and destined to succeed him as emperor. Marcus was about twenty when Herodes arrived in 141. He stayed there for five years, becoming *consul ordinarius*, the consul who started the new year and thus had greater prestige than the consul suffect, in 143. At much the same time, Herodes found a wealthy and well-connected wife, Regilla, who brought with her an estate on the Appian Way and a villa at Canusium in southern Italy. Still a teenager, she found herself married to a man who was over forty. Herodes was acting more as a Roman grandee than a philosopher but had gained the affection of the young Marcus Aurelius, which would stand him in good stead when further troubles came his way.

The couple moved back to Athens in 146 but Regilla died in 160. Again, rumours abounded, that Herodes had paid a freedman to kick his wife when she was pregnant, but a case brought against him in Rome by her brother was dismissed. By now Marcus Aurelius and his brother Lucius Verus were emperors but it was increasingly a troubled period. Herodes suffered his own tragedies as his favourite daughter, Elpinike,* and three adopted sons all died around this time. In Athens, he found himself embroiled in a dispute with the Quintilii family, who held office in the Greek provinces. According to Philostratus, they fell out with Herodes owing to a disagreement over the musical events at the Pythian Games at Delphi. The Quintilii, siding with discontented Athenians, brought an accusation of 'tyranny' against Herodes. When the case came before Marcus

---

* Elpinike, after whom his daughter was named, was an Athenian noblewoman who had many connections to the political elite of the city in the mid-fifth century BC.

Aurelius in Sirmium, the provincial capital of Pannonia, in 174, Herodes did not help himself by losing his temper and insulting the emperor. Marcus, steeped in Stoicism and remembering their close relationship from thirty years earlier, refused to condemn him. Nonetheless the humiliated Herodes moved to Orikos on the coast of Epirus, whose decaying port he is said to have refounded. An *odeion* found by archaeologists and dating from this period may be one of his benefactions to the city.

A letter to the Athenians from Marcus Aurelius survives, pleading for Herodes 'with his famous zeal for education and culture' to be welcomed back to Athens 'to share the good cheer at their religious and secular festivities'. Herodes duly returned to the city and met with the emperor during his visit to Athens in 176, on which occasion Marcus Aurelius renewed their friendship by asking Herodes to help nominate candidates for four posts in philosophy in the city. Now in his seventies, Herodes chose to retire from public life and retreated to his villas near Athens and Marathon. The grammarian Aulus Gellius describes the pleasures of life in the Athenian villa: 'Both in the summer and under the extremely warm autumnal sun, we shielded ourselves from the trying heat thanks to the shade of the ample groves, with their long, gentle promenades, as well as the cool situation of the house, with its elegant baths and abundance of sparkling water...' Here Herodes welcomed young men who wished to receive instruction. After an open lecture he would ask ten of his most erudite students to dine with him. Choosing a small number of compatible students for intense tutorship was common practice among the teachers of philosophy and rhetoric. Herodes' inner circle was known as the Klepsydrion ('the Waterclock Club'), a high-level intellectual discussion group.[*]

---

[*] The Greek *klepsydrion* means literally the stealer of water, hence a waterclock. The name may have been chosen as Herodes may have limited the time for discussion.

Very little of Herodes' rhetoric survives. Some of its subjects are known, however – two orations on the Peloponnesian War and one *On the Constitution*, which discusses the relationship between Sparta and Macedon. It is clear that, like many intellectuals of his time, he knew the history of the Greek past and the language of the First Sophistic so intimately that some classical scholars were misled into believing that *On the Constitution* was composed in the fifth century BC. (Like Aristides, Herodes had a passion for writing in Attic.) According to Philostratus, who had access to sources now lost, Herodes spoke steadily, with clear diction, and showed individuality in his choice of examples. His tone was not aggressive but relied more on subtlety and restraint. Philostratus concluded that 'his type of eloquence is like gold dust shining beneath the waters of a silvery eddying river'. Unlike Aristides he could speak without preparation and had a fund of knowledge from which he could provide examples. To Philostratus he was one of the very best of all rhetoricians.

Philostratus also records the impulses that fuelled Herodes' patronage. He regarded his accumulated capital as 'dead money' which could otherwise be used for the benefit of the people of the cities to which he gave his support. He felt it was his duty to relieve need and prevent individuals from sliding into poverty. One could argue, albeit generously, that his demand for repayment of debts from the Athenians was triggered by a wish to divert his resources to the city as a whole. In breaking with his father's policy of giving cash handouts, Herodes is closer to the example set by the emperor Hadrian of donating buildings to the community rather than money. A building that advertised his presence was for Herodes more satisfying than the adulation of Athens' citizens. But the donation of buildings was, for Hadrian and Herodes, about something more than ensuring their legacy. Both men realised the value of providing fresh water to a city – aqueducts, baths and *nymphaea* provided pragmatic solutions to cities that had outgrown their supplies.

Wells at Alexandria Troas, for instance, were only bringing up muddy water before Herodes gave the city a new aqueduct. In Athens, however, it may be that the citizens felt their city was a sacred space in which new buildings were an intrusion; hence there was a conflict between their feelings of civic pride and the interventions of a wealthy man determined to leave his mark on the city come what may.

The first of Herodes' donations to Athens was his stadium, announced at the Greater Panathenaea in AD 140 and completed for the next festival four years later. Despite its size – it was 204 metres long and 33 metres wide, with seats provided along the natural slopes of hills – Herodes' Panathenaic stadium was a simple building without the elaborate decoration that was common on the Asian mainland. The marble it was built from came from the quarries on Mount Pentelikon that had supplied the marble for the Parthenon 600 years earlier. Herodes had indicated that he wished to be buried at his estate at Marathon, but according to Philostratus, the people of Athens, having forgotten their previous hostility, insisted that he be buried within his Panathenaic stadium when he died in 177. A funeral oration by one of his pupils, Hadrian of Tyre, moved the audience to tears.*

By far the most spectacular of Herodes' donations to Athens was the *odeion*, built on the south-western slopes of the Acropolis. It is recorded as having been a memorial to Regilla and thus dated to after her death in 160. It was huge for an *odeion*, large enough to seat 4,800 spectators and opulently fitted out with a magnificent cedarwood roof. *Odeions* were primarily built to

---

* Tradition records that foundation stones close by the stadium are Herodes' tomb. Much of the original structure of the stadium was lost over the centuries and then overlaid by the reconstructions for the revived Olympic Games of 1896.

hold musical and poetry competitions, and a roof, especially one made of cedarwood, improved acoustics. The Odeion of Herodes Atticus had a large *scena*, the building's structural backdrop, some 28 metres high, which would have been richly decorated and with statues attached. At some point, apparently after it had been abandoned as a meeting place, a devastating fire spread through the building, exploding the marble in the intense heat and bringing down the roof. This may have been part of the destruction inflicted by the Heruli.

Almost as spectacular as the *odeion* was the *nymphaeum* donated to the sanctuary at Olympia by Herodes and Regilla when she was still alive (it is provisionally dated to the early 150s, when it was ridiculed by Lucian's Peregrinus; see pp. 168–9). An inscription on a stone bull reading 'Regilla, priestess of Demeter, dedicated the water and the things around the water to Zeus' confirms the attribution. Two basins were set one above the other on the slopes of Mount Kronos. It is a mystery as to why Pausanias does not mention what must have been an imposing structure, though his preference for older Greek architecture may have been the reason. The upper basin, which was semi-circular, was surrounded by statues, divided between Herodes' family and the imperial family. Zeus presides over them both. [*]
To keep the water moving an aqueduct a kilometre long was constructed to bring water from the Kladeios river, a tributary of the Alpheios river, to a tank behind the upper basin. From here it flowed through a lion-head spout into the basin and was then transferred by similar spouts to the rectangular lower basin, and then into a trough from which it was distributed to other parts of the sanctuary. The donation of the *nymphaeum* at Olympia was obviously a matter of family pride as Herodes' son-in-law and his family kept it repaired.

[*] There has been intense scholarly discussion over the placing of the statues. See the authoritative survey by Judith Barringer in her *Olympia: A Cultural History*, pp. 220–5.

★

How best to sum up Herodes? Brilliant, committed in his patronage, but flawed in character, he often let his emotions get the better of him at a time when a Stoic attitude was expected. Accounts describe how, when his wife and daughter died, philosophers were called in to moderate his outpourings of grief. Yet he also had some insight into his emotions. Aulus Gellius recounts a story in which Herodes, when told by a Stoic that he should rise above his feelings, replied that impulses of the mind also contain useful qualities that should not be repressed. Herodes also complained to Gellius that Stoics had a tendency to suppress their emotions so completely that their minds became lethargic. It is from odd recorded snippets such as these that one can begin to gain insights into a complex character. But perhaps the most important evidence for Herodes' character comes in the form of the monuments he erected to commemorate his dead wife and children. Their statues are known to have graced the opulent *nymphaeum* at Olympia and their inscribed bases have been found in Delphi. These traces of the life of Herodes Atticus suggest a private man who used his patronage for a public display of his feelings for those close to him.

Interlude Four

The Clouds Darken: The Greek World in an Age of Crisis

We are being harassed to the extent of the unaccountable and extorted by those who ought to be protecting the public. Living in the open countryside and not near military camps we nevertheless suffer affliction alien to the golden age of your reign. Traversing the territory of the Appians and leaving the main roads, soldiers, leading men from the town of Appia, and your agents are coming to us and are leaving the main roads and they are taking us away from our work, requisitioning our draft animals and extorting that to which they have no right.

As this contemporary document from Anatolia attests, at the beginning of the third century the peace and prosperity of the Greek world was suddenly threatened.[*] The sequence of benign emperors, Nerva, Trajan, Hadrian, Antoninus Pius, Marcus Aurelius, was broken by Commodus, the dissolute son of Marcus Aurelius.[†] Following Commodus' assassination in

---

[*] It is also remarkable for stressing rights that were expected to be protected by the authorities.
[†] 'If a man were called upon to fix that period in the history of the world during which the condition of the human race was most happy and prosperous, he would, without hesitation, name that which elapsed from the deaths of Domitian to the accession of Commodus.' Edward Gibbon, *The History of the Decline and Fall of the Roman Empire* (1776–88).

192, civil war broke out and a period of unrest ensued which saw no fewer than five men claim the title of emperor. Septimius Severus defeated his rivals to become emperor in 193, initiating the Severan dynasty, which would hold power until 235. There had been other earlier events that disturbed the peace. One of the orations of Aelius Aristides laments a mysterious raid by the 'Costoboci' on the shrine of Eleusis in 170. In the east, the continued threat of the Parthians required imperial armies under Marcus Aurelius' co-emperor Lucius Verus to confront them and regain control but it was at a dreadful price as the armies brought back smallpox with them which spread throughout Anatolia.

After the assassination of Commodus, the governor of Syria, Pescennius Niger, challenged Septimius Severus, who had proclaimed himself as emperor with support from the legions of the west. Niger chose as his 'capital' the ancient Greek city of Byzantium, later Constantinople, which was brutally sacked by Severus after a three-year siege. Niger, having escaped and crisscrossed Asia Minor with diminishing resources, was finally hunted down and killed, but not before the cities of western Anatolia had been dragged into supporting one or other of the imperial contenders. Severus punished the opposing cities, including the major city of Antioch in Syria, reducing them to the status of villages or depriving them of their right to hold games. In the ensuing Parthian Wars, Severus and his successor, his son Caracalla, held off the Parthians, but the passage of the Roman armies to and from the eastern frontier – as the opening quotation suggests – brought significant disruption to everyday life.

Worse was to come. The death of the final emperor of the Severan dynasty, Severus Alexander, in 235, brought further serious instability, with competing emperors and renewed pressures on the borders. The fatal flaws in the structure of the empire had been exposed – it could not fight off several threats at the same time and victories, when they came, encouraged the lucky generals to become usurpers. The so-called crisis of the third century had begun. Over the next fifty years, eighteen emperors claimed some form of legitimacy. Infighting consumed resources that were desperately needed elsewhere. In Persia, the exhausted Parthians had been replaced by a new, aggressive dynasty, the Sassanids, a much more formidable enemy. In 252 the Persians ravaged the province of Syria and sacked Antioch, one of the great cities of the eastern empire. In 260, the emperor himself, Valerian, was captured and humiliated by the Sassanid king, Shapur.

From the northern borders of the empire waves of barbarian tribes fought their way into its eastern provinces and ravaged the prosperous cities of the western Mediterranean. Even the great temple to Artemis at Ephesus suffered damage. The library of Alexandria and scholars attached to it are not recorded after the 260s. In 267, a hitherto unknown people, the Heruli, enjoyed a year of pirating in the northern Aegean and the Peloponnese before reaching Athens and sacking the western parts of the city. Ruined buildings were scavenged to build a new defensive wall (which can still be seen in the agora). It is around this time that there is the earliest mention of the word Goths to describe a loose amalgamation of Germanic invaders brought together as much by the lure of plunder as by ethnicity. In the province of Bithynia, the cities of Nicomedia, Nicaea, Apameia and Prusa were pillaged.

The situation deteriorated further in the 270s. An exchange of letters between two bishops describes 'those [Christians] who have been enrolled among the barbarians and have accompanied them in their irruption in a state of captivity, and who forgetting that they were from Pontus, and Christians, have become thorough barbarians, as even to put those of their own race to death by the gibbet or strangulation'. In 271 the emperor Aurelian abandoned the Roman province of Dacia, conquered a 150 years before by Trajan. The year before, the remarkable Zenobia, queen of the opulent trading city of Palmyra, exploited the weakness of the Romans to capture much of the east including Egypt. Alexandria fell to her in 270. It would take Aurelian until 272 to defeat her.

While traditional education survived – Plotinus, the subject of my next chapter, saw himself as sustaining the Platonic tradition – the economy and stability which had supported it were threatened. A period of hyperinflation under Aurelian triggered the collapse of the monetary system in the Greek east in 275. Orators could no longer travel freely for research or make speeches before city audiences. Inevitably relationships between the elite and the emperors fragmented, as can be seen from the surviving rescripts, the answers emperors gave to their subjects. Two hundred and forty of these are extant from the six years of the reign of Caracalla (211–17), but only eight for the emperors ruling between 268 and 275.

The cities had provided lifeblood for the elite, but in an economy based largely on agricultural productivity they were vulnerable to economic downturn. The fourth century would see the emergence of great villa estates as the wealthy took their resources elsewhere. It became increasingly difficult to find individuals who could afford to serve on town councils. In the 360s the orator Libanius talks of the councils as 'like so many old women, wrinkled, half dead, all rags'. New building ceased. The great aristocratic families of Athens, such as Herodes Atticus', faded from the record and do not seem to have had the resources to rebuild the city after its sack by the Heruli. There is evidence that after the sack philosophers taught in their homes rather than in the grand *odeions* of the city. There are no donations of monuments to Olympia after 270. The imposition of more effective tax collection by Diocletian after 284 ate further into resources.

Yet Diocletian (emperor 284–306) was successful in bringing the disorder to an end. His tax reforms, division of provinces to make them more effective and splitting of the administration between co-emperors, one ruling in the west and one in the east, brought stability to the empire which his successor Constantine was to exploit.

One development which was perhaps inevitable in such a troubled time was a fear that the traditional gods of the empire were deserting it. Imperial decrees insisted that everyone should be seen to be offering sacrifices. This caught out not only recalcitrant pagans but also Christians: Diocletian launched widespread persecution of Christians in the early 300s. Nicomedia in Bithynia, where a church was razed, scriptures burned and individual Christians executed, was one focus of the emperor's religious purges.

The rise of Christianity was an important feature of this period even if Christian theology remained inchoate. Its story can be told through three leading figures of the age: Plotinus, who provided much of the philosophical background which would shape the theology of Augustine and hence medieval Christianity, and the theologians Clement of Alexandria and Origen, whose Christianity cannot be understood without closely examining their background in traditional philosophy. Owing to his influence, I have chosen to deal with Plotinus first, even though chronologically he is later than the other two.

18

The Philosopher: Plotinus (c.AD 205–70)

Plotinus was modest enough to suggest he was simply bringing together the many strands of the Platonic tradition established by the great philosopher 600 years earlier. He considered himself to be the heir of a living philosophical culture, the authority of whose earlier commentators had not been superseded. However, in his reformulation of Platonism, which was termed Neoplatonism in the nineteenth century, Plotinus was the last great philosopher of antiquity but also, thanks to his influence over later generations, the first philosopher of the Middle Ages. His influence was predominant among the Platonist teachers of Athens until their school was closed down in 529, passed into Judaism and Islam and reached Augustine in north Africa (if only through weak Latin translations of the Greek originals) to infuse Western theology. His greatness lies in his endless probing to achieve a philosophy of coherent simplicity, one in which the philosopher did not display arrogance but remained humble before the complexities of explaining the material and immaterial cosmos.

Plotinus was born in Egypt, in the Greco-Roman city of Lycopolis (modern Asyut), in AD 204 or 205. By his late twenties he was studying in Alexandria. Nothing is known of his life before then but he must have acquired a good knowledge of the philosophical schools. Now he wanted to go further. Having first been disappointed by his teachers, he was referred to one Ammonius Saccas who, though little is now known about him, had an excellent reputation in his time. In the fluid spiritual world of the period, Ammonius had turned his back on Christianity to concentrate on Platonism but was ready to include both Christians and pagans in his circle as was often the case in the Alexandrian schools.* While Plato remained the core of his studies, his student Porphyry tells us in his *Life of Plotinus* that 'he followed his own path rather than that of tradition, but in his writings both the Stoic and Peripatetic doctrines are sunk; Aristotle's *Metaphysics*, especially, is condensed in them, all but entire'. Porphyry also tells us that Plotinus 'had a thorough theoretical knowledge of Geometry, Mechanics, Optics and Music'. Among the Platonic dialogues, he warmed in particular to the *Timaeus*, as had Plutarch (see earlier, p. 115).

In this period, Plato and Aristotle were not seen as incompatible. It was thought that Aristotle had known Plato well, that he could aid understanding of parts of Plato's philosophy and fill in gaps in Plato's works. Porphyry, a serious philosopher in his own right, wrote a treatise entitled *That the Schools of Plato and Aristotle Are Only One*. Plotinus also became aware of the rich philosophical traditions of India and Persia. When the Roman emperor Gordian III assembled an army to invade Sassanid Persia in 243, Plotinus managed to attach himself to the expedition in the hope of studying Persian philosophy at first hand. However, Gordian was assassinated after a defeat by the Persians† and the campaign was aborted. Plotinus had to struggle back to Antioch. In 245 he moved to Rome and he stayed there teaching until his death in 270.

---

* As we shall see, the Christian Origen was among Ammonius' pupils and the philosopher Hypatia was still following this tradition 150 years later.
† The sources are unclear. Some scholars believe he was killed in a battle with the Persians who had repulsed the Roman invaders.

In the *Life of Plotinus*, Porphyry paints a vivid picture of Plotinus. He relates how the god Apollo was once consulted over his character and the reply came back: 'Sleeplessly alert, pure of soul, ever striving towards the divine which he loved with all his being, he laboured strenuously to free himself and rise above the bitter waves of this blood-drenched life.' In short, Plotinus was other-worldly, 'ashamed at being in his body', reluctant to talk about personal matters and not interested in any statue or portrait of himself. At times he would become so withdrawn that he appeared lost in a mystical trance. He was a vegetarian. 'He refused such medicaments as contain any substance taken from wild beasts or reptiles; all the more, he remarked, since he could not approve of eating the flesh of animals reared for the table.' He radiated benignity, and many, women as much as men, were attracted to him both as a philosopher and as the future guardian of their children in the event of their deaths. Plotinus was a man of the highest integrity; he supervised scrupulously the money left to each of these charges. He had, it goes without saying, an excellent mind. While he was concentrating on composing a treatise, he could be interrupted to discuss other matters without losing the thread of what he was writing. He went straight to the heart of any philosophical problem presented to him.

As a teacher, he welcomed all opinions and questions, 'a liberty [according to the austere Porphyry] which led to a great deal of wandering and futile talk'. He was at ease with his community. On those occasions when he was a target of insolence he took it calmly and did not retaliate. Even his opponents recognised his greatness of soul. He also had an intuitive grasp of character. Once, when Porphyry was so distressed that he was considering suicide, Plotinus saw the state that he was in, grasped that it was the result of melancholy rather than a rational response and encouraged Porphyry to take a break in Sicily, which did indeed restore him.

1. The Oxyrhynchus rubbish dump (Egypt) has been a fertile source for ancient texts. This fragment is from Homer's *Iliad*.

2. The spectacular library and mausoleum built in Ephesus in memory of the provincial governor Celsus by his son, *c.* AD 135. It formed an elegant backdrop to a street.

3. Busts of philosophers and orators were common in public places, not least among them Plato whose *Dialogues* everyone knew.

4. The historian Polybius: a monument in honour of his support for the Greeks of the Peloponnese in their final settlement with Rome, *c.* 145 BC.

5. Part of the extraordinary text (*c.* AD 120) by Diogenes of Oenoanda (Asia Minor), which summarises the philosophy of Epicurus in 25,000 words.

6. The remarkable first-century AD Sebasteion of Aphrodisias, a Greek monument honouring the coming of Roman imperial rule and a symbol of the harmony between the two cultures.

7. An inscription found at Delphi, possibly a statue base, in which the communities of Delphi and Chaeronea honour Plutarch. (His name comes at the beginning of the second line.)

8. Dioscorides receiving a mandrake root, from the frontispiece of the famous sixth-century copy of *De materia medica*, now in the Imperial Library in Vienna.

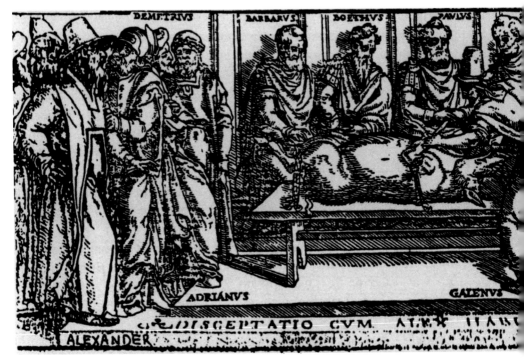

9. A sixteenth-century print of Galen dissecting the nerves of a pig, so demonstrating that the brain, rather than the heart, was the seat of speech.

10. The stadium at Messene in the western Peloponnese. Pausanias' survey shows his adulation of the struggle for Greek freedoms.

12. A statue of the orator Aelius Aristides, a statue now in the Vatican Museums.

11. The magnificent setting of the Greek city of Sagalassos which reached the height of its prosperity in the second century AD. This is the grand entrance to the city.

13. The Roman part of Pergamum was embellished at the beginning of the second century AD under the patronage of the emperors Trajan and Hadrian. A date for the expansion of the Asclepium is usually put about the 120s. It then became a centre for the elite, rather like a spa in the nineteenth century.

14. The Odeion built in Athens by Herodes Atticus in the middle of the second century AD, and still in use today.

15. A neo-classical imagining of Hypatia teaching by Robert Trewick Bone (1790–1840). A typical school of the period would have been far less raucous!

16. A surviving fragment of Origen's *Hexapla* which compares versions of the Greek Old Testament from the early third century AD. One of the great feats of textual analysis.

17. A sixteenth-century rendering of Ptolemy's Earth-centred universe, with his ordering of planets around the Earth, and Heaven beyond the circle of stars.

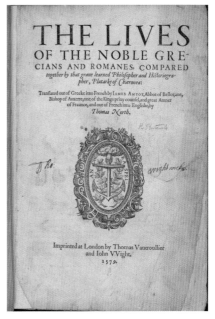

18. A page showing the European bramble from the sixth-century edition of Dioscorides' *De materia medica*. The text is in the original Greek but with later added words in Arabic (upper right).

19. The translation of Plutarch's *Lives* (1579) by Sir Thomas North was used by Shakespeare as a source for his play *Antony and Cleopatra*.

20. Ptolemy's *Geographike* was first printed as a map in the twelfth century in Sicily. This 1482 edition was published just before the European discovery of the Americas.

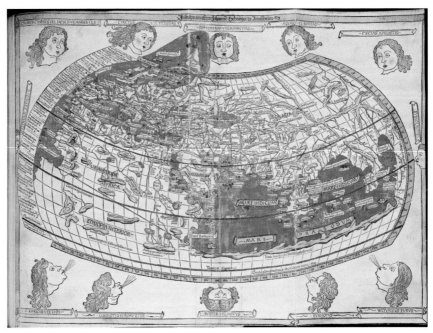

However, Porphyry's most important contribution to philosophy was to assemble Plotinus' teachings in an ordered form, the *Enneads*. Porphyry tells us that Plotinus would never reread what he had written: his eyesight was limited, his writing slovenly, his spelling poor – all he cared about was ideas. So he entrusted Porphyry with putting together his papers and editing his writings. Porphyry divided Plotinus' work into six treatises, each containing nine (*ennead*, 'a group of nine') titled subjects. The divisions he imposed were somewhat arbitrary, but Porphyry's editorial labours ensured that a full exposition of Plotinus' philosophy has come down to us.

And it is a highly complex philosophy. Much of the *Enneads* takes the form of responses to Plotinus' opponents. Crucially, the assembled works recognise the growing importance of a single entity, 'the One' – a development from Plato's hierarchy of Forms or Ideas. In fact, the concept of 'the One' can be taken back even further in the history of Greek philosophy to the pre-Socratic Parmenides (writing *c.*475 BC but the subject of a dialogue by Plato which Plotinus admired) who argued, in one of the earliest pieces of sustained reasoning that survives, that all reality was one, changeless and beyond time. Plato had elaborated this, notably in his influential *Republic*, to place 'the Good' at the summit of the hierarchy of knowledge. 'Below' it are the Forms or Ideas, perfect expressions of, say, Justice or Beauty which, though immaterial, can be grasped by the reasoning mind. Plotinus takes the concept even further. He places unity above diversity, harmony above disharmony. As he describes 'the One', or 'the Unity', in the *Enneads*: 'The Unity was never in any other... it is great beyond anything, great not in extension but in power, sizeless by its very greatness... We must therefore take the Unity as infinite not in measureless extension or in numerable quantity but in fathomless depths of power.' It cannot be fully known by the human mind. 'We do not grasp it by knowledge, but that does not mean that we are utterly void of it... We can and do state what it is not while we are silent as to what it is.' However, some people have the capacity to conceive a sense of 'the One'. 'We can but try to indicate, in our own feeble way, something concerning it... Those divinely possessed and inspired have at least the knowledge that they have some greater thing within them though they cannot tell what it is; from the movements that stir them and the utterances that come from them they perceive the power, which is not themselves, that moves them.'

So a minority can sense the presence of 'the One' and it is a benign presence. Plotinus provides a beautiful metaphor for it later in the third section of Book V. He imagines a choral dance, whose performers are circling round a conductor. When they face towards him, they can sing and dance in harmony. When they turn away they lose their harmony. So the concentration on the centre brings peace and beauty. As described by Plotinus, this art of contemplation of 'the One' seems to resemble a form of mysticism. Porphyry records that Plotinus achieved this state on only four occasions. 'He has risen beyond beauty; he has overpassed even the choir of the virtues; he is like one who, having penetrated the inner sanctum, leaves the temple images behind him.'

'The One' possesses a divine simplicity and self-sufficiency. In its complete transcendence resides what is perhaps the most important of Plotinus' contributions to later religious thought. Its purpose is to generate without losing anything of itself, just as the Sun generates heat and light without losing anything of its power. Plotinus talks of 'the One' endlessly overflowing. But what does it generate? Here Plotinus introduces the concept of Intellect (Greek *nous*). The Intellect is an active force concerned with containing within itself all the Platonic Ideas and the thinking applied to them at the same time. It is also conscious that it emanates from 'the One'. As a result it bustles with intellectual energy and so is inevitably complex compared to the simplicity of 'the One'. *Nous* is close to Aristotle's First Principle, the Unmoved Mover (pp. 44–5). However, unlike the Unmoved

Mover, which is self-sufficient, the Intellect is totally dependent on 'the One' for its existence and always eager to return to it. Just as Plato believed that his Ideas existed eternally, so do the Ideas within the Intellect. Each one is distinct but can be grasped by the reasoning mind which gives access to the totality of the Ideas. Unlike 'the One', the nature of the Intellect can at least be conceived by the human mind. The philosophical problem that remains is how can 'the One' create the multiplicity of the Intellect. One analogy might be that white light can break up into a spectrum of colours.

Since the Intellect remains immaterial, how does it have any relationship with the material world? Here Plotinus introduces a third element, the Soul. The Soul is a force present within the cosmos but it is also rooted in each individual body and the body depends on it for its continued existence. As it is generated by the Intellect, it contains within it some memory of the Ideas; these are inherent in each human being even if the individual is not conscious of them.* Plotinus provides an example. When you are reading a scroll, you are so taken with *what* you are reading that you are not aware of the fact that you are reading. As the *Life* by Porphyry tells us, Plotinus was able to conduct a conversation with an outsider without losing the deep thread of his philosophical thoughts. They were always part of him, within his soul.

Like the Intellect, the soul of an individual is drawn two ways by contradictory impulses. Plotinus calls them the 'lower' and 'higher' parts of the soul. It can engage in philosophical thinking (the 'higher') or it can concentrate on the sensory experiences of the body (the 'lower'). The latter impulse activates desire but it can also control desire. In this sense the individual soul is an agent of change within the temporal sphere. It can decide what time the body is to get out of bed, when and what to eat and when to go to sleep. Its interaction with the material

---

* This had been the subject of Plato's dialogue the *Meno*.

world is what gives an individual their personality. In short, the relationship between the soul and the material world can actively define the way an individual sees things and responds to them. It has free will, although certain desires impel it to move upwards towards the Intellect. Plotinus obviously would prefer the soul to engage in thinking but it must satisfy the desires to some extent, otherwise the body would die from lack of food or sleep. In this, although the *Enneads* contain a number of ethical responses to the Stoics for their materialism, Plotinus is close to the Stoic philosopher Epictetus in separating the two impulses of the soul and preferring one over the other. Orientation towards the Intellect is crucial if one is to be truly oneself.

So we come to matter, which Plotinus characterises as essentially passive. It lacks intelligibility. There is no ultimate value of any kind in matter. Plotinus makes the point by imagining a prisoner in gold chains. The gold may be of value for some but for the prisoner it is worse than valueless. The soul has, however, a generative power. It can, says Plotinus, shine light into darkness. It must maintain that light (which comes from its 'higher' part), rather than become lost in the darkness of matter. By being in the material world, the soul can apply its knowledge of the Ideas to the objects it 'sees' around it. So while there is an Idea of Beauty existing eternally in the Intellect, the soul can apply this knowledge to objects of beauty it can see or hear. However, the soul's appreciation of material beauty, a face, a landscape, a piece of music, will always be inferior to the Idea contained within the Intellect. The senses can also be deceived unless they are informed by the 'higher' part of the soul. As Plotinus put it: 'He that has the strength, let him arise and withdraw into himself, forgoing all that is known by the eyes, turning away forever from the material beauty that once made his joy. When he perceives those shapes of grace in bodies, let him not pursue them; he must know them for copies, vestiges, shadows and hasten away towards that they tell of.' Plotinus avoids the contradiction that has transfixed Christian theology, of a benign creator being responsible for evil in the world he has created, by arguing that evil arises from a deficiency of the potential goodness of matter.

The task of each individual is, therefore, to create a unity for the soul which integrates the two impulses but which remains rooted primarily in the Intellect. Plotinus gives advice as to how this might be achieved, through the cultivation of virtue, through the use of dialectical reasoning and the act of contemplation. Contemplation should be orientated towards seeing the ultimate unity of One, Intellect and Soul. Achieving this will be a mystical experience, beyond any contact with the material world. Then the soul will be self-sufficient, above the transitory desires and misfortunes of everyday life.

The 'lower' part of the soul, that which interacts with the material world, is not doomed. It can gain inspiration from the actions of virtuous individuals so long as the soul accepts that these are diminished forms of the true virtue to be found in the Intellect. It will, however, have a hunger to understand the Intellect. There is always the possibility of redemption as, however much the 'lower' part of the soul becomes entangled in the world of matter, it will never lose the knowledge given to it by the Intellect. This strand of his thought has led to Plotinus being criticised for his seeming obliviousness to the day-to-day struggles that most mortals experience. His assumption that a means of escape is always present is another indication of his other-worldliness.

Plotinus died in AD 270. As he aged, his voice lost its power, his sight worsened and he developed ulcers on his hands and feet. He moved to Campania, south of Rome, where he was cared for on the estate of a friend. His last words were reportedly: 'Try to bring back the Divine in myself to the Divine of the universe.' Porphyry, who was in Sicily at the time, was told that at the moment of Plotinus' death a snake appeared from under his bed and slithered away through the wall.

The originality of Plotinus lay in the picking and choosing, accepting or rejecting elements of the Platonic and Aristotelian texts he quarried to create his own system of thought – albeit within a Platonic framework. He was influential in setting out a philosophy of a transcendent One who could be sensed but of whom little could be said. For Plotinus there is a distinction between what is eternal and beyond time and the activity of the soul in the material world which is within time. One offshoot of Plotinus' thinking, developed by the Christian theologian known as Pseudo-Dionysus (flourished c.AD 500), is negative or apophatic theology, describing God, alias 'the One', in terms of what he is not.

Plotinus always appealed to mystics. His claim that an individual would always be adrift if they did not respond to the hunger of the soul for completeness with the Intellect proved to be an important contribution to later theology. His three entities, 'the One', the Intellect and the World Soul, could be seen as a Trinity, although they are, of course, hierarchical compared to the Christian formulation of the Trinity, in which Father, Son and Holy Ghost are of equal power.

There are many differences between Plotinus and what would emerge as the monotheistic religions of Christianity and Islam. Christianity and Islam taught of a God who actively created the universe and continued to exercise influence over it. This 'the One' could not do. It generated only an immaterial entity, the Intellect. Likewise Plotinus had no place for a Son sent in human form by God the Father. He believed that the soul of each individual had the power to assert itself over the material world without the need of a redeemer. The gap would widen. At the end of the fourth century in the Latin west, Augustine of Hippo would suggest that, through the original sin of Adam and Eve, human beings were diminished and therefore reliant on the grace of God to save them. This became central to Christian orthodoxy and so eliminated any connection between the latter and the texts of Plotinus.

A contemporary of Plotinus, the Christian Cyprian of

Carthage, martyred in AD 257, coined the phrase 'There is no salvation outside the Church', which later became dogma in the Roman Catholic Church. Plotinus, in contrast, hoped that individuals would prioritise the 'higher' part of the soul over the 'lower' but there was no official requirement to do so. This allowed his philosophy to be of importance to Judaism and Islam as it was to Christian theologians. It was a philosophy for all from which all religions could take insights.

19

The Platonic Theologian: Clement of Alexandria (c.AD 150–c.215)

Greeks schooled in the culture of learning known as *paideia* shared a common culture which extolled virtue and ethical ways of living. This meant that for the educated Greek, the transition to Christianity in the second century AD was not as dramatic as it would later become. Whether delivering a Christian sermon or a pagan oration, the technique and presentation would be the same. As the scholar Michael Frede has put it: 'It is extremely difficult, if not impossible, to distinguish between the Christian position [God] and the position of Plato ['the Good'], Aristotle [the 'Unmoved Mover'], the Stoics [usually Zeus eternally driving forward the cycles], and their followers in later antiquity and thus the vast majority of philosophers in late antiquity.' We have just encountered Plotinus' distinctive attempt to reconcile these conceptions of transcendence. However, everything became more complicated with the emergence of a Christian Trinity of God the Father, Jesus the Son and the Holy Spirit alongside angels and souls who had reached heaven, especially when there were pagan trinities in Greek and local cultures. The theologian Clement of Alexandria taught that Christianity did not offer an alternative to pagan culture but was rather the culmination of it. Modern scholarship has revised the old view that paganism and

Christianity were always in opposition to each other. There was a fluidity in the way that Christians used Greek philosophy to bolster the credentials of their own religion.*

Clement was as much at home within the milieu of Platonism and Stoicism as Dio was (see pp. 207–8). While Dio found in 'reason the only sure and indissoluble foundation for fellowship and justice', Clement claims that reason was amplified by the *logos* ('reason' or 'the Word') appearing in human form as described at the beginning of St John's Gospel.† This embrace of Greek philosophy, alongside Christian ideas, contrasted with some of Clement's Roman contemporaries such as Tertullian of Carthage who required Christians to reject 'Athens' and the culture of *paideia* outright. It helped, of course, that the New Testament was in Greek and the Hebrew Scriptures had been translated into Greek, the Septuagint, in Alexandria, as early as the third century BC. The early Church Fathers in the east did not have to battle with a foreign language and had access to a vast array of texts which they could hardly ignore. As a result, Greek theology would always be more sophisticated than its Latin cousin.‡

Little is known of Clement's life. He was born into wealth in the middle of the second century AD. His Greek is so good that he was probably educated in Athens and he has certainly absorbed *paideia*. As he memorably put it: 'The wealth of refined learning is like some kind of spice mixed in with an athlete's food.' A later reference to him as Titus Flavius Clemens suggests that his family were Roman citizens. Like many of his class he began

---

* One of the best examples of this is Basil of Caesarea's (AD 330–79) *Address to Young Men on How They Might Derive Benefit from Greek Literature* which urges the young to master Greek literature before they progress to Christian theology.

† The fourth of the canonical gospels dating from around the end of the first century AD.

‡ Augustine could not access the Greek texts so he developed his own distinctive and influential theology for the west.

travelling to find teachers who inspired him, visiting Greece, Italy, Coele-Syria (now Syria/Lebanon) and Egypt before finding Pantaenus, head of the catechetical school in Alexandria, who 'engendered purity of knowledge in the soul of his hearers'. After his conversion, Clement followed Pantaenus in becoming the head of the school and took on a missionary role, actively attempting to convert pagans to Christianity, notably through his text *Protreptikos*, 'the exhortation to conversion'. He describes himself as 'a true priest of the church and a true deacon of the will of God' rather than having a formal ecclesiastical office. This was still a troubling time for Christians – their rejection of the rituals of conventional religion made them vulnerable. Septimius Severus launched a persecution of Christians in Alexandria in 202 which forced Clement to take his library of scrolls to Caesarea in Palestine, where he died in about 215.

During his time in Alexandria, Clement would have been amazed by the massive presence of the Serapeum, the temple to the Greco-Egyptian god Serapis which had burned down in 181. The devastated site overlooked the city from its highest hill. Rebuilding on a grand scale, which began almost immediately, is a reminder of the power and wealth that sustained 'pagan' cults, even one adopted as here by the Greeks from a foreign culture.*
When it was completed, c.215, the temple itself contained a vast statue of Serapis and dominated a precinct which contained other temples, lecture halls and a library that appears to have housed overflows from the celebrated library of earlier times. This and the *Mouseion*, a study centre for favoured scholars, still functioned and lecturers would come from across the Greek world to speak there. While Alexandria was a Greek foundation and the Greek population was dominant, there were also significant Jewish and Egyptian communities with their own quarters. There were moments of tension and violence

---

* The Ptolemies used the cult, an amalgam of various deities, notably Osiris and Apis, as a means of bridging the gap between Greeks and Egyptians.

between the communities but among the elite there was a common culture which appears to have transcended religious differences. In fact until the persecution of 202 there is every sign that Christians from the Greek elite could mix easily with their pagan and Jewish fellow citizens. Until the intrusions of an 'African' emperor,* Clement could freely follow his intellectual and religious concerns.

Yet the Christian community was still small. There does not appear to have been a bishop in charge of the church but Clement knows of poorer Christians and is aware of earlier Christian teachers whose views differ from his own. Even though it was now 170 since the crucifixion of Jesus, Christian beliefs were still diverse and fluid in communities, largely of Greek speakers, scattered through the empire. The challenge of bringing the doctrine of an Aramaic-speaking Jew into the Greek world had been immense and only hindsight over the eventual 'triumph' of Christianity makes it appear a coherent and inevitable process. Some key decisions had, however, been made by the middle of the second century. A major debate had been conducted over whether the dramatic story of Christ and his resurrection had been so revolutionary that Judaism and its scriptures had been superseded. This had been the message promulgated c.AD 140 by a popular and wealthy preacher named Marcion, from the southern Black Sea port of Sinope. Marcion had been rejected by the mainstream Christian communities and the decision had been made to preserve the Hebrew scriptures alongside the emerging canon of New Testament texts. The argument was illustrated by a text of c.AD 155–60, the *Dialogue with Trypho the Jew* by the Christian apologist Justin Martyr, in which Justin argues, against Trypho, that the Hebrew scriptures, what Christians refer to as the Old Testament, had passages foretelling the coming of Christ and so needed to be preserved. In about 180, the bishop of

---

* Septimius came from Leptis Magna, in what is now modern Libya.

the Greek community of Lyons, Irenaeus, produced a coherent text *Adversus Haereses*, 'Against the Heretics', originally written in Greek, which talked of a unified church with its own texts (consisting of only four gospels and some letters of Paul) and orthodox beliefs passed down from the apostles. The *Adversus* was later to become authoritative but at this time no church hierarchy existed with the power to enforce any one version of Christianity. While Irenaeus argues that tradition is passed on through ordination, from the apostles onwards, Clement dwells more on the evolution of an intellectual tradition and appears to rely on his *paideia* as giving him authority as a teacher.

Two other major works of Clement's survive, the *Paedagogos*, a teaching manual for newly converted Christians with Christ as the 'teacher', and the *Stromateis*. The three works suggest a progression, from initiation into Christianity, the use of Christ as a teacher, and then a much deeper analysis of *gnosis*, or knowledge, in the *Stromateis*.* The *Stromateis*, often translated as 'Miscellanies', is a rambling work. Clement seems to have planned it as such. 'So, in a meadow, the flowers blooming in their variety, and in a garden, the plantations of fruit trees are not separated according to species from those of other kinds… and are pruned neither in arrangement nor expression, but deliberately scattered, all mixed up, the pattern of our *Stromateis* has been designed for the sake of variety, just like a meadow.'† It is within the *Stromateis*, however, that Clement makes the argument for using Greek philosophy as a foundation for Christianity. He talks of the bees who work methodically across the varied flowers of the fields, picking and choosing which flowers to feed off to produce a single honeycomb; the chosen flowers are the philosophy, the honeycomb the Christian soul.

Just as the bees gathered widely from the fields, so Clement

---

* *Gnosis*, the word used by Clement to define true knowledge, should not be confused with the esoteric writings of the Gnostics.
† Contemporary enthusiasts for rewilding would approve of the analogy!

drew heavily on earlier texts. In his surviving writings he makes over a thousand references to other writers and to 348 different classical authors, citing Plato 600 times and Homer 240 (from virtually every book of the *Iliad* and *Odyssey*). While Irenaeus hardly mentions any 'pagan' Greek authors at all, Clement draws a quarter of his references from them. 'I am not talking about philosophy as Stoic, or Platonic, or Epicurean, or Aristotelian, but whatever is well expressed by each of these sects, teaching righteousness along with an understanding following from piety; this eclectic whole I refer to as philosophy.' In fact, as we will see presently, Clement favours Plato and the Stoics above other thinkers. The lure of an immaterial divine figure transcended any Old Testament references to God as a human figure. 'You must not entertain the notion at all of figure and motion, or standing or sitting, or place, or right or left, as pertaining to the Father of the universe, although these terms are in scripture.' The theologian Origen, as we will see in the next chapter, was to take this 'spiritual' interpretation of the Bible even further.

One new source proved very influential for Clement. In the rich intellectual diversity of Alexandria, he came across the works of philosophy of Philo the Alexandrian, who lived c.25 BC–c.AD 50. Philo was Jewish but he mixed with the Greek elite and his brother had even held office in the city. He was widely read in Greek philosophy and studied the scriptures in their Greek Septuagint translation, which he believed to be an exact rendition of the original. While he was a contemporary of Jesus he does not appear to have known of him.*

Philo wrote widely on philosophical issues. His *On Animals* is a dialogue in which he rejects the view put forward at length by his nephew Alexander that animals have reason – rather they

---

* Philo coined the word *polytheos*, polytheism, to distinguish Greek religion from Judaism.

follow their own natures through instinct.* A dialogue on the nature of divine providence again involves a discussion with Alexander on whether providence exists. Alexander denies that it does; too much of the material world has no meaning and if there was a divine providence it would surely have been arranged differently. Philo counters these arguments one by one and the dialogue concludes by Alexander agreeing to come back to hear the positive arguments for providence. Philo appears to be using dialogue to emphasise his own philosophical superiority – as a wise older man he can counter any argument made against him. It is within this context, humans as superior rational beings under the aegis of divine providence, that Philo's examination of scriptures takes place.

Philo's extensive writing on Judaism centred on the books of Genesis and Exodus, which he believed provided moral and spiritual guidance to their readers. He takes literal passages and explores at length their allegorical meaning. Philo has absorbed Platonism and he attempts to reconcile the attributes of his God and the Forms of Plato. While God exists it is not easy to discern his presence but he is the One of Plato, the source of all goodness and the author of a benign creation. Philo is not always clear as to how God works through the world. *Logos*, 'the principle of reason', is one of his emanations but Philo refers to other abstract powers including virtue, temperance, continence (Philo argued that asexuality was an ideal) and 'helpers' such as angels. While Plato saw the Forms as having an identity independent of the Good, Philo treats them as an intrinsic part of the Creator. Similarly, he attempts to equate the account of the Creation given in Genesis with the 'divine craftsman' of Plato's dialogue *Timaeus* (see p. 115). Somehow the goodness of God's creation has infused the prophets, Abraham, Isaac and Jacob, although Philo's hero is Moses. Moses is Plato before Plato – he

---

* Alexander was an important figure in his own right, procurator of Judaea, AD 46–8.

had grasped the reality of the immaterial world before Plato and Plato was only Platonic because he had absorbed his philosophy from Moses. This was an important breakthrough in that Plato could now be seen not as an original philosopher but as the heir to an existing tradition rooted in Judaism. Having absorbed the various schools of Greek philosophy, Philo was able to reject Epicureanism for its atheism and materialism, accept Plato and realise that the Stoic insistence on temperance offered fruitful guidance for a virtuous life.

Clement could take much from this. He makes 300 references to Philo in his works. If 'the One' had given the human race a shared mind, then Judaism could make a contribution to it and, for Clement, Philo is the philosopher who demonstrates this. Clement adopted the idea from Philo that Greek philosophy is dependent on an earlier Judaism. Philo had characterised Moses as a legislator, High Priest and prophet; Clement also gives him high status, but regards him primarily as a politician and philosopher. Clement replaces Moses as the High Priest by giving the title to Jesus. As regards the *logos* and the Holy Spirit these are close to God but are 'first born powers and first created'. The crucial point was that the *logos* was a later creation.

The difficulty lay in finding the links between Moses and the prophets and the Greeks. Clement has to create an appropriation. He draws on legends that Homer was originally from Egypt and would have picked up earlier traditions there. As he puts it in Book One of the *Stromateis*, 'Well then, let it be that the "thieves and robbers" are the philosophers amongst the Greeks [and those] who took portions of the truth from the Hebrew prophets before the advent of the Lord without acknowledgement, but appropriated the doctrines as if they were their own.' The results according to Clement were mixed. In some cases the Greeks distorted and debased the teachings of the Jewish prophets, in others they developed their own 'spirit of understanding'. In this last category, Clement would place Plato. He claims that

Plato grasped the concept of a supreme god, which was then elaborated by the Christians.

Clement also drew on the Stoics. One of the most fundamental contributions of Stoicism is the ideal of universality replacing the traditional allegiance of a Greek to a specific city. In his *De Otio*, the Roman Stoic Seneca sums it up clearly: 'Let us understand two commonwealths: one, great and truly common by which gods and human beings are embraced, in which we look neither to this corner nor to that, but measure the boundaries of our state by the sun; the other, the one to which the accident of our birth has consigned us: this may be that of the Athenians, or of the Carthaginians, or any other city which does not extend to all people, but only to certain individuals.' Christianity measures 'the boundaries of our state by the sun', in other words is universal. Clement also valued the Stoic stress on moderation, which was compatible with his ideal of Christian living. In a minor work, *Who is the Rich Man Who Shall Be Saved?*, he stressed that wealth was not evil in itself but could be misused to cause evil effects. This was a typical Stoic belief, though critics felt that it allowed Stoics to sustain a conservative status quo. Clement nailed the Sceptics with the philosophical conundrum of their being certain that nothing was certain and rubbished the Epicureans for their rejection of the divine (Epicurus, 'the leading light of godlessness') and their materialism.

So what is the value of philosophy for Clement? It lays the groundwork for Christianity. 'If Greek philosophy does not even possess the full extent of the truth and is too weak to perform the commandments of the Lord, yet even so it prepares the way for the truly royal teaching, somehow or other chastening and forming the character in advance and preparing the one who extols providence for the reception of the truth.' Divine providence, another concept of the Stoics, ensures that the tradition is sustained from Judaism to Greek philosophy and so on to Christianity. Now philosophy has been made redundant.

'It seems to me, since the Word [*logos*] himself has thus come from heaven to us', writes Clement, 'that we do not need to go for human teaching any more by carefully studying Athens and the rest of Greece, and even Ionia [in other words traditional *paideia*]. For if our teacher [Christ] is he who filled all things with his holy powers, with creation and salvation and the provision of good, with law-giving and prophecy and teaching, the teacher now instructs in all things, and the whole universe has become Athens and Greece by the Word [*logos*].'

Yet how did Clement make the intellectual leap that was needed to replace philosophy with Christianity? Traditionally, educated Greeks were dependent on a core of hallowed texts and so resistant to innovation. Christianity was revolutionary in that it believed that 'first created' *logos* had in fact been sent by God in the form of a human being who had supernatural powers, in the making of miracles and in the ability to transcend a humiliating form of death to reappear as a living being before rising into heaven. Clement tended towards Docetism (*dokesis*, 'apparition'), the belief that, although the *logos* appeared to be a human being, Christ was an ethereal body, beyond suffering in the flesh. Belief in Jesus as the Christos, the messiah, much talked of in the scriptures, demanded some kind of intellectual leap, especially for Greeks. It was provided by the concept of *pistis*, 'faith'.

In the epistles of St Paul, *pistis* is set against 'the wisdom of the wise'. The relationship between faith and reason has been debated theologically over the centuries but Clement is a pioneer of an approach that was to become prominent in the Middle Ages. He took a phrase from Isaiah (7.9): 'Unless you believe, you will not understand.' In other words the leap of faith provides the essential key to deeper understanding. Clement sets it out brilliantly in the *Stromateis*. 'Faith like a grain of mustard seed bites beneficially into the soul so that it grows in it magnificently until the reasons concerning the highest realities rest on it.' In the *Stromateis* (Book Five, Chapter Six), Clement contrasts earlier Greek philosophers who rely on their senses for knowledge with Christians who know through faith.

Like most of the Greeks brought up in the world of *paideia*, Clement is an optimist and appreciates rather than denigrates the senses. As he puts it in the *Paedagogus*: 'Do not put a wreath around my head. For in the springtime in the dewy soft fields, with variegated flowers blooming, it is a beautiful thing to spend one's time, just like the bees, cherishing a pure and natural scent.' In Book Three of the *Stromateis*, he takes a neutral position on the wholesomeness of sex, accepting it as a natural and welcome part of married life, the natural precursor to having children. The individual should live a life of continence but this should be no different from continence in any other sphere of life. Clement displays none of the prurience against any form of sexual intercourse seen in so many of the Church Fathers. Unlike Augustine in the Latin west, this was not a man weighed down by a sense of his own sinfulness. Conversion to the *logos* was a moment of joyful liberation. 'Let Christ be to you continuous and unceasing joy', he advised those newly baptised. 'For what other work is fitting for him who is wise and perfect than to sport and be glad in the enduring of good things and the disposing of what is good, celebrating with God.' He believed that the final decision of salvation or damnation in the afterlife was not immediate but somehow the soul could make some form of progress towards salvation. The later, medieval, concept of purgatory was present, in embryonic form, in Clement's thought.

Orthodoxy had not yet been imposed on the Christian communities and the legacy of Clement, like his pupil Origen, was later tarnished by the declaration of the Trinity as a non-negotiable doctrine at the Council of Constantinople in AD 381. Both Clement and Origen had seen the *logos* as subordinate to God, the 'first created' for Clement, not as eternally part of the Godhead as would become orthodox in 381. According to Photius, the formidable ninth-century patriarch of Constantinople,

Clement 'degraded the Son to the rank of a creature' and was thus heretical. Within traditional Christian circles Clement was viewed with ambivalence as having been seduced by the charms of pagan philosophy. Clement VIII (pope 1592–1605) removed him from the list of saints. An alternative view is that Clement kept Christianity receptive to a much broader tradition of learning and he should be valued for this.

20

The Biblical Scholar: Origen (c.185–c.253)

Your natural ability enables you to make an esteemed Roman
lawyer or a Greek philosopher of one of the most notable
schools. But I hope that you would entirely apply your ability to
Christianity. Indeed in order to bring this about, I beg of you to
take from your studies of Hellenic philosophy those things such
as can be made encyclic or preparatory studies to Christianity...
Apply the things that are useful from geometry and astronomy
to the explanation of the Holy Scriptures, so that, as the
philosophers say about geometry, music, grammar, rhetoric, and
astronomy (namely that they are assistants to philosophy), we
may say such things about philosophy in relation to Christianity.

Thus wrote the third-century Christian theologian Origen
to Gregory, a student of his in Caesarea (Palestine), who was
wavering, as students do, over his choice of career. Origen had
absorbed from his fellow Alexandrian Clement the conviction
that Christianity was the culmination of pagan Greek philosophy
and that study of the pagan philosophers should be encouraged.
In his work as the first prominent interpreter of the scriptures,
Origen also adapted many techniques that had evolved in literary
Alexandria to deepen his understanding of the texts. He was a
formidable scholar. A story tells of how Origen once wandered
into one of Plotinus' lectures and Plotinus' heart sank when
he realised that his 'student' already knew it all. Like Clement,

Origen was writing before doctrinal orthodoxy had been defined by the church. In the sixth century he was to be anathematised (and thus rejected by the Orthodox Church).

Origen was born probably in AD 185, so he was twenty years older than Plotinus. He is largely known from an adulatory biography by the church historian Eusebius which scholars have analysed to sort out truth from exaggeration and fantasy. Sadly the work contains few of the personal observations that enliven Porphyry's *Life of Plotinus*. Eusebius mentions that he has seen a hundred letters from Origen but none of them (other than the one to Gregory quoted at the beginning of this chapter) survive. His father had been martyred, probably in the persecution initiated by Septimius Severus in 202, and it was said that Origen would have followed him if his mother had not hidden all his clothes. (He refused to go out to see the authorities naked.) Then, still aged only seventeen, and, already immersed in the scriptures, Origen began teaching at one of Alexandria's Christian schools. His religious convictions did not, however, deter him from following pagan teachers. He studied with Ammonius Saccas, the teacher of Plotinus, who, as we have seen, had renounced his Christian background in favour of paganism, and, like Clement, was a follower of the Jewish philosopher, Philo. This aroused the condemnation of Demetrius, bishop of Alexandria, and Origen appears to have set himself up as an independent philosopher without renouncing his Christianity. This enabled him to travel – he reached Rome in 212 and the province of Arabia in 213 or 214. At this time he was not formally ordained and maintained his individuality of approach among the other Christian groups of the city.

In 215 the emperor Caracalla visited Alexandria and brutally put down protests against him. A clampdown on intellectuals forced Origen to flee to Caesarea Maritima in Palestine where he would eventually make his home. Here he was ordained by the local bishop. Back in Alexandria Demetrius was furious. It may have been then that a story that Origen castrated himself was put about by Demetrius who, taking Deuteronomy 23 ('No one who has been emasculated by crushing or cutting may enter the assembly of the Lord') literally, believed that it should have barred him from being a priest.* Having escaped Egypt and taken up residence in Palestine Origen compared his experience with the exodus of the ancient Israelites.

In Caesarea Origen began teaching pagans interested in Christianity and he did so through the medium of philosophy. It was now that his reputation as a scholar started to grow. Porphyry listened to his lectures and assured his readers that Origen was at home with Plato and Aristotle, Stoicism and Pythagoreanism. He regretted, however, that Origen had subjugated his classical learning to Christianity. Origen's pupil Gregory neatly summed up his approach. Origen 'picked out and placed before us everything that was useful and true in each of the philosophers... while counselling us not to pin our allegiance to any one philosopher, even if all men swear that he is all knowing, but to attach ourselves only to God and the Prophets'.

Following the death in 235 of the emperor Alexander Severus who had been tolerant of Christians, there began an era of increasing persecution under his successor Maximinus Thrax and Origen had to go into hiding. On the death of Maximinus in 238 he was able to resume his teaching and there are records of visits to Athens and Rome. He may have met Plotinus in Rome. Yet he failed to evade the persecutions of the emperor Decius, promulgated in 250, during which he was imprisoned and tortured. He survived two years of brutal incarceration but his health was so destroyed that he died, probably in 253.

Origen's study of the scriptures was always a prominent feature of his theology. His approach was informed by skills that had been developed in the Alexandrian scholarly community. There were four recognised elements of textual criticism. First,

---

* The church historian Eusebius records in his *Ecclesiastical History* (VI.8) that the story comes from Demetrius when he was nearing death. It may have been an invention as a result of Demetrius' hostility to Origen.

the decoding of the text itself, which may have been corrupted by careless copying; then, the provision of any background knowledge needed, such as the history or geography behind the narrative; next, criticism of the text as a piece of literature including its use of grammar; and finally, an assessment of its moral and aesthetic value. A 'final' text of Homer, for instance, had been assembled from the various texts available in the library. One problem with the Homeric epics had been their depictions of gods acting immorally. Their actions were now interpreted as symbols of spiritual truths so as to maintain Homer as a moral teacher. (Plato would have none of this and excluded the epics of Homer from his ideal state.)

Origen was the first scholar to submit the scriptures, both the Old and the New Testament, to this rigorous brand of textual criticism. He used the same symbols as the Alexandrian librarians when correcting his texts. He believed that the scriptures were divinely inspired, through Christ passing on the will of the Father. Thus they were deserving of serious scholarly attention.

The most extraordinary example of this is the edition of the Old Testament produced by Origen and known as the *Hexapla*, 'the sixfold'. Origen took the original Hebrew version of the scriptures, placed a Greek transcription of the Hebrew letters alongside it and then four Greek translations. By placing them in columns he was able to spot any divergences. The Septuagint was one of the translations; the others were well-known attempts to translate the original Hebrew or to edit the Septuagint when the text did not reflect or reproduce the original Hebrew. The process of comparison raised a host of issues: the original Hebrew had been further standardised since the Septuagint translation, there had been careless recopying, and translators had made their own additions when the Hebrew was unclear.*

---

* Among other symbols, Origen and his associates used an asterisk (*asteriskos*, 'little star') when a Hebrew phrase was not found in the Septuagint. As we have seen, its use had been developed some centuries before by the astronomer Aristarchus of Samos (born *c.*310 BC).

Origen accepted that his Hebrew was not good enough to solve all these problems but, by comparing other translations, he hoped to create an authoritative version of the Septuagint. It was a formidable task. It is estimated that, working over a period of twenty years, Origen would have needed 6,000 papyrus sheets in fifteen codex volumes. Only a single copy of the work was produced – the challenges of making other copies would have been overwhelming – and the final version was lodged in the bishop's library in Caesarea. It disappeared during the Arab invasions of the seventh century, but by this time it had been consulted and some parts had been copied.

By the third century, Christian scholars had begun to see the complete body of the Hebrew scriptures as telling a coherent story of God's involvement in the material world, with each text intimately connected to the others. What they needed was an overall interpretation using examples from one book to illuminate narratives from another. Like Clement, Origen was influenced by Philo in believing that passages in the Bible reflected deeper spiritual meanings. This was, of course, close to Platonic philosophy, which taught that the immaterial world contained truths unknown to those whose imagination and reason was only concerned with what they could see around them. For Origen in his *Commentary on John*, salvation is the entry of the soul from the material world into 'an invisible world, a world which is not seen, and an intelligible world on whose appearance and beauty the pure in heart will look'. The path there is essentially one already mapped by Plato (and Plotinus).

While Origen accepted that the stories of the Testaments often offered insights for the ordinary Christian, he saw himself as far too sophisticated to accept literal interpretations of scripture. Writing on Genesis, he queries whether 'anyone could be so unintelligent as to think that God made a paradise somewhere in the east and planted it with trees, like a farmer, or that in that paradise he put a tree of life... a tree you could derive life from by eating its fruit with the teeth in your head'. Some deeper understanding was needed. Links needed to be made. Thus, for example, the rituals of sacrifice in the Old Testament find their fulfilment in the sacrifice of Christ on the cross. The Song of Songs is not the story of a carnal love between a man and a woman but is interpreted by Origen as an allegory of the relationship between the soul and God. So when Psalm 80 orders readers to suck honey from the rock, the honey can be interpreted as the sweet words of Jesus. Origen's reading makes the Old Testament a Christian rather than Jewish text and so marks an important moment in the development of Christianity. Rather than responding to critics such as Celsus (of whom more below) that the scriptures and gospels were full of discrepancies, Origen believed that they simply required more sophisticated interpretations. As he put it in his *First Principles*: 'Divine wisdom took care that certain stumbling blocks to the historical meaning should take place by the introduction into the midst of the narrative of certain impossibilities and incongruities.' As a result Origen was untroubled by discrepancies. As the text is sacred, the interpreter must simply work harder to find a meaning that is worthy of God, which is the ultimate aim. Divine inspiration would help him in his task. Once the relationships between the scriptural texts of the Old and New Testaments had been blended, he said, it would be like the harmonious music of a harp.

The text of Origen that best illustrated this was his *First Principles*. He probably began work on it quite early in his life. History has not been kind to the *First Principles*. The original Greek text has largely vanished and has to be reconstructed from a Latin translation by the fourth/fifth-century monk and theologian Rufinus of Aquileia. However, Rufinus was so determined to refute the charges of heresy later made against Origen that he may have distorted the original text.

In *First Principles*, Origen set out his philosophical system. As with Plotinus, it is a hierarchical one, with three elements which Origen terms the Father, Christ and the Holy Spirit, who proceeds from Christ as Christ does from the Father. While the Father is the universal force, the power of Christ, the *Logos* or wisdom of the Father, extends to rational human beings and that of the Holy Spirit to those who have achieved salvation. The Father has created the scriptures but they are promulgated through the *Logos*, Christ. Christ had appeared on Earth as a man but, just as there were deeper spiritual meanings in the scriptures, so the spirituality of Christ could be discerned behind his human appearance. In a memorable phrase, Origen describes him as the yeast that is added to the dough of the law of Moses and the prophets. 'The light contained in the law of Moses but hidden by a veil shone forth at the coming of Jesus.' The death and resurrection of Christ showed that there were spiritual truths to be found in the words of the prophets and so the link between Old and New Testaments was confirmed.

So how did Origen see creation and its aftermath? Originally, at an undefined moment before time, the Father created a finite number of souls. Ideally they stay close to their creator in permanent adoration of him. Yet – and this point was crucial to an understanding of Origen – each had their own freedom and they could choose to drift away from the Father into the material world, where they would be imprisoned in fleshly bodies. Only Christ, the supreme representation of rationality, would realise that his true home was with the Father. While Plato was the most profound influence on Origen, as he had been for Philo, he also absorbed an important teaching of the Stoics that, in the end, all things will be restored to their original state. Just as the Stoics believed in the eternal revolutions of the cosmos, according to which one era dissolved into the next but then reappeared much as it had been before, so Origen taught that eventually all souls would be reunited with the Father. Like Plotinus' 'the One', He would offer the eternal possibility of reunion. The freedom of the embodied soul lay in using reason to discern that its true home remained with the Father. 'The power of choosing between good and evil is within reach of all.' Some would take many lives to find the path to God, but each reincarnation offered hope of a new beginning to the ascent to virtue. Origen used the term 'regeneration' as a 'new coming to be, when a new heaven and a new earth are created for those who have renewed themselves'. In the individuality of each soul struggling in its own way, Origen has been credited with the invention of the human personality, a personality which can take initiatives. To the outrage of his readers, Origen suggested that even Satan had the power to be reconciled but his nature was such that he would probably refuse. Origen's hell offered the possibility of purification before the final reconciliation of all peoples.* Notions that suffering could be eternal were a product of the imagination, 'a description of those who through their immersion in the darkness of deep ignorance have become separated from every gleam of reason and intelligence'. Such a view isolated him from conventional Christian thinkers, for whom the eternity of suffering in hell was an ever-present reality.

In another key work, Origen responds to an attack on Christianity by the second-century Greek philosopher Celsus. The original text of Celsus, *The True Word*, has been lost but Origen's text is intact and something of Celsus' sarcastic denigration of Christianity can be reconstructed from quotations of his that Origen used. Celsus was a conservative, in most part a Platonist, who was offended by the radical nature of Christianity and its success in gaining adherents. He defended the polytheism of pagan philosophy by claiming that there was indeed one supreme force, but that it had been given different names by different cultures and peoples. The Zeus of the Greeks is the same as Amun of the Egyptians. He used the analogy that the world's oceans comprise a single unity but are made up of many different seas. Celsus claimed that this polytheism was an ancient tradition common to all nations and had ensured the stability of society. He believed that the Jews had already abandoned the

---

* This was known as the doctrine of universalism.

old traditions and that Christians, by worshipping a Jew who had been executed in the most humiliating circumstances, were further undermining society. Moreover, Christians relied on the angry God of the Old Testament, their New Testament being full of discrepancies; they were also superstitious, and many of their beliefs had been plagiarised from other sources. Celsus was particularly incensed by the way in which Christians dropped out of society and he called for them to revere the emperor and take a full part in public affairs. Despite its coarsely sarcastic tone, scholars regard *The True Word* as a well-researched piece of work. Celsus is clearly knowledgeable about the texts he criticises. It was not an attempt to sway committed Christians but rather a warning to those who might be tempted to convert.

Origen was asked by a wealthy Christian named Ambrose to launch a counterattack.* His work, known by its Latin name, *Contra Celsum*, was probably composed in the late 240s, perhaps seventy or eighty years after *The True Word* had been written. Origen's primary aim is to prove that Christianity is as sophisticated as any other philosophy, in fact even more so as it contains wisdoms others do not have. He argues that those with a training in Greek philosophy are, in fact, more able to assess the truths of Christianity than barbarians. One of Origen's tactics is to counter Celsus' claims that were based on one school of philosophy with counterclaims made by an opposing philosophy without needing to have recourse to the scriptures. In fact, scholars have been able to clarify Stoic doctrines taught by Chrysippus from Origen's comments on them. Henry Chadwick describes how Origen's comparison of the unity of divine and human natures in Christ with a red-hot iron, where the iron and the fire become indistinguishable, was borrowed from Chrysippus' explanation of how the soul permeated the body. Yet Origen's analogy would reappear in Christian texts for generations to come.

---

* Ambrose is also known to have provided scribes to record Origen's writings.

Origen accepts that some Christians are superstitious or take the scriptures literally, but he refutes Celsus' claim that they are necessarily ignorant. Many Christians, he says, are well read in other philosophies and they have not kept their own doctrines secret, but these are far better known than those of other philosophies. When Celsus challenges the Christians for their worship of an ordinary man, Origen replies that the impact of Christ has been much greater than that of Plato or victorious Athenian generals. The only way that God could manifest himself among human beings was by sending a messenger who, while remaining spiritual, would appear in human form. He introduces an argument that was to become prevalent, namely that Christ appeared at a moment of political stability, the *Pax Romana*, during which his message would be free to travel across the Mediterranean. When Celsus argues that Origen's use of allegory is simply an attempt to cover up the barbarities of the scriptures, Origen replies that the Homeric epics had been similarly interpreted for their spiritual truths. Whatever accusations can be made against Christians for their superstitions can be met with examples from other philosophies. Origen argues that Christianity is a more spiritual religion than Greco-Roman paganism. Rather than join the army, Christians proclaim the virtues of peace. Nor are they encumbered with the burden of temples, altars and extravagant processions, which Celsus considered vital for a functioning society. When Celsus accused Origen of borrowing from Plato, Origen responded that, according to Philo, Plato had been the heir to the Jewish prophets (see earlier, pp. 261–4). *Contra Celsum* is regarded as the most sophisticated defence of Christianity of the early Christian centuries.

Origen is considered as much a giant in early Christian theology in the East as Augustine is in the West. Yet in many ways he was the greater thinker in that he was rooted in the Greek tradition of thought in a way that Augustine, who knew little

Greek, could never be.* Christianity needed a strong intellectual background to give it coherence and Origen provided it. While he borrowed from earlier philosophical traditions, his theology was a personal one, of much greater depth than that of his fellow Christians. He was often critical of alternative interpretations and the readiness of other Christians to read scriptures literally. Like Clement he was endlessly optimistic in his hope that all souls would eventually be reunited with the Father and that there would be no eternal punishment. This would leave him in trouble when orthodoxy was consolidated in the following century and the threat of hell emphasised. He could hardly be blamed for using his imagination to understand spiritual truths but Christianity was developing new authoritarian forms and the barriers were narrowing. This is the theme of our next interlude.

* Augustine was to have the advantage as there would be no Western theologian of his stature for 600 years and this allowed him to become embedded in Latin Christianity.

Interlude Five

Constantinople and the Promulgation of Christian Orthodoxy

The founding of Constantinople by the emperor Constantine in 330 shifted the political and cultural focus from Rome, which was now in decline, to the ancient Greek city of Byzantium as an alternative imperial capital. Within two hundred years of its foundation, Constantinople would be capital of its own Greek-speaking empire and would remain so for over a thousand years. It would be from Constantinople that the doctrine of the Trinity would be proclaimed as orthodoxy in 381, so limiting the free discussions among Christians and pagans that were explored in the last two chapters. A ban on all pagan shrines and festivities followed in the 390s, a crucial step in shaping the intellectual climate of the Byzantine empire over the following centuries.

The instability of the empire described in Interlude Four (see pp. 241– 5) had been brought to an end by the emperor Diocletian (r. 284–306). Diocletian had reformed the system of government, parcelling out the empire between four rulers (the Tetrarchy), improving the taxation system and fighting back against Rome's external enemies. A defeat of the Sassanid Persians in 297 settled the eastern border for generations. But the Tetrarchy did not last. Constantine, son of one of the Tetrarchs, Constantius I, was proclaimed emperor by his father's troops in 306[*] and soon won control of the western empire after defeating a rival emperor, Maxentius, at the Battle of the Milvian Bridge just north of Rome in 312. The following year Constantine and Licinius, who held power in the east, jointly issued the Edict of Milan which offered toleration and patronage to the Christian communities.

In 324, Constantine defeated Licinius, thus making himself sole ruler of the over-extended Roman empire. He announced that he would found a new city to commemorate his victory, but there was no doubt that his choice of Byzantium, on a promontory overlooking the Bosphorus, was inspired by the need to have a secure base from which to defend the eastern parts of the empire. Byzantium was relatively close to both the Danube and Euphrates borders, to the north-west and east respectively, both of which were vulnerable to attack from Rome's enemies. Roads ran from the city to the east and west (the Via Egnatia). A fine harbour (the celebrated Golden Horn) meant that the city could be supplied by sea if roads were disrupted. A new harbour on the coast of the Sea of Marmara started during Constantine's reign, but only completed after his death, enabled bulky grain ships from Alexandria to dock. However, one drawback for travel from the city was that the flow from the Black Sea made it hard to progress northwards along the Bosphorus.

Before long, Constantine realised that having given toleration to Christianity, he was faced with disputes between alternative interpretations of the nature of Christ. Was he subordinate to the Father and a later creation, as most earlier Christians, such as Origen, had believed, or in some way eternally subsumed into the Godhead with no specific moment of creation? In 325 Constantine presided over a council of bishops in the imperial palace at Nicaea which, under his urging, declared that God the Father and Jesus the Son were 'consubstantial', one in substance with each other. This was not yet a declaration of a Trinity, the

* This was in York.

assembled bishops simply recording that they 'believed in the Holy Spirit'.

Officially the debate over the nature of Christ was settled in this so-called Nicene Creed. However, it had required an emperor with the aura and immense powers at his disposal to compel the Council 'to unanimity and concord'.[*] In the years that followed, subordinationism remained powerful, even though there were several different ways of formulating it. A council of bishops meeting in 357 at Sirmium, in the Balkans in modern Serbia, put forward the traditional subordinationist view. First they criticised the notion of 'substance' as being unscriptural. Then they stated what appeared to them to be obvious: 'No one can doubt that the Father is greater than the Son in honour, dignity, splendour, majesty, and in the very name of Father, the Son Himself testifying, *He that sent Me is greater than I.* (John 14:28.) And no one is ignorant that it is Catholic doctrine that there are two Persons of Father and Son; and that the Father is greater, and that the Son is subordinated to the Father.' Constantine's son Constantius II (r. 337–61), a subordinationist, maintained toleration between pagans and the growing numbers of Christians.[†]

But subordinationism was not to prevail. By the middle of the fourth century the empire had been again split into east and west by Constantine's three sons and in 378, Valens, the emperor of the east, was killed in a devastating defeat of the Roman legions by the Goths at the Battle of Adrianople (see further p. 293). The new emperor, Theodosius, a tough Spanish general, followed the Nicene Creed, which was much more popular in the west. Aware of the many dissensions among Christians, and determined to assert his authority, he issued a decree, first from Thessalonica and then from Constantinople itself, that all bishops should

---

[*] The words are those of Theodoret of Cyrus in his *Ecclesiastical History*.

[†] As already noted Constantine's father had been Constantius and he was incorporated into a dynasty making his grandson 'II'.

follow a Father, Son and Holy Spirit 'of equal majesty'. Those who demurred were to be denounced as 'insane and demented heretics' and would lose their sees. The creed passed by a hand-picked council of bishops in Constantinople in 381 reasserted the Father and Son as 'consubstantial' and described the Holy Spirit as 'proceeding from the Father'. Although there was no mention of the Holy Spirit being of one substance with the other two figures this was essentially a Trinitarian creed which would prevail in the mainstream Christian churches to this day.*

Other than it being his own belief, why had Theodosius chosen this alternative doctrine? He must have been aware that he needed to distinguish the Greek Church from the 'barbarian' tribes who had by this time been converted to Christianity of the subordinationist kind. This had been achieved. But it was also a matter of asserting imperial authority and eliminating the image of a Jesus who had been executed by a Roman governor, Pontius Pilate. One could hardly applaud a revolutionary who had challenged Roman authority. The crucifixion had to be downplayed. The success of Theodosius can be seen in the iconography that followed. By 390, Christ is shown in the Church of San Pudenziana in Rome as a magistrate sitting in authority. By 410 on a wooden panel on a door in Santa Sabina, also in Rome, he is shown with his arms outstretched and no cross behind him. By 500, in the Archiepiscopal Chapel in Ravenna, he is shown dressed as a Roman soldier. The transformation is complete and, with Constantine having told the historian Eusebius he had seen a vision of a cross in the sky proclaiming *In hoc signo vinces* ('In this sign you will conquer') before the Battle of the Milvian Bridge, Christian mythology now included an exhortation to spread the religion by force. It would be centuries before images of a suffering Christ reappeared.

From the mid-380s reports of a more aggressive Christianity

---

* As I have argued in my book AD *381*, the First Council of Constantinople was an important turning point in the history of European thought.

emerged. Groups of monks began smashing up temples and statues. By the 390s Theodosius, de facto ruler of both eastern and western empires,* was well established and confident enough to take the next step, the banning of all pagan shrines and festivals.† The Olympic Games, held according to tradition every four years from 776 BC, may have been celebrated for the last time in 393. At Aphrodisias, a church arose out of the ruins of the city's temple to Aphrodite and throughout the empire other pagan buildings, notably bathhouses, were ravaged. The pagan mosaics of the library at Sagalassos were defaced and the excavators attribute this to Christians. The Christianisation of cities gathered pace with new churches built and, in larger cities, a bishop's palace. The bishops now became the most important local authority figures, possessed of increasing administrative powers.

There was an important assumption behind all these developments: that religion needed to be brought into some kind of order and one coherent definition of doctrine imposed as the only acceptable form of belief. Never before in the classical world had a single religion been defined and imposed as a doctrine. At a time of imperial breakdown Theodosius' proscription marked a new emphasis on imperial authority. Scholars disagree as to whether the Nicene formula would have emerged as dominant in any case, but it seems sensible to assume that the debates were so sophisticated and abstruse that no consensus would have been possible without an imperial edict. One is reminded of Claudius Ptolemy's statement (p. 152) that theological agreement on 'the first cause' is impossible 'because of its completely invisible

---

* On Theodosius' death in 395, the empire split once again into east and west and this was to prove a permanent division. The eastern empire would emerge as the Byzantine empire which was to last until 1453.
† The outreach of an emperor was limited and so there are reports of pagan shrines continuing to operate after the 390s even into the fifth and sixth centuries.

and ungraspable nature'. Other than the short reign of the pagan emperor Julian (r. 361–3), the fourth century was one of a markedly imperial Christianity. By the sixth the Byzantine emperors were regarded as divine figures.

However, as Edward Watts writes in his *The Final Pagan Generation*, one can overestimate the impact of Christianity as destructive of pagan values. Three prominent figures, who struggled to maintain the old *paideia* – and whose 'fourth century was the age of houses full of gold coins, elaborate dinner parties honouring letter carriers, public orations before emperors, and ceremonies commemorating officeholders' – are the subjects of our next chapters.

21

The Court Orator: Themistius (c.AD 317–c.388)

In his summing-up of the new imperial authoritarianism of the fourth century, the classical scholar Christopher Kelly concludes: 'It was clearly in the interests of all jockeying for power and position or preferment to cheer loudly as the glittering procession of a godlike emperor passed them by.' Themistius was just such a man, a court orator, adept at shifting his allegiances between different emperors, both Christian and pagan, while claiming that he was a philosopher in the old tradition. There has been extensive scholarly debate over whether he was simply interested in maintaining his position and status within the imperial court or whether he adopted a more active role as an imperial propagandist. He is a good example of how *paideia* could still be exploited by an ambitious pagan to lend him credibility at a time when Christianity was becoming the dominant religion.

Themistius was born in about 317 in Paphlagonia, on the southern coast of the Black Sea. His father, Eugenius, was a teacher in Constantinople, himself the son of a philosopher, and it was here that he instructed the young Themistius in traditional *paideia* and philosophy. Yet Eugenius was also an enthusiastic landowner. He involved himself in planting and watering programmes in order to make his estate more productive. 'In agriculture', he is recorded by his son as saying, 'one could find the only kind of rest that is suitable for a philosopher.'

Until the late 340s Themistius travelled from city to city in Asia Minor offering his services as a rhetor while hoping for a permanent post. On his travels, he wrote a number of commentaries on works of Aristotle – something of a rarity at this time. However, his writings showed him to be, like many of his contemporaries, as much at home with Plato as with Aristotle. He believed in a hierarchy of spiritual forces which included the emperors sent by 'the Divine' as the culmination of the political hierarchy. Rather than withdrawing into himself to achieve a reclusive spirituality, as a philosopher such as Plotinus did, Themistius felt that he ought to participate actively in society, perhaps a reaction to his readings of Aristotle, who was always more concerned with the material world than Plato.

Themistius' breakthrough came in 347 when he was asked to make an oration before the emperor Constantius II. It was an astonishing coup for a man who had so few apparent connections, but he must have had some influential supporters even if their names are not recorded. Such speeches in the presence of emperors were not panegyrics or pleadings for patronage or privileges, but straightforward and frank expositions of philosophy in which the speaker had the opportunity to show himself to be a man in control of his desires and unabashed by the prospect of talking before an emperor. Thus Themistius told Constantius that it was no good 'wearing the crown on straight' when one's character was shameless or clothing one's body 'in fine and colourful raiment while exhibiting a mind bare of virtue'. In speaking in such terms Themistius – a man largely unknown to the emperor – was running quite a risk. The fact that he was prepared to gamble his life and future career in this way shows an impressive level of self-confidence.

Themistius prepared the oration meticulously.* He appears to have known of Dio's orations on kingship (see pp. 216–7) and he used some of the same rhetorical strategies as his predecessor, but he also showed that he was prepared to break conventions, not least in omitting the traditional expressions of the orator's inadequacy for the task ahead of him. Soon he was forging ahead into the philosophy of Aristotle and Plato and showing how the philanthropic virtues they proclaimed as the essence of a good leader were appropriate to Constantius. This was skilful rhetoric, in which Themistius was using his profound knowledge of literature and history, and it earned him the praise and respect of his contemporary and fellow rhetorician, Libanius. The speech before Constantius set him on a path for the next forty years; he treated every new emperor to the same accolade – that they represented the ideal virtues of Plato and Aristotle.

And the oration certainly paid off in political terms. In 355, Themistius was made a member of the Senate in Constantinople by Constantius. In a speech explaining the choice, Constantius praises Themistius as 'the spokesman of the ancient and wise men and the hierophant [the interpreter of sacred mysteries] of the innermost shrines and temples of philosophy'. Such a man 'shall improve the souls of those who dwell in her [the Senate] and raise up the gymnasium of virtue along with all the other buildings'. The civil service was expanding and places were available both for those of the traditional aristocratic elites and for newcomers from provincial families. The privileges that went with Themistius' new position included free supplies of grain and other food items. The relationship between emperor and orator also appears to have gelled on a personal level, since Constantius is known to have commissioned a bronze statue of Themistius in his honour. He also trusted Themistius to accompany him on a largely ceremonial embassy to Rome as the official leader of

---

* It is known by its title *Peri philanthropias*, as its main theme is to urge the emperor to exercise philanthropy.

the delegation. In this capacity, Themistius delivered a speech[*] in which he praised Constantius before the Roman senate.[†] He enthused that Constantius was indeed a philosopher-king recognised as such by a genuine philosopher. In the same oration Themistius presented Constantinople, still, of course, a relatively new foundation, as a well-established but subordinate ally of the ancient capital of the empire which was benefitting from the care of Constantius.

But Themistius began to face problems of image. Was he truly a philosopher when he appeared to be so embedded in material things? Or was he in fact a sophist, his oratory a cloak for personal ambition? Criticism was directed at him and Themistius fought back. He claimed that he took only a few of the perks of his senatorial job and that when he received grain he used it to feed his needy students. Rather than dressing up in the extravagant costume of a senator, he wore the sober garb of the philosopher.

Nevertheless Themistius played an active part in the routine duties of a senator. He is recorded as recruiting and scrutinising candidates for posts in the civil service (of which there were many for each vacancy) and this role was expanded by Constantius after Themistius' successful speech in Rome. Begging letters to Themistius from Libanius survive in which Libanius requests favours for his students by, for instance, reducing the heavy fees that admission to official posts required. It is not clear how far Themistius cooperated with granting these demands and what he might have gained personally had he been successful in pursuing them. What *is* clear is that he was becoming one of the most prominent officials of the regime, a man whose support was sought after, and who was able to build up his own following among the new senators. Themistius also appears to have gained

---

* It is known as *Oration 3*.

† In a famous description of the visit to Rome the historian Ammianus Marcellinus praises Constantius for processing through the city showing no sign of emotion as its splendour was revealed.

one of the salaried posts of teacher in Constantinople and as a result claimed not to need to charge his students fees. His generosity ensured that his fame as a teacher spread.

There were other ways in which Themistius made himself politically useful. While Constantius was a subordinationist Christian, he was not a fanatical one. Despite some reports of pagan temples being damaged during his reign, the destruction does not seem to have been widespread. The imperial bureaucracy grew inexorably during the fourth century, drawing in many of the men who in earlier times would have remained with their city assemblies. In the 350s most of them would still have been pagans. If the administration was to be effective the religious affiliations of its members needed to be sensitively handled and Themistius appears to have eased his way into acting as a go-between for a Christian emperor who could not afford to alienate his senior civil servants. In an age when *paideia* still had immense prestige and elitist Christians used much of the same terminology as the pagan philosophers, Themistius was clever enough to use words and phrases common to both. He was able to exploit the growing monotheism of the previous decades, for instance, by using the word *Theos*, 'God', which was recognisable by pagans and Christians alike. *Philanthropia*, 'love of mankind', the subject of his first speech to Constantius, had its roots in Stoicism but had also been adopted by Christians (in the writings of Clement and Origen, for instance). Themistius used this term often. He also avoided mentioning the debates over the precedence of Jewish or Greek philosophy (see pp. 261–4) which were dividing the two religious traditions.

While Themistius and Constantius were close, the imperial courts of the fourth century were tense places. Intrigues abounded and it was not unknown for leading officials to vanish between one reign and the next. Executions of fallen men were not uncommon (one might compare the situation with that of the English court of Henry VIII). Perhaps the most remarkable achievement of Themistius was to remain at the forefront of the imperial administration for a further four reigns.

Constantius' death in 361 saw the accession of his cousin Julian, who had been employed in fighting off barbarian invasions in the north. Julian championed the revival of pagan cults, especially the more mystical forms of Neoplatonism, and denigrated Christians. The Christian advance might have been reversed if he had not died on campaign in the east in 363. Having fallen out with Constantius before the latter's death Julian then proceeded to remove many of the late emperor's officials. While Themistius is recorded as having given a speech of welcome to Julian, he did not feel close to him even though he retained his position as a leading member of the Senate. Julian appears to have felt that Themistius was too much of a philosopher to play a role in public life. It is notable that Libanius appears to have asked him for fewer favours during Julian's reign. These years also brought sadness to Themistius' personal life. The funeral oration he made following the death of his father reveals the emotional impact the death made on him. But greater sorrows were to come, with the death of his wife and only son. By 359 he had remarried, and when Libanius congratulated him, Themistius replied that his main concern was now to have more children.

Julian's successor Jovian, proclaimed emperor by Julian's troops after the latter's death on campaign against the Sassanid Persians in 363,* restored Christianity. Themistius dealt shrewdly with the transition of power. An oration survives from the beginning of 364 in which he congratulates Jovian on becoming consul at the start of the new year. While Themistius had never been denounced by Julian, Themistius now claimed that Jovian had welcomed him back into imperial favour. Once again he stressed the importance of philosophy, thanking Jovian for his restoring it to the imperial palace. The humiliating peace with

---

* This was Themistius' version; other sources suggest it was more of a *coup d'etat*.

the Persians that the emperor Jovian had negotiated in 363 was greeted by Themistius as a victory.

The main thrust of the speech, however, was to applaud religious toleration. With a Christian emperor ruling over a still largely pagan landed class represented in the Senate, Themistius was ready to urge Jovian to give toleration to both paganism and Christianity. He argued that there are things that even an emperor cannot constrain, notably virtue and reverence for the divine. 'Since the deity has created a suitable disposition toward piety as a common feature of human nature, he has decreed that the manner of worship be left to the decision of each individual… The author of the universe takes pleasure in diversity.' Themistius goes on to claim that it is an unalterable law of God 'that the soul of each and every man be set free in regard to what it believes to be the way of paying reverence to God'. If a body was killed for its beliefs, 'its soul will escape, carrying away in its flight freedom of opinion'.

It is impossible to believe that Themistius would have made such a strong plea for toleration unless it accorded with Jovian's own views. It was quite clear that Julian's championing of his own version of paganism had been a failure and now balance had to be restored. The Christian bishops were demanding a revival of their influence and must have hoped that the new emperor would back them. However, precarious as his position was so early in his reign, Jovian could not afford to alienate the traditionalists who still made up much of his administration. Whatever Themistius' own beliefs, and they can hardly have been in favour of the continued expansion of Christianity, his prime objective was to ensure he embedded himself in the favour of the new regime. What he would not have expected was that, not much more than a month after making his speech, he would soon have to establish an allegiance to a new emperor.

When Jovian died in February 364 without ever making it back to Constantinople from the Persian front, Valentinian, a successful general, was acclaimed as emperor by his troops and appointed his brother Valens as co-emperor in the east. The brothers' family originated in Pannonia, in the Balkans, and both were Latin speakers. The earliest chance for Themistius to make a speech of welcome to Valens was probably in late 364, when the empire had been officially divided and Valens had arrived in Constantinople. It is known that the emperor was present in the Senate when the speech was given and had, in fact, given his own speech in Latin to the body the day before.

Themistius trod carefully. Power sharing in the empire had not been a success. Diocletian's Tetrarchy had been subverted by Constantine, who reverted to a system of dynastic succession by leaving the empire to his three sons. But this had not worked well, the eldest son, Constantine II, and his brother Constans fighting each other over portions of the empire. So Themistius had to emphasise the brotherly love between Valentinian and Valens in the hope that this time division would not end in civil war. He could also dwell on the short reign of Jovian, suggesting that his death followed from his lack of divine support. Valens and Valentinian on the other hand had been proclaimed from above, the army which had elevated them acting as agents of God.

The God that Themistius describes in this oration is one acceptable to both pagans and Christians. He has, Themistius tells his audience, three supreme attributes, eternal life, superabundance of power and benignity towards mankind. There was nothing here that either pagans or Christians could disagree with. So once again Themistius could plead for religious toleration and his stance may have been agreed with Valens beforehand as a means of securing the new emperor breadth of support. He followed his customary path of denouncing Valens' predecessor. Having earlier applauded Jovian's treaty with the Persians as a victory, Themistius now declared it to be a defeat. Another theme of the oration is Valens' care for the city of Constantinople which he had promised in his initial speech. Themistius naturally supported him. The expansion of

Constantinople had created a desperate need for more water to be provided for the city. Valens followed earlier traditions of patronage in commissioning an aqueduct, much of which still stands today.

By 375, Valens was facing a growing crisis on the Danube border as groups of Goths migrated into the empire. At first he had welcomed the incursions, hoping that if the Goths were brought under control they could provide recruits for the armies and, if they settled, they could be taxed. Yet it was soon clear that their numbers were too great; the Goths went on the rampage searching for food, and the only way of containing them was by military confrontation. There were problems also further east where the Sassanids were threatening Armenia. Valens had made it his priority to defend this border and he had travelled there with Themistius, a sign of how effectively the orator had established a relationship with the emperor. With so many enemies confronting Valens, he urgently needed more manpower and it was lucky that Themistius was at hand when Valens needed a senior official to cross the empire to Rome and plead for more troops from the western emperor. Themistius set off, travelling day and night, sleeping under the stars, as he later described his desperate mission. He arrived in Rome sometime in 376. The emperor Valentinian had died the year before and Themistius had to deploy his oratory on Valentinian's son Gratian, the new emperor. He employed his usual flattery, proclaiming that Gratian embodied the values of leadership endorsed by Plato. His oratory brought some success in that Gratian must have realised that only a joint effort by the emperors would defeat the Goths and he agreed to release some troops. In fact Gratian's response proved inadequate. Many westerners believed that the threat from the Goths had been exaggerated. They were wrong. In 378 Valens and his legions were surrounded by a large force of Goths at Adrianople in Thrace, and the eastern emperor was killed in a defeat signalling that the growing military power of the 'barbarians' was all too real.

Yet another time Themistius was faced with a new emperor, the Spanish general Theodosius, appointed by Gratian in January 379. Themistius was now in his sixties but his oratory was still effective enough to ensure his survival. He dwelt on the inexperience of Valens compared to his replacement. He emphasised his closeness to the new emperor, even presenting himself as the guardian of Theodosius' son Arcadius. This was a clever ploy. Any enemies he had could hardly risk attacking him if, in so doing, they risked drawing the ire of the emperor. Once again Themistius sold himself as bringing philosophy into the palace. 'I am able to contribute words that are more peaceful than Homer's... would anyone not permit me, according to my custom, to cull virgin blooms from the meadows of Plato and Aristotle, which no blade has touched, and to weave crowns of human happiness for the king?' His clever presentation of the new emperor as a man of culture was once again an intrinsic part of his success.

Theodosius had been chosen by Gratian over Gratian's half-brother who was only eighteen. Theodosius was thirteen years older than Gratian and was more experienced in war. He was also a determined character as his initiatives in church affairs would soon show. While he was new to the east, it was inevitable that with time he would emerge as the stronger of the two emperors and in his first oration before the emperor in 379, when Theodosius, travelling eastwards to Constantinople on the Via Egnatia,* had reached Thessalonika, Themistius framed him as such. He emphasised that while Gratian had been declared emperor simply because he was the son of his father, Theodosius had earned his place because of his great natural abilities. Themistius predicted a bright future for the new emperor. He

---

* This essential road linking west and east had first been constructed in the second century BC. Starting as a continuation of the Via Appia, it crossed what is now Albania, Greece and Turkey on its way to Constantinople and the extensive road network of the eastern provinces.

assumed that Theodosius would be able to defeat the Goths and restore peace. 'Now fighting spirit returns to the cavalry and returns also to the infantry.' Theodosius would, according to Themistius, continue to make Constantinople the equal of Rome with new buildings and an enlarged senate.

However, it was not so easy. Theodosius suffered another defeat by the Goths in 380 and then came to accept that there had to be a negotiated peace. In an oration of January 381, Themistius cleverly switched from promoting Theodosius as a man of war to praising him as an effective civilian leader and then, subtly, playing again on Theodosius' experience, presented him as the more powerful of the two emperors. Just at this time, Theodosius was using the council of bishops he had summoned to Constantinople to declare that Constantinople was second only to Rome in the religious hierarchy. It was a bold move and one which earned Theodosius and his successors the enmity of Jerusalem, Antioch and Alexandria, all of whom claimed a more significant Christian heritage.

The peace that Theodosius had effected with the Goths in 382 appears to have been an acknowledgement that they could not be defeated (one of the terms agreed was that the Goths should be allowed to live under their own laws), but it was presented by Themistius as a *deditio*, a surrender by the Goths. At this time no one could envisage any relationship between Romans and barbarians other than that of conqueror and vanquished but the reality was that the empire was now on the defensive against forces that it was unable to defeat. In his oration, Themistius had to accept that the Goths had not been dispersed but he claimed that this was a deliberate policy, since it would make them easier to tax and recruit as soldiers.

In his speech of January 383, Themistius acknowledges that 'my body is worn out and old age advances, now is the time to lay aside my writing tablet'. However, Theodosius would not allow him to rest. Soon after this oration he was appointed urban prefect of Constantinople, a senior position, the primary concern of which was the competent administration of the city. The post offered enormous opportunities for exercising power and making money. It was normally held for a year but Themistius would last only a few months. His acceptance of the role triggered much of the same public opposition that had greeted him when he had been appointed to the Senate. Ambitious young men – the post would normally have been held by a man in his forties or fifties – must have been frustrated by the appointment. The old questions arose: how could such a promotion be reconciled with the life of a philosopher? As his critics complained, he had been offered the post before but had turned it down for this very reason. But Themistius once again retaliated. There were many cases of philosophers accepting public office, he said, and taking on the post offered him the chance to bring 'divine principles' into the secular world. Furthermore, any criticism of him was surely an indirect criticism of the emperor for appointing him. Yet, if, as he had argued, Theodosius was the ideal philosopher-king on the model of Plato, surely it was right for a philosopher to serve him. When he had previously been offered the post, the offer had come from a less worthy emperor. He listed other more minor offices he had already held as if he now deserved what was almost the most senior post in the administration. These rigorous, well-argued defences showed that Themistius' ability to compose and sustain a speech before an audience remained undiminished.

Nothing is known of the response of Themistius' critics to his defences. Very soon after his early retirement from the post, he withdrew from the scene. No more orations of his are recorded after early 385. It is telling that he fades from view just when Christianity was becoming more aggressive. In 384, the new praetorian prefect, Maternus Cynegius, had unleashed a programme of temple destruction. Paganism was on the defensive and, as we have seen, Theodosius was to ban all pagan cults in the early 390s. This was not a climate in which a pagan philosopher could prosper. There is one reference to Themistius still being alive in 388 but that year is normally seen as being his last.

Peter Heather and David Moncur in their fine study *Politics, Philosophy, and Empire in the Fourth Century: Select Orations of Themistius* describe Themistius as 'a talisman, a symbol that the importance of traditional Hellenic values was being recognised by Christian emperors in a period of huge cultural change'. He was faced with a succession of vulnerable Christian emperors who desperately needed to secure their positions. What was remarkable was they came to rely so heavily on a pagan philosopher and there is every evidence that his relationship with each (with the possible exception of Julian) was a close one. Themistius manipulated every new challenge both to his advantage and to that of each emperor. He even gained the respect of Gregory of Nazianzus, the Cappadocian-born bishop whose sermons in Constantinople in 380 are one of the most erudite defences of the doctrine of the Trinity.* One could also argue that he initiated a new form of political philosophy which urged the ruler to incorporate the virtues of the great philosophers into his method of rule.

---

* Gregory was briefly archbishop of Constantinople, appointed as such by Theodosius following his declaration of the Trinity. He did not survive long, easily overcome by the turmoil of the ensuing First Council of Constantinople.

22

The Last of the Pagan Orators: Libanius
(AD 314–393)

Athens was still a major cultural centre in the fourth century AD, even though the city had been in economic decline for some 600 years. The original landed families whose wealth had sustained the city were no more, and in one humiliating moment there were such limited resources to pay a grain ship that a teacher had to ask his wealthy pupils to contribute. After the disruptive invasion by the Heruli (in AD 267) the teaching schools appear to have continued without interruption but a major social change seems to have taken place around this time. Violent behaviour in the city, largely between rival groups of students who identified themselves with a particular teacher, became commonplace. There are reports of teachers flaunting their status by processing through the streets with the favoured pupils crowding around them. There were even cases of less scrupulous pedagogues meeting prospective students arriving at the port and getting them to sign up (and presumably pay) for classes on the spot. On a number of occasions the governor of the province had to intervene. In 339 he dismissed three of the professors who held state-funded chairs when their students got out of hand. However, protests forced him to back down and reinstate them. In future, such disciplinary action took place only when the teachers themselves demanded that one of their colleagues be censured. Increasingly, teaching moved from public buildings to private homes. Excavations in Athens have shown what appear to be teachers' houses of the period with halls attached. We encountered earlier the arrangement by which some students paid a 'listener's' fee and were able to move from one teacher to another. But this system atrophied.

Much of what we know about student life in fourth-century AD Athens comes from a student from the provinces. Libanius was born in Antioch, in the province of Syria, in 314. His family prided themselves on their wealth, education, rhetoric and patronage of festivals and games but problems with the family finances and the death of his father held him back and it was not until he was twenty-two (in AD 336) that Libanius arrived in Athens to study rhetoric. It was the culmination of a dream. 'Like Odysseus, I think that I would have looked past even marriage with a goddess for a glimpse of the smoke of Athens.'* In his *Autobiography*, Libanius described how he had given up the normal pleasures of boyhood to concentrate on studying the great speakers of the past. He was quickly disillusioned by the rowdiness of his fellow students and was contemptuous of any who did not share his enthusiasms. While he always retained an admiration for the cultural heritage of Athens, he had to admit that 'because of old age, they [many teachers] would need to sleep peacefully with their bellies full'. His favoured mentor from earlier times was Aelius Aristides, whose orations he studied in detail and often used as models.

Libanius showed himself so accomplished a speaker that he was offered one of the professorial vacancies created by the sackings of 339. Behind the scenes it is clear that he was an obsessive networker. At twenty-five he was ten years younger than the holders of the other chairs but, of course, Libanius lost his chair when the original holder was reinstated. Next he moved

---

* This refers to Odysseus' dalliance with the goddess Circe.

to Constantinople before being appointed to the chair of rhetoric at Nicomedia between 343 and 348. He travelled widely, relishing the chance to speak of the ancient glories of Athens and show that he was deeply immersed in the traditional culture of *paideia*. In 349, he composed a panegyric to two sons of Constantine, the joint emperors Constans and Constantius II. This proved so successful that he was summoned to Constantinople to take up a prestigious chair of rhetoric. He found the atmosphere of the city so politically tense, however, that he asked to be able to move to his native city of Antioch where he spent the rest of his life, from 354 to 393. He remained fond of Nicomedia and was devastated when a massive earthquake followed by a tsunami in 358 destroyed the city and killed one of his closest friends among thousands more who were trapped in collapsed houses.

Libanius was awarded Antioch's only chair in rhetoric when he arrived in 354. The post and the standing of his family (he talks of his grey-haired mother and a brother who was already a grandfather, as well as his old friends from school) ensured he would always be a member of the city's social elite. One of his uncles, Phasganius, was particularly influential in acting as a patron and helping him settle in. Secure in this family backing, Libanius was never afraid to criticise the governors of the city and its town council. Some of his most cutting speeches deplore the treatment of the impoverished of the city. In one case he highlights the wretched state of prisoners who were immured for so long that they died before their cases could come to court. Owing to the nature of the post, Libanius was excused from other official responsibilities in the city. This meant that his impact on municipal matters was limited and he was often frustrated at being ignored. From the point of view of patronage, he would have been better off close to the imperial court in Constantinople.

Yet Libanius loved Antioch more than he did Constantinople. Some of his most famous orations provide a panorama of a sophisticated city. 'Don't we have a mild climate, delightful baths, a wonderful market, a spring glistening with flowers, a summer that is bright with the colours of fruit trees and that with its perfumes makes the city into a meadow.' He described the Orontes river, whose waters were fed through the city's fountains, and the long colonnades following the line of the streets, which were, he said, like flowing rivers themselves. The city had a diverse population, Greeks, Jews, Syrians, Romans, with Syriac as a native language within the city and Aramaic outside. So there was a bustling atmosphere of different minorities. Antioch had recovered from the destruction wreaked by the Persians a hundred years earlier and remained an important base for the defence of the eastern frontier.

Libanius has left a vast body of works: formal orations, declamations prepared as models for his students, thoughts on the speeches of the Athenian orator Demosthenes, and over 1,500 letters. The latter make him a major source of evidence for the nature of the relationships between a rhetor and his professional contacts. Libanius was clearly a superb networker. Not surprisingly he was a traditionalist. He was supremely confident in his use of Attic and deeply learned in the classical texts. He was acclaimed for the elegance of his writing. Aware of how Christianity was threatening the *paideia* of earlier centuries, Libanius was saddened by this development. With the decline of city life, the opportunities for traditional rhetoric also appear to have been diminishing. It was far better, said some, to learn Latin and make a fortune in Rome. As all Roman law was first promulgated in Latin (as was the Theodosian Code issued in Constantinople in 438*), a career in law did indeed require a good command of the language. In one of his orations, Libanius

---

* This famous law code, an amalgamation of laws passed since 312, was issued jointly by the emperors Theodosius and Valentinian III. The Code privileged orthodox Christianity and no fewer than sixty-five decrees against 'heretics' were included.

lamented the spread of Latin in the east and claimed that he did not know any at all.[*]

Libanius was a contemporary of Themistius and, as we have seen, the two men corresponded. However, their objectives were very different: Libanius was an orator. 'To me, as with the nightingale, singing is enough,' as he engagingly put it. Themistius prided himself on being a philosopher, an important distinction. When one of Libanius' students wished to progress from rhetoric to philosophy, Libanius recommended him to Themistius. Themistius loved being close to power and on a visit to Antioch in 356, he claimed that he missed the limelight of Constantinople. Libanius, on the other hand, had no interest in becoming a senator and dealing with emperors.

The two also differed in their attitudes to the emperor Julian. Although Libanius had never taught Julian, their paths had crossed in Constantinople and they had corresponded even before Julian became emperor. Once Julian had come to the throne in 361,[†] Libanius embraced him for his restoration of paganism in a way that Themistius had failed to do. Julian had arrived in Antioch on his way to fight on the eastern frontier and was distressed that Antioch had not given him and his restoration of paganism more fervent approval. He relied heavily on Libanius for support, which Libanius provided in a manner more typical of Themistius. In a response to a letter of approval from Julian, Libanius wrote: 'I feel that, even if I sipped nectar, my joy would be no greater than now, when an emperor, whom Plato sought long ago and found at last, has commended my resolution and admired my oration.' He was uncompromising

---

[*] Evidence from the church councils of the east show that virtually no bishops spoke Latin and had to have Latin texts translated for them. A rare inscription on a statue base from c.AD 400 has been found in Aphrodisias honouring one Oecumenius as 'expert in the laws' who has 'blended the Italian muse with the sweet-voiced honey of the Attic'.

[†] Julian was a legitimate successor as he was the son of a half-brother of the first Constantine.

in his support for Julian's renunciation of the Christianity into which he had been born. 'You quickly threw aside your error,' he told the emperor, 'released yourself from darkness and grasped truth instead of ignorance, reality in place of falsehood, our old gods in place of that wicked one and his rites.'

A few months later Julian was dead, killed in battle, and two of Libanius' orations, an emotional lament (*monodia*) and a more formal funeral oration, show a profound sense of grief. Libanius' hopes of building a closer relationship with an emperor and so enhancing his status had been dashed. In one of his letters he writes that his ambitions have now become 'weaker than shadows'. In the *Monody* he laments the disaster of Julian's death – it leaves an empire lawless and abandoned by the very gods that Julian had venerated. Libanius dwells on the achievements of Julian, moral, cultural, military and political, and then describes a personal depression so overpowering, he says, that he cannot even write.

In the funeral oration, composed over the winter months of 363–4, Libanius expands on Julian's charisma and intellect. 'He was the only one of the young men who came to Athens that went away having imparted instruction rather than received it… there was always to be seen around him, like a swarm of bees, a crowd of young and old, philosophers and rhetoricians.' Julian would have loved to have stayed in Athens, Libanius tells us, but his cousin Constantius' call to duty on the northern frontiers impelled him to take up command there. Once he became emperor he needed to reform the court and Libanius' account provides a vivid picture of its teeming day-to-day life. 'On looking into the state of the imperial court, and seeing a useless multitude kept for no purpose, a thousand cooks, and hairdressers no fewer, cup-bearers yet more numerous, swarms of waiters, eunuchs in number beyond the flies around the flocks in spring, and of all other descriptions an indescribable lot of drones… he expelled them forthwith.' Libanius ignores the problems resulting from Julian's programme of restoring paganism. 'Reconciling the gods to the earth, he resembled a ship-builder who again equips a great ship, that has lost her rudders, with new ones… and yet what greater action can one name than his praising the gods, and that noblest gift of the gods, literature.' It is obvious that for Libanius an emperor cannot also be a Christian and thus abandon Greek culture with its traditional gods. Libanius concludes with a vivid description of Julian's last campaign and death. His adulation for Julian may have affected Libanius' status with subsequent emperors. In his later letters, no longer able to boast of influence with the court, he dwells on past rather than present triumphs. But it is instructive to look in detail at Libanius' role as a teacher.

Antioch was second only to Athens as a centre for rhetoric and Libanius was determined to make his school the best. He brought fifteen students with him from Constantinople and, on his arrival back in his home city, delivered his *dokimasia*, the ritual declamation that showed he had benefitted from studying in Athens. According to Libanius, this was such a resounding success that he soon he had fifty pupils signed up – the cause of some ructions with the existing teachers, and a reminder of just how much competition there was for students. Always sensitive to opposition, Libanius was furious if any of his students transferred to another teacher and was often unfairly critical of his competitors. There is evidence from his *Autobiography* that he faced accusations of scandalous behaviour which he blamed on malicious rumour-mongers. Scholars disagree on how far Libanius' *Autobiography*, which presents him in a consistently flattering light, is a reliable account of his career.

In one of his orations, delivered in 382, Libanius boasts that in his career he has taught students from every part of the eastern empire – even from beyond the Euphrates and into Armenia. Typically they would arrive at the age of fourteen – but a later start was possible, as we have seen with Libanius himself in Athens. Syrians seem to have constituted the largest group among his students, but Cilicians were also prominent, and every province of Anatolia provided their share. Others came from Arabia and Palestine. Few were known to Libanius before their arrival and he had to make an assessment of each one. Many students brought him gifts and it is unclear to what extent they formed part of the fees that were expected. Libanius prided himself on not charging students from poorer families, although even those less fortunate must have paid for a conventional education before he admitted them to his class. The students would still have to find living expenses. Some of Libanius' most persuasive letters are those pleading for support for a worthy student. It is clear that there were philanthropists who would help in such cases.

Despite his reservations about the spread of Christianity, Libanius was quite happy to take on Christian students as long as they accepted teaching from a pagan perspective as was still practised by many. The case of Basil of Caesarea Mazaca (in Cappadocia) provides a good example. Basil had been briefly a student of Libanius in Constantinople and a letter survives from Libanius which praises him for his elegant letter writing. After a career in law and teaching rhetoric, Basil was baptised a Christian and expressed regret for his 'devotion to the teachings of a [pagan] wisdom that God had made foolish'. He then enjoyed a distinguished career as bishop, theologian and charity worker. Even so, probably in the 370s in his old age, Basil wrote a tract entitled *Address to Young Men on How They Might Derive Benefit from Greek Literature* in which he encouraged Christian students to master pagan philosophy before they studied theology.* He recommended students to his old teacher. This was typical. Many of Libanius' letters show how he kept up a network of correspondents who might help to sustain his school. He was particularly pleased when a father whom he had taught sent his sons to study with him – and even more so when a boy could already recite Homer or reproduce some of the speeches

* The 'Address' was to become especially popular among Renaissance humanist scholars.

of Demosthenes by the time he arrived. Reports would be sent back to fathers, telling of the progress of their sons.

The transition in a Greek education from the grammarian (see pp. 26–8) to the teacher of rhetoric was an important one. While the grammarian dealt with the detailed examination of texts, the rhetor was more interested in their flow. Once he had assessed the accomplishments of a new student, Libanius would begin with a study of Homer's *Iliad*. The curriculum then followed a standard pattern, to which Libanius faithfully adhered. What mattered was the skills the teacher brought to his commentaries and here Libanius came into his own. He made such a sophisticated analysis of the speeches of Demosthenes that later Byzantine scholars referred to him as 'the second Demosthenes'. Plato vied with Demosthenes as the best writer of Greek prose and students engaged with his *Dialogues* at an early stage of their education. Euripides was the favoured playwright, Thucydides the preferred historian. Libanius was regarded as such an outstanding teacher that many of his declamations were recorded and then entered other teachers' reading lists. Students are said to have joined his classes after reading his declamations elsewhere.

The purpose of all this textual study was to develop the ability to compose one's own text and deliver it. The student began gradually, often using Libanius' declamations as a model. The written text would be revised again and again and then practised aloud. Learning how to use one's voice and presence was crucial to the process of transforming a text into an oration that would be persuasive and respected for its originality. Libanius once complained that students were rehearsing so loudly during the night that they kept the neighbours awake. Finally, probably in the third year – but earlier for the most brilliant pupils – a student would be ready to speak in front of the whole school. Libanius would then offer his own observations. He was a demanding and critical teacher, so this must have been a daunting moment for the students. But any successful rhetor would have to perform in public so this test of the student's ability at public declamations was compulsory. Three years seems to have been a normal period of study, though often students would stay on for further practice or progress to one of the prestigious schools in Athens for the finishing touches. Remembering his own disturbed time in the city, Libanius was often irritated by their apparent rejection of his teaching. The satirist Lucian ridiculed those who kept studying over 'whole Olympic cycles'. Those staying for shorter periods, one or two years, might still pick up enough experience to be able to speak in the law courts or in city assemblies.

Libanius would provide references for his 'finished' students. In a stroke of good fortune for their prospects a man named Modestus, who had been a prominent official in Antioch, had moved to Constantinople as city prefect. In a spate of requests to Modestus to offer places for his students, Libanius admitted 'adding more cargo to an overburdened ship'. His highest recommendation was that a student would be 'great defending people on trial or great in the same position where I am'. His recommendations show that above all he valued character, graciousness, self-control, diligence and, of course, skill in public speaking. Libanius firmly disapproved of the growing practice of purchasing offices. He despised those who flaunted their wealth.

As we saw in the life of Themistius, Theodosius appointed a new praetorian prefect, Maternus Cynegius, who in 384 initiated a programme of demolishing temples. When Cynegius embarked on a tour of inspection of the provinces of Syria, Mesopotamia and Egypt between 386 and 388, it was monks and bishops among his entourage who carried out the assaults on pagan shrines. Theodosius appears to have acquiesced in the destruction. Libanius decided to respond to these events in the form of an oration addressed to the emperor (although it seems it was never delivered in person). This oration is a rare surviving account of how a pagan saw the growth of Christianity. Prudently,

Libanius chose not to denounce Christianity or Theodosius himself but rather the 'monks' who were wrecking ancient sites that had seen centuries of worship. He astutely argues that it is imperial law that they are breaking.

> But those black-garbed people… run to the temples, bringing with them wood, and stones, and iron, and when they have not these, hands and feet… the roofs are uncovered, walls are pulled down, images are carried off, and altars are overturned: the [pagan] priests all the while must be silent upon pain of death. When they have destroyed one temple they run to another, and a third, and trophies are erected upon trophies: which are all contrary to [your] law.

He demands that the emperor rein in his unscrupulous subordinates. Although he does not mention Cynegius by name, the praetorian prefect is clearly his target.

As he grew older Libanius became more bitter. Whether this was because of ill health, or his feeling that the old traditions were being challenged, or the growing concentration among teachers on making money, he was increasingly disillusioned by his students and their failure to dedicate themselves to their studies. He talked of himself as a farmer whose seed falls only on stones. One of his gripes was that his traditional policy of not charging poorer students fees was being exploited by those who had the resources to pay. There is evidence from other teachers and centres of education that students were indeed becoming more restless in this period, more ready to move from one teacher to another if they were dissatisfied. The older tradition that one might stay with the same teacher over a number of years was fading.

In 387 rioting broke out in Antioch after news of new taxes reached the city. Many of Libanius' students fled but there was a more enduring outcome of this unrest. Sacrilege had been committed when rioters defaced statues of the emperor. Theodosius immediately closed the hippodrome and theatres

(Libanius cynically suggested that the closure of the places of entertainment was why the students had left!) and accused the town council of failing to keep order. Further punishment appeared imminent. When Flavian, the elderly bishop of Antioch, left for Constantinople to plead with Theodosius to show compassion, the city waited in trepidation for the emperor's response. Flavian was successful and Antioch was pardoned, though many of its privileges were temporarily withdrawn.

It must have been humiliating for Libanius not to have been chosen to lead the delegation to Theodosius himself but it was a sign of how the climate was changing. In the city itself, John Chrysostom, a brilliant orator (*chrysostom*, 'of the golden voice'), once a pupil of Libanius who said John would have been his successor 'if the Christians had not taken him from us', preached a series of sermons which resonated with the Christian population. John suggested that this was what the Last Judgement would be like, so constructing a Christian narrative from the traumatic events.* Libanius must have been hurt by a former pupil rousing such emotions. His surviving orations of the year suggest he was determined to reassert rhetoric used in support of traditional values but now rhetoric was being diverted to new causes and soon afterwards Theodosius would ban all worship at pagan shrines so draining the lifeblood from Libanius' world.

In these last years of his life, Libanius continued to write letters to prominent contacts in the imperial administration, but he was plagued by migraines and his sight was failing. He had had a son, Cimon, by a live-in companion, and Cimon's death in 392 prostrated him further. (He blames his failing eyesight on his continual weeping at Cimon's death.) It was a sad ending to an active and productive life. Yet after his death his orations were greatly treasured by Byzantine scholars, who preferred their

---

* The pagan art of rhetoric could easily be transferred into the Christian sermon. It is often forgotten that Augustine was the city orator in Milan before his conversion.

austere style over the more flamboyant examples of his rivals. His reputation would remain high for centuries and he provides us with a mass of evidence for the cultural life of the empire of Late Antiquity.

23

The Neoplatonist Philosopher and Mathematician: Hypatia (c.AD 355–415)

Philosophers still occupied their distinct role in the Greek world as late as the early fifth century, even though by now pagan learning was under threat from the Christian Church. Philosophers stood apart from the tensions and chaos of the late antique cities, reflecting on the importance of virtuous public duty and ready to share advice without charging for it. Earlier subjects of this book, such as Dio Chrysostom and Plutarch, are examples of men sustained by private wealth who spoke of good government and concord within and between cities. So in 415 there was nothing unusual in Orestes, the Roman prefect of Egypt, whose palace was in Alexandria, consulting the most respected philosopher of the city, in this rare case a woman, Hypatia.

Hypatia was born about 355. Her father, Theon, a mathematician who had written texts on Euclid and Ptolemy, appears to have made mathematics a substantial part of Hypatia's education. This was not unusual in that Plato had taught that mathematical logic was the gateway to a deeper understanding of his philosophy, but Theon took the subject to a much more advanced level. Theon and Hypatia would have known of the *Collectio*, a comprehensive textbook on mathematics by Pappus, an early fourth-century Alexandrian,* which consisted of eight books covering such subjects as geometry, mathematical proofs, astronomy and mechanics. Pappus was primarily a geometer and the last Greek who is considered to have done original work in the subject, although later Byzantine scholars considered him to be as much a philosopher as a mathematician. He expected his readers to have access to other mathematical texts which they could consult alongside the *Collectio*. Among them was Ptolemy's *Almagest* (see pp. 155–7).

Hypatia eventually began to produce works of her own. She wrote a commentary on Books Three to Thirteen of the *Almagest*, which appears to have been a revision of her father's work on Ptolemy. In this sense she is as much an astronomer as a mathematician as is evidenced by the fact that she was later consulted by a student on how to build an astrolabe. There are much later sources which suggest that she also worked on the brilliant, and still forbidding, work on conics by the third-century BC geometer Apollonius of Perga and the *Arithematica* of Diophantus, a mathematician of the third century AD. As both these scholars worked in Alexandria, and Apollonius is mentioned specifically in Pappus' *Collectio*, this is not impossible. The authors of such commentaries had the intellectual sophistication needed to understand the original text and to provide clarification of it for new readers. It is clear that Hypatia was by now working at the highest level, beyond what her father had ever achieved. Whether or not Pappus, Theon and Hypatia deserve to be called philosophers rather than mathematicians, they certainly had a broad intellectual understanding of both disciplines and the degree to which they reinforced each other.

Theon had established a teaching school in Alexandria. From the 380s, however, he seems to have ceded the day-to-day running of the school to Hypatia. By the 390s she was firmly

---

* Nothing is known of Pappus' life but a mention of an eclipse of the Sun which took place in Alexandria in AD 320 places him there.

in charge and her students were able to study both philosophy and mathematics. She had access to the commentaries on Aristotle of Alexander of Aphrodisias and Porphyry's works on Plotinus. In keeping with tradition, her teaching included an emphasis on virtuous behaviour. Despite her reputed beauty, she maintained her virginity, as was often the case with philosophers. (Plato, Epicurus and Epictetus himself had never married.) As we have seen, Plotinus' was not the only brand of Neoplatonism to flourish at this time. There was a rival school developed by Iamblichus (*c.250–c.330*), a Syrian philosopher and pupil of Porphyry, which relied on revelations and rituals that invoked divine spirits and which proved popular in Alexandria. Centred on the Serapeum, which was equipped with a shrine and teaching rooms, this school was overtly antagonistic to Christianity. Hypatia, however, continued to follow the less aggressive doctrines of Plotinus.

It is lucky that the letters of one of the pupils at Hypatia's school survive. Synesius was a wealthy Libyan from Cyrene, already a Christian but avid to know more of pagan philosophy. Hypatia welcomed him and other Christians. He repaid the compliment. Synesius had visited Athens out of curiosity but found that the teaching there was sterile. Writing to his brother, he says: 'in our time, Egypt nourishes the fruits it receives from Hypatia, but Athens, which used to be the city of the wise, now has only its beekeepers to keep it happy'. A certain fluidity still existed among the diverse Christian traditions of Alexandria; many Christians followed Clement and Origen in recognising the value of Greek philosophy. We have already encountered the *Address to Young Men on How They Might Derive Benefit from Greek Literature*, by the Cappadocian father Basil of Caesarea, while Plotinus' analysis of the divine was not far from Christian concepts of a threefold structure of God. Hypatia does not seem to have made any compromises with Christian dogma in her teaching; instead she focused on the relationship between the material world and the divine, as had been the concern of Greek philosophers for 750 years. By refusing to teach the philosophy of Iamblichus, she also had no need to enter pagan temples for the rituals he practised and so avoided any impropriety for her Christian students.

Synesius' letters refer to an inner circle of Hypatia's devotees – a group of favourite students selected by their teacher as being most dedicated to philosophy. Synesius talks of purification and contemplation of the divine in a form that would be as relevant to pagans as to Christians. Letters to the other students he met at the school describe the bonds created between them. 'Since we live the life of the mind', he wrote to an individual named Herculian, 'we are bound by a divine law that requires us to honour one another.' Another letter refers to the difficulty in sharing the advanced philosophy taught by Hypatia with those who had not attended the school community. The implication here is that one most undergo an initiation into divine knowledge. One senses a Platonic emphasis on the higher part of the soul being beyond physical passions and so resistant to sex and intemperate lifestyles. Hypatia certainly set an example here. Long after he had left the school, Synesius asked for her endorsement of works he had written whose quality had been called into question by critics. He asked for her reassurance when he experienced personal traumas such as the death of his children or the onset of illness.

Yet times were changing. The Christian community in Alexandria was growing. While Christians valued Plato, and he can be seen as providing the intellectual backbone of Christian theology, the empiricism of Aristotle was now disparaged for being too materialist and Epicurus rejected for his godlessness. The variety of schools was now diminishing. Hypatia's school appears to have been among the last that sustained the wide breadth of learning of Alexandria's heyday, not least in preserving the importance of mathematics. By the 380s Christians were becoming more assertive. Theodosius had declared the Trinity of Father, Son and Holy Spirit, the Nicene formula, as the only acceptable doctrine and this had been endorsed by the Council of Constantinople in 381. Aggressive monks were taking the initiative in sacking temples and shrines in Egypt and Syria. In Alexandria tensions grew after the selection of the Nicene Theophilus as patriarch of the city in 385.* In 391 the Christian emperor Theodosius banned all pagan cults, including visits to temples and sacrifices.

Theophilus was not going to miss the opportunity for a display of Nicene Christian triumphalism. When he discovered pagan cult objects in a disused Mithraic shrine he paraded and mocked them. His provocations led to riots and the pagan rioters seized the great and previously impregnable complex of the Serapeum. Olympus, a teacher of Iamblichus' philosophy, rallied the occupants with eloquent defences of the cult of Serapis and, according to Christian sources, atrocities were committed against Christians. There was a stand-off and the emperor was called on to intervene. Theodosius effected a compromise: the rioters should leave the Serapeum and would be allowed to go free provided they renounced all pagan activities. The rioters duly dispersed and many of the remaining pagan teachers left the city. Theophilus now changed both the ethos and physical structure of the city by building churches where temples had once stood. The hallowed statue of Serapis was torn apart by the Christians who had reoccupied the Serapeum, and a shrine containing relics of John the Baptist and the prophet Elisha took its place. But this was only the start. In a decree of 408, the emperors of east and west commanded that 'if any images now stand in the temples and shrines, and if they have ever received or do now receive the worship of pagans anywhere, they shall be torn down'.

Hypatia was not directly involved in these events as her school

---

* 'Patriarch' is a title, derived from the Old Testament, given by tradition to the bishops of Rome, Constantinople, Jerusalem, Alexandria and Antioch.

did not include pagan rituals, but she must have realised that the freedom to express her philosophy was under threat. In fact, she was prepared to move openly around the city as philosophers had always done and she appears to have had a calming influence. Respect for Hypatia's intellectual supremacy together with her personal integrity gave her a formidable reputation. The fifth-century church historian Socrates Scholasticus noted that 'everyone was awestruck and admired her more because of her overwhelming prudence'. Another later historian, the Athenian Neoplatonist Damascius (AD 458–550), recorded how 'the governors always greeted her first when they came into the city'. Her sex would have barred her from any form of public office, but the evidence suggests that, unlike Themistius, she would have refused it anyway and retained a role as a philosopher only. What was remarkable was that she could occupy a public position which allowed her to display her learning at large in Alexandria. Some reports suggest that the Christian Synesius made sure that the authorities respected her school. As a woman with male pupils Hypatia was unique.

Theophilus died in 412. By this time, a hundred years after Constantine had given it toleration and patronage, Christianity was well established and bishops had become important figures. Many were from elite backgrounds, they led the most important communities in the cities, and their ascetic lifestyles added to their authority. Between the fourth and sixth centuries bishops would assume ever greater political powers. A key turning point came in 409 when the bishops were given the task of selecting the *defensor civitatis*, the official who spoke on behalf of the socially disenfranchised. Later bishops were required to be involved in the distribution of grain and even, in 530, to serve on the committees carrying out the city's annual audit. During the same period the clergy was required to support the emperor and his administrations through their prayers. Claudia Rapp provides a summing-up in her authoritative study *Holy Bishops in Late Antiquity*; the bishops 'had become spokesmen of their cities, advocates for the concerns of the general population, community leaders with the ability to agitate the population into action'. While secular building projects had ceased, the building of churches and bishops' palaces had boomed.

Yet this is to paint a too idealistic picture. Many bishops were men of virtue and learning, but others were opportunists, eager for the fruits and status of office. The term of office of a bishop was for a lifetime, in comparison with the short reigns of city magistrates or governors of provinces, so these positions were worth competing for. There were often major outbreaks of violence after the death of a bishop, with candidates from rival factions struggling to replace him. The theologian Gregory of Nazianzus (pp. 329–90) told of 'a frightful brawl' in his native town of Sasima in Cappadocia, 'a no man's land between two rival bishops'. A similar brawl took place in Alexandria. Theophilus had hoped that his nephew Cyril would succeed him as patriarch but he had a rival in the form of an archdeacon, Timothy, who organised his supporters during the months that Theophilus lay dying. On Theophilus' death, three days of fighting erupted in the streets. It took the commander of the imperial troops based in the city to quell the unrest and declare Cyril the rightful bishop.

Cyril turned out to be ruthless in suppressing dissent. By 414, the churches of his opponents had been closed. When he accused the city's Jews, who represented some 20 per cent of the population, of being supporters of Timothy, he provoked further unrest. Riots between Jews and Christians broke out. A church was burned to the ground and it was alleged that those Christians attempting to put out the flames were killed. Cyril retaliated by massing his supporters, raiding synagogues and driving Jews from the city.

It fell to the prefect (governor) of Egypt, Orestes, to restore order. Both Cyril and Orestes appealed to the emperor, Theodosius II, the grandson of Theodosius I, who was still a boy. Orestes had already ordered Hierax, one of the supporters of

Cyril, who it was claimed had infuriated the Jews, to be arrested and tortured. Now, while he waited for a response from the emperor, Orestes refused to negotiate with Cyril. In retaliation Cyril stormed into the governor's palace clutching a copy of the gospels, arguing that religion should prevail over secular power. Orestes remained unmoved. Cyril then called in 500 monks from nearby monasteries in support. However much Cyril wanted these monks to be no more than a show of his strength, they proceeded to surround Orestes' carriage and one of them, Ammonius, threw a stone at Orestes' head and wounded him. Orestes was lucky to be saved by a group of Alexandrian citizens who were angered by the intrusion of the monks. Ammonius was arrested, tortured and killed. Cyril promptly declared him a martyr, although this seems not to have convinced the populace, who recognised that he had assaulted Orestes.

Orestes considered his position. He was ultimately responsible to the emperor for keeping good order in Alexandria and would be judged on this basis. He needed advice and it was now that he turned to Hypatia, who, as a pagan, had played no part in the religious disputes between rival Christian factions. While Orestes gathered Hypatia and a group of advisers from the elites of religious communities of the city for discussions, Orestes understandably deemed it inappropriate for him to attend Cyril's services. This served to whip up further the fury of the partisans who supported Cyril. Yet they found themselves trapped. Any direct assault on Orestes would lead to charges of treason with the possibility of imperial retaliation of the most brutal kind. It was in this strained and toxic atmosphere that the feeling grew among Christians that Orestes was being badly advised by a pagan woman who had perhaps used magic on him.

A local church official named Peter now chose to form a band of supporters to confront Hypatia. It was March 415, a month when the ports were still closed for winter and many of the poor were dependent on the church for handouts. Recruiting a crowd was a straightforward business, although Peter seems to have had no idea how it could be used. While Alexandria had long been an unstable city, it was rare for a mob to kill the target of their frustrations. The last such murder had taken place in 361 when an unpopular bishop had been killed. But crowds are easily inflamed and Hypatia would pay for her readiness to be out in public. Peter's gang came across her travelling through the city in her carriage and thereafter things lurched swiftly and viciously out of control. Hypatia was dragged from her vehicle, taken to a church on the seafront, then stripped and killed by being flayed with discarded roof tiles. Her body was then burned.

The city and the world were horrified. Hypatia's brutal murder had not only ended the life of a respected and honoured individual, it also marked the extinguishing of a symbol of elite philosophical learning. The opinion of almost everyone who recorded the event was that, while Cyril played no direct part in it, he had created the climate that allowed it to take place. The emperor ordered that Cyril's bodyguard, the *parabalani*, the toughs who surrounded him, were to be removed from his entourage and placed under Orestes' control. It was apparently only by bribing the emperor's officials that Cyril did not suffer more serious punishment. Orestes vanishes from the record – he may have resigned. A few years later Cyril is still found dominating the city council of Alexandria. He died as late as 444.

While the murder of Hypatia may not have been specifically aimed at destroying her school and the intellectual tradition that it represented, this was the result. Very often a teacher would groom a successor over a number of years but Hypatia had no teacher or member of her family to replace her. The fruitful practice of teaching pagan philosophy (Neoplatonism in particular) alongside Christianity in Alexandria died with her. Some pagan schools remained but none of any repute. In fact, it was Athens that saw a revival of classical learning; lists of known students there record many who came from Alexandria. The year 529, when the Christian emperor Justinian closed the

Platonic schools of Athens, and the remaining philosophers left for Persia, might be seen as the final closing of the door on more than a millennium of Greek intellectual tradition.

Meanwhile there was a shift of academic study towards the confines of the monasteries. Monasteries have been given a somewhat romanticised reputation as preservers of learning but they in fact had cut themselves off from the 'pagan' traditions of scholarship. As I hope that this book has shown, these were highly sophisticated and had sustained extraordinary achievements across many academic disciplines over the centuries. The benefits of Mediterranean travel that had done so much to enrich learning were, inevitably for monks, severely restricted. The definition of a non-negotiable theological orthodoxy in 381 and at subsequent church councils narrowed debate further. A statute of 425 promulgated by Theodosius II ordered the removal 'from the practice of vulgar ostentation all persons who usurp for themselves the name of teachers and who in public schools and rooms are accustomed to conduct with them students whom they have collected from everywhere'. The atrophy and eventual extinction of these schools was a major cultural loss. Edward Watts in his *City and School in Late Antique Athens and Alexandria* provides his own conclusion. 'By the seventh century, local conflicts about the role of pagan teachers had largely passed. There were few such teachers left and even fewer who taught Christian students. This slow fade into irrelevance represents pagan intellectual culture's sad final moment.'

24

Afterlives

The texts considered in this book were all composed in Greek and originally on papyrus. They were thus vulnerable to fire, damp and decay if they were not selected for copying. Once the Christian Byzantine empire had emerged in the sixth century AD they were also liable to be discriminated against for their paganism. Several of my subjects surmounted this latter hurdle easily. There was no religious reason to discard Dioscorides' work on the healing properties of animals, vegetables and minerals in his *De materia medica* (to give it the Latin name by which it is best known). It survives in a sumptuous edition from AD 512 which was dedicated to a Byzantine princess, Anicia Juliana, the daughter of one of the last western emperors, in thanks for her funding of a church in Constantinople. It is richly illustrated, with 383 full-page illustrations of plants.

Such a treasure would inevitably be influential, not least as a medical text as its name suggested; it was lent out to a hospital in Constantinople, and was used as a model for gift copies to the emperors' fellow rulers. The original was consulted by many visitors who left their mark by transcribing the names of the plants in their native languages. Examples include Arabic, Old French, Hebrew and Latin. By 1406 the volume was in the monastery of St John Prodromos in the suburbs of Constantinople and it survived the Ottoman conquest of the city in 1453. Moses Hamon, one of Suleiman the Magnificent's Jewish physicians, owned it in the 1550s and it was bought by the ambassador of Maximilian II, the Habsburg Holy Roman Emperor. It is now in the Imperial Library in Vienna.

Many other copies of the *De materia medica* survived and it became a standard herbal of the Middle Ages. The Christian scholar and statesman Cassiodorus (*c*.485–*c*.580), from Calabria in southern Italy, who spent his last years accumulating and copying Greek and Latin texts, recommended Galen and Dioscorides to his monks. 'If you cannot read Greek easily, above all else consult the *Herbarium* of Dioscorides, who described and illustrated the herbs of the fields with amazing exactness', as he put it. Throughout the Middle Ages it was a go-to medical text in the Byzantine, Arabic and, later, Latin worlds.

Dioscorides' plants were selected largely from the eastern Mediterranean and beyond but his influence was such that early botanical gardens attempted to stock his recommendations. An edition of *De materia medica*, the *Herbarium vivae icones* ('Living Portraits of Plants') (1530–6) with superb woodcuts by Hans Wieditz, a pupil of Dürer, was immediately recognised as setting a new standard in illustration. Another edition of Dioscorides by the Sienese physician Andrea Mattioli was the bestselling natural history book of the sixteenth century. Yet Mattioli was assailed by scholars who noted discrepancies in the original text, partly because Dioscorides was illustrating plants he may have never actually seen himself. The geographical range was expanding too. Carolus Clusius, who studied botany in the medical school at Montpellier, set off in the 1560s to Spain and Portugal where he found 200 plants that had never before been recorded. Then there was the extraordinary variety of plants from the New World. By the 1590s, the 700 original specimens of Dioscorides had expanded to 6,000 and new methods of classification were in hand. Despite the enormous respect in which Dioscorides was held, and his presence (with Theophrastus, 'the father of botany') on the frontispieces of many herbals into the nineteenth century, he became increasingly redundant as a scholarly source.

Another of my subjects who transferred easily to the early medieval Christian world, despite the avowed agnosticism of his work *On My Own Opinions*, was Galen. Galen's reputation was already well established at the time of his death (*c.*216). His numerous surviving texts only enhanced his authority. The Christian Origen commented positively on his *On the Usefulness of Parts*, in which Galen sets out the divine purpose of each part of the human body. By the sixth century a corpus of his works, the 'Sixteen Books', was brought together (probably in Alexandria) and was influential for centuries as an introductory guide for medical students. By 550 it had been translated into Syriac; it would be lectured on by one Agnellus in Latin in Ravenna in the early seventh century; and it was translated into Arabic by the tenth century. A ninth-century Christian physician in Baghdad, Hunain ibn Ishaq, was able to list 129 texts of Galen that had been translated into Syriac or Arabic.*

The authority of the 'Sixteen Books' was such that they eclipsed any alternative approaches to medicine. The 'Books' consisted largely of those elements of his writings which summed up Galen's conclusions and they ignored the heavy emphasis on empirical observation that had been such an important feature of his professional life. Gradually other texts of Galen reappeared, many of them in Arabic translations of the original Greek. The more intellectual Arab commentators recognised that these original texts offered new insights. One of the most important outcomes was the *Canon Medicinae* of Ibn Sina (980–1037, known in the Latin west as Avicenna), a reasoned amalgamation of Galenic medicine with underpinnings from Hippocrates and Aristotle. Translated into Latin, it became a staple of the

---

* As recently as 2005 a single manuscript of the Greek version of Galen's *On My Own Opinions* was discovered.

medical curriculum in the medieval university, not least because it replaced Galen's agnosticism with monotheism.

Galenism became so deeply embedded that physicians and surgeons who had mastered the basic texts assumed that he was authoritative. Humanist scholarship was more critical.* The star here was Niccolo Leoncino (1428–1524), doctor and translator of Greek manuscripts at the court of Ferrara, who knew Greek well enough to spot the inadequacies of the Latin versions. He saw that Galen had been so badly mistranslated that the Latin texts described diseases that never existed and Galen's portrayal of herbs was misleading. Leoncino spotted the same problems with Latin translations of Dioscorides. Scholars needed to go back to the original Greek texts of Galen and Dioscorides and these began appearing in Venice in the early sixteenth century. In 1525, the famous Aldine Press in Venice produced an almost complete Greek edition of those of Galen's works that were known. It was a rushed job, which resulted in numerous errors, but it remained the standard edition for centuries for those who could read Greek. The Aldine edition not only included Galen's works on philosophy, showing these to be a fundamental part of his approach to his medical practice, but also his works on anatomy. Some of these were already known – Mondino de Luizzi was inspired by them to begin dissection of human bodies in Bologna about 1315 – but during the sixteenth century there developed a craze for ritualistic displays of dissection in the Italian universities. The students gathered around a corpse, a surgeon cut it open and a professor described what could be seen. While enthusiasts for Galen assumed he was always correct, more percipient observers could see that the human body did not match his descriptions of the Barbary apes that he had relied on. A challenge to his authority was about to take place.

* The Renaissance humanists were those scholars who revived the study of *humanitas* from classical sources, in Latin and later Greek.

It came from Andreas Vesalius. Vesalius had been born into a family of physicians in the Habsburg Netherlands in 1487. After his own medical training, he became professor of anatomy and surgery at Padua in 1537 and was able to dissect bodies there. He quickly noticed that what he could actually see inside human bodies was different from what Galen had described from Barbary apes and, moreover, that Galen had misunderstood the functions of many organs. In his *De humani corporis fabrica* ('On the Fabric of the Human Body') of 1543, Vesalius was confident enough to discard Galen and reproduce accurate drawings of the body. His analysis of organs led to further advances and the eventual discovery of the circulation of blood and the motion of the heart by William Harvey, first revealed in a work of 1628.[*] Vesalius remained conservative in that he followed the order of dissection according to the sequence that Galen had advocated and Galenism retained an influence in the medical professions as a whole well into the nineteenth century. Bloodletting – a remnant of the doctrine of the four humours, in which balance had to be achieved by removing excess liquid – whose efficacy had been preached by Galen, was one survival.

In contrast to Lucian of Samosata, whose attack on Christianity in his *The Death of Peregrinus* (pp. 167–9) ensured that he was not respected in either the Christian East or the West, Plutarch had been writing before Christianity had become widespread and so his works were never accepted as inimical to Christianity. His essays on ethics, the *Moralia*, were quarried for Christian sermons by early Christian writers. (Clement of Alexandria was one such who used him.) As a result Plutarch was fully accepted by Byzantine scholars. The eleventh-century metropolitan Johannes Mauropus went so far as to claim that among the

---

[*] Harvey had learned his medicine at Padua, one of the few universities in Italy that accepted Protestants.

pagan philosophers only Plato and Plutarch would 'be saved from the wrath of Christ'. Yet it was not until 1300 that the Byzantine scholar-monk Maximus Planudes, an enthusiast for original Greek texts, assembled almost all the works of Plutarch that we know today.

Three manuscripts of Planudes' compilations survive. One of these came to the west from Constantinople in the collection of the Greek scholar Manuel Chrysoloras in the late fourteenth century. Chrysoloras, who held the first chair in Greek in Florence, was determined that the Latin west should know of the close relationships between Greeks and Romans in earlier times in the hope that they would respond together to the threat to Byzantine civilisation from the Ottoman Turks. So Manuel Chrysoloras placed particular emphasis on the *Parallel Lives*. Latin translations of the original Greek followed, notably those of the humanist Leonardo Bruni (1370–1444), who concentrated on the generals and statesmen of the Roman republic to underpin his own glorification of the Florentine republic of which he was chancellor. Bruni was also inspired by the *Histories* of Polybius, which, he felt, encapsulated the ideals of republicanism which he championed.

It was when the whole of the *Parallel Lives* appeared in print in Latin from 1470 that Plutarch really came alive. (This was also the moment when historians such as Polybius and Arrian entered the Renaissance consciousness through Latin translations.) These early editions spread widely and fostered many more. The clarity of Plutarch's prose and the wealth of anecdotes he told about his subjects brought him a mass of readers who used him, albeit uncritically, as an entry into the ancient world. Two further translations were particularly popular: the elegant French edition of Jacques Amyot (1572) and the English translation of Thomas North (1579), which itself depended heavily on Amyot. The first inspired Michel de Montaigne, who made at least 400 references to 'my very own Plutarch, so perfect, so outstanding a judge of human actions' and 'a philosopher who teaches us what purity is' in his *Essais* (1580). North's translation was an important source for Shakespeare's *Coriolanus*, *Antony and Cleopatra* and *Julius Caesar*. So, while historians note the dangers of regarding the *Lives* as reliable history, many of Plutarch's vivid portrayals – the barge with which Cleopatra enticed Mark Antony, the drama of Caesar's assassination, the exploits of Alexander – shaped European consciousness of the classical world in a fundamental way.

Plutarch's *Lives* were of special relevance to the Founding Fathers in what was to become the United States. The text had already been an important component of classical education in the American colonies and, even for those who could not read Latin, there were many English editions available. In the context of the American Revolution against British rule, Plutarch's account of the Greco-Persian Wars inspired the belief that a coalition of republics could take on a centralised monarchy and win. The *Life* of Themistocles, who organised the Athenian response to the Persian invasion of 480, was especially popular. Following independence, Plutarch's *Lives* of Demosthenes and Alexander were used to promote the importance of a strong alliance of states against a potential 'Macedonian' takeover, so helping shape the emerging American Constitution. As Plutarch had put it in his *Life* of Aratus, one of the leaders of the defeated Achaean League in its struggles against Sparta in the third century BC: 'Small cities could be preserved by nothing else but a continual and combined force, united by the bond of common interest.' The *Lives* of the Romans that Plutarch had chosen were quarried for their stress on virtue. Those who threatened the Roman republic, such as Julius Caesar, were deplored and his assassins, Brutus and Cassius, applauded. In virtually every political debate, heroes and villains from the *Parallel Lives* were used as common currency.

The *Moralia*, Plutarch's essays on ethics and other subjects, were overshadowed by the interest in the *Lives* but they had their own adherents. The essayist and philosopher Ralph Waldo

Emerson, for instance, favoured the *Moralia* over the *Lives*. 'If the world's library was burning, I should as soon fly to rescue the *Moralia* as Shakespeare and Plato, or next afterwards.' Emerson warmed in particular to Plutarch's defence of the immortality of the soul.

Among the other discoveries of Maximus Planudes was a copy of Ptolemy's *Geographike* tracked down in the library of the Chora Church in Constantinople. It was not the first rediscovery of the work. One had already survived in the Arab world, where the original Greek text had been translated in the ninth century. A map based on the *Geographike* was drawn up by the cartographer Muhammed al-Idrisi at the cultured court of the Norman king of Sicily, Roger II, but in the age of the Crusades it failed to travel to the West. Planudes' copy, in contrast, was presented to the Byzantine emperor Andronikos II Palaiologos, who ordered his mathematicians and transcribers to create maps from it, three of which survive. One of these was taken to Florence by Manuel Chrysoloras and by 1410 a Latin translation had emerged.

The appeal of the *Geographike* was that, with longitude and latitude established in the text, locations of which geographers had become aware since Ptolemy's day, such as Scandinavia, could be added to it. By 1500 the *Geographike* was so superior to anything else on offer that it was supplanting the Christian *mappae mundi* (medieval maps of the world, often with Jerusalem at the centre) and the medieval portolan maps (nautical maps based on compass bearings). Yet its supremacy was short-lived. By 1520, when the full extent of Africa was known and the New World discovered, it was becoming redundant. Ptolemy had stretched his known world so far round the globe that the Americas could not be fitted in. Such, however, was Ptolemy's prestige that the Flemish cartographer Gerard Mercator produced a fine copy of the *Geographike*, misconceptions and all, as a tribute to him as late as 1578.

In 1439, another *Geography*, that of Strabo, had appeared in Italy, in the baggage of the Byzantine scholar Gemistos Plethon, who had travelled there to attend the council of Greek and western churches held in Florence that year.* While Ptolemy had provided no more than the positions of 8,000 locations, Strabo provided actual descriptions of the cities and regions he covered and he was thus immediately of interest to the humanists, who were avid for knowledge of the classical world. Among them was Cyriacus of Ancona (1391–1452), 'the father of archaeology', who had wandered the Mediterranean collecting inscriptions and surveying ruins. His commentaries on his findings were added to the first Latin translations of Strabo in the 1450s. The importance of Strabo was highlighted by a scholar at the court of Ferdinand of Naples in the 1480s. 'By describing the people, the nations, events on sea and on land in every province, the harbours, the seas, the mountains, the rivers and the springs, he [Strabo] adequately supplemented that which had been missing in the other cosmographers.' By the sixteenth century Strabo had become a more important influence than Ptolemy. The Aldine Press was on hand to provide a definitive version of the original Greek text in 1516 and the *Geography* became one of those texts that was considered essential for those training as courtiers or statesmen.

As well as Ptolemy's *Geographike*, his major work, the *Almagest* (see pp. 155–7), came under fire. The *Almagest*, as its Arabic name, 'the Greatest', suggests, had been translated into Arabic in Baghdad in the ninth century. Before then, Islamic astronomy had depended on Persian and Indian texts but Ptolemy was clearly superior to these. Commentators began to provide overviews of his findings. Perhaps the most famous of these was Nasir al-Din al-Tusi (1201–74). His *Redaction of the Almagest* was written in Maragha in Iran in the thirteenth century. Ten times

---

* The council failed to heal the schism between the Greek and Latin churches, which persists to this day.

as many copies of the *Redaction* survive as of the *Almagest* itself, suggesting that many scholars could not cope with the breadth and complexity of the original.

The *Almagest* provoked two concurrent responses. One was to recalibrate the positions of stars now that over a thousand years had passed since the time of Ptolemy's original observations. The other was to cast doubt on Ptolemy's methods: al-Tusi himself would list sixteen fundamental problems with the Ptolemaic system in a work of 1261. He also made his own observations of the heavens from the observatory he had constructed in Maragha. By 1271 he had compiled a *zij*, a collection of astronomical tables, following the format of Ptolemy's *Handy Tables* (p. 156). Al-Tusi claimed to be able to construct an alternative planetary system that also correlated with Ptolemy's observations. His work sparked off an intense debate, not least over the artificiality of the equant (p. 155), and it may even be that Copernicus 'can be looked on as, if not the last, surely the most noted follower of the Maragha school'.

Medieval European astronomy was a good deal less curious than that of the Islamic world. Fragments of learning supported the belief that the Earth was a sphere and that it was at the centre of the universe. European astronomers also distinguished between the planets which were moving and the fixed stars beyond. But it was not until the tenth and eleventh centuries that Islamic astronomy started to filter through to the West. The astrolabe, known from Hellenistic times, and used by the Arabs to measure the altitude above the horizon of a celestial body, arrived in Europe in the tenth century. Ptolemy's *Almagest* appeared in two separate translations, one from the Arabic and one from the Greek original, in the twelfth century. As their Islamic counterparts had done, European astronomers immediately saw the *Almagest* as being far more comprehensive than any rival. However, despite astronomy being one of the seven liberal arts studied at medieval universities, in the words of modern historians of astronomy, few students were able to absorb it. 'The typical medieval Arts student was no mathematical astronomer and certainly there was no place for observation in his astronomy course.'* Tables of the motions of the planets based on Ptolemaic principles had been adopted from Arabic models in Toledo after the city had been 'liberated' from the Arabs in the eleventh century, and these were recalibrated in the 1270s using the same principles. The so-called Alfonsine Tables speeded up the process of calculation and enabled predictions of future planetary movements to be made from the western European sky. †

Medieval astronomers were hampered by the difficulties of transferring symbols and numerals from one manuscript to another. Few transcribers had sufficient knowledge to do it so the *Almagest* became more and more unreliable as errors were repeated in subsequent copies. Georg Puerbach's *Theoricae novae planetarum* ('New Theories of the Planets'), the first printed treatise on astronomy (1472), which explained how Ptolemy's works had underpinned the planetary tables, became a bestseller. The *Theoricae* was published by a student of Puerbach, Johannes Muller of Königsberg, better known as Regiomontanus, who then compiled a shorter version of the *Almagest*, the *Epitome*, which corrected the errors that had crept in to the original and presented its reduced text with clarity. The *Epitome* made the *Almagest* truly accessible for the first time in the West. Indeed, it was the version that Copernicus used.

Copernicus' *De Revolutionibus* ('On the Revolutions of the Heavenly Spheres'), which had a heliocentric system in contrast to Ptolemy's, was published in 1543, as its author was dying. Copernicus' mathematical solutions were complex and it was some time before more accurate observations, and the invention

* The first European observatory was Tycho Brahe's Uraniborg in Denmark, late 1570s.
† The Alfonsine Tables were named after the Christian king Alfonso X of Leon and Castile in whose court they were compiled.

of the telescope, could comprehensively challenge Ptolemy's system. Even then, conservatives fought rearguard actions as Galileo, the champion of the telescope, was to find to his distress in the seventeenth century. Ptolemy was eventually superseded but he still deserves the accolade of the modern historian of science, the late John David North:

> All told, there are very few scientific writers, whether from antiquity or any other historical period, whose work so strongly influenced posterity as did Ptolemy's. Through him the mathematical models of the astronomical sciences passed into the domain of the natural sciences generally, and this must be counted as one of the most significant of all events in the entire history of western science, even outweighing in importance the technical brilliance of Ptolemy's individual results.

As we have seen, the austere Christian world of Byzantium disapproved of Lucian of Samosata, and it was only during the Renaissance that a more tolerant attitude to pagan texts allowed him to flourish. He is said to have been the first author whose works were taught by Manuel Chrysoloras when he arrived in Florence in 1397. By 1440 there were as many Latin translations of Lucian's works as there were of Plato and Plutarch and an Aldine edition in the original Greek appeared in 1503. Lucian appealed for his light-heartedness and plays on words but it was the sheer variety of his works and subjects that ensured his popularity. His satires could be adapted to make attacks on contemporary figures, not least the clergy.

It is not surprising that one of Lucian's most devoted admirers was the scholar Desiderius Erasmus (1486–1536). Erasmus praised him as a 'relentless persecutor of all superstition', a position that aligned neatly with Erasmus' own satirical attacks on the wealth of the church and its pretentious clergy. Erasmus could read Lucian in the original Greek but was responsible for more Latin translations of the original texts than any other Renaissance humanist. The first of these appeared shortly after the Aldine edition of 1503. Erasmus teamed up with his friend Thomas More to create an edition of Latin translations in Paris in 1514.* Yet there were still many who resented Lucian's attack on Christianity and his works were placed on the papal Index of Prohibited Books. Schools run by Jesuits banned him completely.

Despite these condemnations, Lucian continued to flourish. He could be used in many contexts. He was conscious of the clash of cultures and how easy it was for an elite to adopt mannerisms that in themselves give access to privilege. He ridiculed pretensions and challenged conventions in a brilliantly witty way. The eighteenth-century Enlightenment intellectuals, Voltaire, Diderot, Jonathan Swift and the Scottish philosopher David Hume, also warmed to him.

And what of the orators who played such a prominent part in city life during the Roman period? As the Greek cities of Asia Minor atrophied after the sixth and seventh centuries, the auditoriums and audiences that had sustained the art of rhetoric disappeared. Performances were now in front of Christian congregations and had a very different purpose. Schools of rhetoric survived in Constantinople and Gaza and a small selection of the orations of Dio of Prusa, Aelius Aristides and Themistius were preserved. We know that the orations of Aristides were used as models alongside the *Dialogues* of Plato in a school in Constantinople in the twelfth century, for instance. Very little survives of Herodes Atticus' orations. His legacy lies in his buildings. In the West, Greek rhetoric was not known until the fifteenth century when there was a renewed interest in public speaking. Then

---

* Thomas More's *Utopia*, a depiction of a fantasy island, is believed to have been inspired by Lucian.

Greek-speaking scholars could read the surviving orations in the original.

The shock of the Ottoman conquest of Constantinople in 1453, when manuscripts were burned in the mayhem of the sack of the city by Mehmed II, resonated through the West. The humanist Enea Silvio Piccolomini (later Pope Pius II, r. 1458–64) was in despair. 'Alas, how many names of great men will now perish! Here is a second death for Homer and for Plato too. Where are we now to seek the philosophers' and the poets' works of genius?' We shall never know which orations were lost in the sack of Constantinople, but the great works of the classical period remained prominent. So, among the Renaissance humanists, it was the earlier Greek orators such as Demosthenes and Isocrates who were favoured while Aristotle's text *On Rhetoric* was the most influential discussion of the techniques of oratory (as was Cicero's *De oratore* for Latin speakers).*

An exception can be made for Libanius, who, as we have seen, had many of his writings and orations preserved. Even in his lifetime, Eunapius, a pagan commentator, had included Libanius among the subjects of his *Lives of Philosophers and Sophists*. Eunapius was disparaging about Libanius' character, casting him as a flatterer, but he could not avoid applauding Libanius' erudition and wide reading. The Christian writers who increasingly came to dominate the scene deplored Libanius' adulation of the pagan Julian (pp. 302–4). However, they were ready to adopt those of his orations which dealt with secular subjects. In the school of rhetoric in Gaza its sixth-century leader, Choricus, used Libanius' declamations as models for his own students. But then an extraordinary transformation in Christian perceptions of Libanius took place. The documentary evidence is obscure, but it seems that forged letters of Libanius

---

* Isocrates (436–338 BC), a persuasive rhetorician, was the great champion of Panhellenism, the belief that the Greeks should form closer cultural and economic bonds.

to Basil the Great and Christian pupils such as John Chrysostom suggested that Libanius had been an important influence on them. The transformation of Libanius gathered pace with the appearance of a life of Basil in which, after the death of Julian, Libanius visited his former student, now an eminent theologian, and converted to Christianity. This hagiographical legend now travelled to the Latin west where medieval religious plays would portray the rhetor of Antioch as a saint.

The approach of the Renaissance humanists was very different. They were interested in the original works of Libanius, not least because he had written Greek so beautifully. In the fifteenth century manuscripts were collected in the East to transfer to Western libraries. Cosimo de' Medici, for instance, acquired a codex of Libanius' declamations. The Aldine Press once again played its part by including Libanius' texts on Demosthenes in a 1504 edition of that great Greek orator. This was the first time Libanius had appeared in print. Meanwhile, some small-scale Latin translations of selected works of his were completed, but it was not until the eighteenth century that full editions appeared. That by Johann Jacob Reiske (1716–74), an enthusiast for Libanius, was published posthumously in 1791–7 and included sixty-three of the sixty-four speeches known today, and most of the declamations. Unfortunately Libanius suffered from the derision in which Gibbon and others held the Greek literature of late Roman antiquity and he was not well regarded in the nineteenth century. A formidable new edition by the German scholar Richard Foerster (1843–1922), which included every work of Libanius that was then known – letters, declamations and orations – appeared in twelve volumes between 1903 and 1927. Over the centuries a number of forged speeches of Libanius had accumulated and Foerster applied his critical skills to weeding them out. His edition remains the standard work. Libanius could now emerge as a brilliant writer of Attic prose and a major source for everyday life in the oratorical schools of late antiquity.

*

The original works of Plato were little known in the West before the fifteenth century. The Neoplatonism of Plotinus and his biographer Porphyry was the most important conduit for Platonism, yet their complexity and the many swirling currents of theological thought make it impossible to reach any coherent notion of the influence of Plotinus on his successors. Plotinus bequeathed a hierarchy of realities, from the One, which could be equated with the Christian God, through to the material world, and a tendency towards mystical understanding of the divine. The Latin theologian Augustine (354–430) read some of Plotinus in Latin translations and while he could not accept the One, the Intellect and the Soul as equating with the Trinity, it appears that Plotinus' spirituality was of immense importance to him. His discussion of the transcendence of 'the One' is taken from Plotinus, as are the moments of his mystical experiences (as at the moment of the death of his mother, Monica, described in *The Confessions*). Augustine adopts from Plotinus the idea that one must purify oneself mentally before being receptive to God and the idea of the impossibility of the individual separating him/herself from the divine presence. Augustine also follows Plotinus in accepting evil as the absence of good rather than a force in itself. Scholars have also noted a profound engagement with Plotinus in Augustine's view on time and eternity and the notion of a spiritual community. As Augustine had no equal for several hundred years and so achieved theological dominance in Latin Christianity, it is also possible to trace some of these Neoplatonist ideas in the work of medieval scholastic philosophers.

In the Greek world, so-called Pseudo-Dionysius, an anonymous theologian who for centuries was believed to be the Dionysius named in the Acts of the Apostles as a follower of the apostle Paul, but who was writing in the fifth or sixth century, was profoundly influenced by Plotinus. However, he has such a wide-ranging mind, so deeply embedded in the theological and mystical writings of his time, that it is difficult, as it is with Augustine, to separate out the various contributions of Plotinus to his thought. Certainly Pseudo-Dionysius borrowed directly from Plotinus the analogy of a sculptor cutting away from a block anything that is not intrinsic to an image. It followed that God/the One could be defined, as it was for Plotinus, in terms of what it is not. Pseudo-Dionysius also adopts from Plotinus the concept of the divine procession, the idea that 'the One' transmits downwards. Plotinus remained an influence in the Byzantine world, although there always remained a tension between his own philosophy and that of orthodox Christianity.

We have already encountered Gemistos Plethon in the context of his bringing Strabo's *Geography* to Florence in 1439, but he made an altogether more significant contribution to the history of ideas as an authority on Plato and Plotinus, whose works he introduced to western Europe. Plethon was so obsessed with Plato that he was considered by many to be a pagan rather than a Christian. The works were passed on via the Medici family to the Florentine Marsilio Ficino (1433–99), who translated them into Latin.

Ficino's translations were so respected that they remained a standard text for centuries. His *Platonic Theology* (1469–74) was a sophisticated summing-up of Plato's philosophy, especially his arguments for the immortality of the soul. Ficino also translated the *Enneads* of Plotinus (the Latin edition appeared in 1492) and was aware of the distinction between Plato's original work and the developments that Plotinus had made. For Ficino, Plotinus marked a more mature development of Platonism. Like Augustine and Pseudo-Dionysius, Ficino believed that Plotinus and Christianity could be integrated and he went back to the works of Augustine to see how it might be done.

Plotinus could now hardly be ignored. In the seventeenth century, with the rise of the material scientists, he was called upon to reassert contemplative thinking as a rational possibility.

The erudite English classicist and theologian Ralph Cudworth (1617–88), for instance, one of a loose grouping known as the Cambridge Platonists, argued along the lines of Plotinus that 'it is evident that wisdom, knowledge and understanding are eternal and self-subsistent things, superior to matter and all sensible beings and independent of them'. Cudworth was particularly concerned with refuting the secular philosophy of Thomas Hobbes and the Christian Stoics such as Justus Lipsius,* who had become an influence in the late sixteenth century. He relied heavily on Plotinus' defence of free will in his *Treatise on Freewill*, published posthumously in 1848. The Cambridge Platonists concentrated on finding rational defences of the immaterial soul and were among the first to explore the nature of consciousness.

Plotinus continued to be important to anyone who was attracted to mysticism. His greatest twentieth-century champion was the French philosopher Henri Bergson (1849–1941). Bergson emphasised the importance of intuition ('the possibility of a supra-sensible intuition', as he put it) and openness to spiritual feeling. Plotinus was one of the rare philosophers with whom he felt an affinity. Bergson lectured on the *Enneads* and quoted from them in many of his writings. He attracted attacks from scientists and rationalists such as Bertrand Russell, but his lectures were a sell-out. Bergson was a hero to many Catholic intellectuals, although the Vatican considered him to be too much of a pantheist to be acceptable. (Bergson himself never claimed to be a Christian.)

And so to the Christian theologians. I noted in Chapter 19 (see pp. 266–7) that Clement was caught out by the imposition of orthodoxy 150 years after his death. He was condemned as a

---

* The Flemish scholar Justus Lipsius (1547–1606) attempted to reconcile Christianity and Stoicism in his *De Constantia* (1583).

heretic in the ninth century but on the basis of passages in his texts that are now lost. It is only recently that his works have been reassessed by Christian scholars and his value in creating links between Greek philosophy and Christianity recognised.

Origen was a more profound and accomplished scholar than Clement and thus a particular target of theological counterattacks. It was hard to criticise him for his saintliness and commitment to the faith but he was fiercely condemned for the perceived heresies in his writings. The first assault came from Eunapius of Salamis, who had obsessively compiled a list of heresies in the 370s. Origen was excoriated for supporting a subordinationist concept of Christ and using allegory too broadly in his interpretation of the Bible. Later he was criticised for his renunciation of the eternity of hellfire for those condemned, his advocacy of pre-existent souls and his belief in free will. The querulous scholar Jerome acknowledged the greatness of Origen as a teacher but, when accused of heresy for this support, turned against him. Jerome was furious when, in 397, his contemporary Rufinus produced a Latin translation of Origen's *First Principles*, which, he claimed, Jerome had approved.* Such ambivalence was common. The volatile patriarch of Alexandria, Theophilus (in office from 385 to 412 – see Chapter 23, pp. 315–6), wavered between accepting and condemning Origen before concluding that he could read him, 'picking out the roses from the thorns'. The controversy subsided but the writings of Eunapius persisted in casting doubt on the orthodoxy of Origen.

Controversy broke out again in the sixth century and Origen was anathematised at a church council called by the emperor Justinian in 553. Once again it was the Renaissance scholars who came to the rescue. The Greek scholar Basilios Bessarion (1403–72), who came over, with Gemistos Plethon, to the Council

---

* Having been doctored by Rufinus to remove sensitive issues, it is the only version of *First Principles* to survive.

at Florence and later moved to the West, brought a mass of manuscripts with him.* Among them was Origen's *Contra Celsum*, which was translated into Latin by Bessarion and then printed after his death in 1481. It was acknowledged at the time as the finest defence of Christianity by an early Church Father. Shortly afterwards, the Renaissance scholar Giovanni Pico della Mirandola caused a sensation when he argued that Origen was more likely to have been saved than burned in hell.

Not surprisingly it was the independent-minded Erasmus who became Origen's champion. Erasmus was the first Latin theologian to recognise that in many ways the Greeks had a much more sophisticated approach to theology than the Latins: 'the great [Greek] Christian writers of the past were able to treat even the most arid subjects with a beautiful prose'. While he was above all attracted to the brilliance of Origen's mind, Erasmus valued him because he was the theologian closest to the origins of Christianity. He stated that he learned more from a single page of Origen than from ten of Augustine. The most comprehensive Latin translation of Origen's works was published by Erasmus in 1536. In the great debate over free will with Martin Luther, Erasmus used Origen's argument, that each soul had the freedom to decide whether to reconcile with God, in his counterattack. Origen was also a favourite of the Cambridge Platonists.

Three of my subjects have come into their own more recently. The story of the intellectual Hypatia's death may have been transferred into Christian martyrology to provide the basis for the legend of Catherine of Alexandria, who remains a saintly mentor for Italian students about to take exams. With the Enlightenment and increasing criticism of Catholicism, Hypatia was highlighted by intellectuals such as Voltaire as a voice of reason extinguished by religious obscurantism. Commentators could not agree, however, on whether to attribute responsibility

---

* He donated them to the city of Venice where Aldus Manutius was able to exploit them for his definitive version of Greek texts.

for her murder to Bishop Cyril or Peter the presbyter who led the mob which killed her. Gibbon in his *The Decline and Fall of the Roman Empire* placed the blame directly on Cyril. Another strand of her legend emerged with the growth of neoclassicism in the early nineteenth century. As Greek civilisation was idealised, Hypatia was portrayed as the last exponent of a great tradition. She was romanticised in an immensely popular anti-Catholic romance, *Hypatia, or Old Foes with a New Face*, by the English author Charles Kingsley in 1853. Women's movements of the twentieth century paid her appropriate reverence, while her scientific importance was highlighted by the naming of asteroids and Moon craters after her. Representations of her had become so far removed from historical reality that I was pleased to be able to refer to E. J. Watts' grounded life of a remarkable and fascinating woman.

The first Latin translation of the Stoic Epictetus' *Discourses* as recorded by Arrian appeared in 1497. In *De Constantia* (1583), the compilation of Stoic texts by Justus Lipsius, Epictetus was one of the Stoic philosophers whom Lipsius felt was compatible with Christianity. More recently Epictetus has come into fashion in relation to mindfulness. He was an important influence on the psychotherapist Albert Ellis (1913–2007), a pioneer of cognitive behaviour therapy. The US Admiral James Stockdale (1923–2005), who was shot down over Vietnam in 1965 and suffered a gruelling seven years of captivity, claimed that Epictetus saw him through. Epictetus' distinction between what can be changed in one's beliefs about an issue and what cannot be changed has become an influential aphorism.

Pausanias experienced almost total oblivion until the fifteenth century when error-full copies of his *Guide* emerged. Unlike many of his contemporaries, he had never been a public intellectual and no one seems to have known anything about him. The *Guide* was like nothing else in Greek literature but its author had never fully explained its purpose. Nevertheless, the Aldine Press published its own Greek edition in 1516 and there are enough references to it by later travellers to Greece to suggest most visitors knew of it. It was extensively used, for instance, for plotting the ancient monuments of Athens by the British soldier and topographer Colonel William Leake (1777–1860), who published his *Topography of Athens* in 1821. Pausanias then fades from the sources. By the middle of the nineteenth century he was subject to the academic disdain with which so many of his generation were viewed. Conservative classical scholars such as the German scholar Ulrich von Wilamowitz (1848–1931) even suggested that Pausanias had never visited the sites that he described. Yet Pausanias found a champion in the anthropologist James Frazer, famous for *The Golden Bough* (1890), who saw the *Guide* as a repository of mythology and thus of religious experience. Then, as serious archaeological work began in the Peloponnese and the very inscriptions and sculptures described by Pausanias emerged, archaeologists gave him increasing respect. Cultural historians began to examine Pausanias within the context of travel writing, the description of landscape and the nostalgic association with buildings of the past. This is now a rich area of scholarship.

The Greek society portrayed in this book was an elitist world, dependent on wealth that was often inherited, and a sophisticated tradition of education. It is rare to find a society which was intellectually stable but also vibrant and fertile. What makes the Greek intellectual culture of the Roman period particularly fascinating is the breadth of interests and its emphasis on originality of content and expression in public rhetoric.

The stability of this world was secured by a conservative colonial power which, after the horror of conquest, respected many of the features of Greek civilisation and protected them. With the exception of one of my subjects, Hypatia, it was a world closed to women and underpinned for Christians and pagans alike by slavery. This is not to say that intellectual life for the elite was without its tensions – it was highly competitive and there was much apprehension over social acceptance. It was not easy to hold one's own in a speech for critical audiences. Many of those orations that survive have done so simply because they are considered among the most accomplished of the genre. There must have been many which fell flat and ended in humiliation for the speaker. As the texts of Lucian showed, it was easy to criticise the pretensions of those who endeavoured but failed to succeed in public life.

Greek society flourished within opulent cities. Until the third century, the leading citizens and the emperors, notably Hadrian, prided themselves as benefactors so there was a process of continual rebuilding and embellishment. As Strabo noted, the Greeks chose the setting, while the Romans provided the sewers, paving stones and aqueducts. The ruins of these cities reveal them to have been majestic places to live in or to visit. Even the audience halls and theatres were constructed to provide effective acoustics. Anyone lecturing in Athens would have enjoyed the stunning backdrop of the Acropolis and its hallowed tradition as the birthplace of so much sophisticated philosophy and other intellectual achievements. The monuments and statues at Delphi in its mountain setting and Olympia in the lush valley of the Alpheios would have been dramatic and awe-inspiring for any visitor.

I have tried through the selection of my subjects to show the breadth of Greek intellectual life during the years of Roman rule. In addition to those disciplines with strongly philosophical underpinnings, the subjects embraced by the writers and thinkers of this Greco-Roman era include history, biography, botany, physics and even travel and satire. Others concentrated on rhetoric with the creation of original compositions that must have been inspiring to listen to.

One of the most important features of Greek thought was an intense sense of spirituality. Most of my subjects believed in some kind of 'beyond' either through a named god or gods or in more abstract philosophical terms of 'the One'. Plato was a critical influence: everyone, even those following other kinds of philosophy, appears to have known his works well. As has been seen, most of my subjects refer to their own spirituality, but Pausanias provides us with a remarkable broad snapshot of religious observance in the second century AD, recording a mass of shrines that were still functioning, many of which had histories that were centuries old. A fourth-century catalogue of buildings in Alexandria listed 2,500 temples. Christianity introduced an institution run by authority figures, the bishops, and a canon of texts, with the possibility of hellfire if one did not conform. In the fluid world of early Christianity, orthodoxy was always shifting according to the personality and status of theologians; the boundaries between acceptance and non-acceptance became ever more problematic. The court philosopher Themistius appreciated this and talked of religious toleration in a way that would not reappear until the sixteenth century. But that is another story.

Acknowledgements

I first came across the 'Greek mind' during an intensive school education in the classics which included studying Homer, Herodotus, Thucydides and some of the fifth century BC playwrights in the original Greek. I became aware even then of the vibrant and expansive intellectual tradition these remarkable texts provided. A different approach came when, at the age of twenty, I spent a summer working as an archaeological assistant on the ancient site of Knidos, one of the most prosperous and intellectually lively Greek cities of the Mediterranean.

I still have a letter to my parents from the summer of 1970 relating how I was taking so long to visit the shrine at Delphi because I had a Blue Guide (the famous Stuart Rossiter edition) that seemed to have something to say about every stone. Little did I know that over thirty years later I would become Historical Consultant to the Blue Guides and contributor of two articles to the successor of the guide I was using in 1970. Over the years I have visited many more cities in Greece, Sicily and Turkey and have written extensively on ancient Greece (*The Greek Achievement* and *The Closing of the Western Mind*). I also benefitted from my long experience as teacher and examiner in critical thinking skills with the International Baccalaureate's Theory of Knowledge course. It reinforced my appreciation of the quality of the best classical Greek minds in assessing evidence and providing coherent arguments across the disciplines.

Children of Athena was a book lurking at the back of my mind as I came to realise that the high standards of education and the fertility of the Greek mind continued into the Roman period. There has been a great deal of academic work on this period but few studies aimed at the general reader and there was a gap to be filled with biographies of the main thinkers. The book started in lockdown and relied heavily on online resources, supplemented by my own library and the good services of the Cambridge University Library. I am especially grateful for two readers, Anthony Stanton and Christos Nifadopoulos, himself holder of a Cambridge PhD on Greek literature of the second century AD, who provided many suggestions to improve a draft text. Paul Cartledge and, in the US, Stan Prager read selected passages and, as usual, provided, psychological support when I had reservations about such a project.

With a draft accepted by Head of Zeus, I again relied on the meticulous editing of Richard Milbank. Richard has read every word and has offered advice on revising many awkward passages. The text has been improved immensely under his care and I am very grateful to him. We were thus able to provide a respectable final text for the excellent copyediting skills of Alison Griffiths. Ellie Jardine has been instrumental in organising a final text. She brought together the pictures which had been initially researched and gathered by Aphra Le Levier-Bennett. The overall production manager has, again, been the ultra-efficient Clémence Jacquinet. I also have to thank, Henrietta Richardson and Hannah Bright at Midas PR, Philippa Hudson for the final proofreading and Isobel Maclean for the comprehensive index.

Children of Athena will be published in the US by Pegasus in New York. I am grateful to publisher Claiborne Hancock for taking on this edition and his colleagues Maria Fernandez as Production Manager and Julia Romero for the US publicity.

The book is dedicated to my son Barney who is the most philosophically orientated of my children. Since my original choice there is now his fiancée, the lovely Catherine, and baby Anna who is already at one fingering the piano of her composer father. I wish *eudaimonia*, 'flourishing' on them all.

Bibliography and Notes on Sources

Prologue

'The Banquet' comes from Lucian of Samosata's *A Feast of Lapithae* (see The Lucian of Samosata Project under Chapter 12 below).

Chapters 1 to 3

Standard works on the Roman empire are many. I have found Martin Goodman's *The Roman World 44 BC–AD 180* and David Potter, *The Roman Empire at Bay: AD 180–395* (both second editions), which cover the period I deal with in this book, to be especially useful. Readers might also find the relevant chapters in my *Egypt, Greece and Rome*, third edition, helpful, since it covers the Roman empire until the coming of Christianity.

On the specific content of this book, particularly useful has been Susan Alcock's *Graecia Capta* for mainland Greece itself and, for Asia Minor, Christian Marek's *In the Land of a Thousand Gods*, this being a fully comprehensive history of the peoples of the Roman empire in the East. Fergus Millar's *The Roman Near East, 31 BC–AD 337* offers a scholarly survey, while Ian Worthington's *Athens after Empire* describes the fate of Athens during this period.

Irene Vallejo's *Papyrus, The Invention of Books in the Ancient World* gives a good survey of printed material in Roman times and the Library of Alexandria is dealt with *passim*. Lionel Casson's

Libraries in the Ancient World has held its own as a general survey. Also important are Simon Swain, *Hellenism and Empire, Language, Classicism and Power in the Greek World* AD 50–250 (e.g. Chapter 1, 'Language and Identity'), and Gregory Snyder, *Teachers and Text in the Ancient World, Philosophers, Jews and Christians*, which has a great deal of material on what teachers actually taught in this period. See also 'Student Life', pp. 51–8, in Edward Watts, *The Final Pagan Generation*. Chapter 4 of *The Oxford Handbook of the Second Sophistic** by Lawrence Kim deals with Atticism as – at a more comprehensive level – do Chapter 5, 'Greek in the Roman Empire', and Chapter 6, 'Spoken *koine* in the Roman Period', in Geoffrey Horrocks' study of the Greek language.

Turning to Greek philosophy and philosophers, Jacques Brunschwig and Geoffrey Lloyd's (eds.) *Greek Thought, A Guide to Classical Knowledge* has comprehensive texts on all the important schools: Cynicism, p. 843, Scepticism, p. 937, Stoicism, p. 987. Daniel Richter and William Johnson (eds.), *The Oxford Handbook of the Second Sophistic*, contains a wide range of articles on the philosophy of the period (especially Chapters 33 to 37 on Stoicism, Epicureanism, Scepticism, Platonism and Aristotelianism). Kendra Eshleman's *The Social World of Intellectuals in the Roman Empire* is thought-provoking. Peter Adamson's *Philosophy in the Hellenistic and Roman Worlds* is a major survey of the subject and, like all of Adamson's remarkable *A History of Philosophy Without Any Gaps*, is comprehensive for this period (and available in chronological podcasts – interested readers should browse the titles of those relevant to this book). Ted Brennan's *The Stoic Life* is stimulating. George Kennedy's *A New History of*

---

* The term 'Second Sophistic' was coined by Philostratus in his *Lives of the Sophists*. He was harking back to the fifth century BC, the great age of Athens and its intellectuals, but concentrated on oratory and public performance. The term 'Second Sophistic' has been extended by later scholars to the second century AD as a whole, which is why it appears in titles of scholarly books.

Classical Rhetoric is a very good introduction, especially Chapter 11, 'The Second Sophistic'.

For the Oxyrhynchus Papyri, Peter Parsons, *The City of the Sharp-nosed Fish*, is excellent. For the Herculaneum papyri, the website of the Herculaneum Society (Herculaneum.ox.ac.uk) has the latest news. The inscription of Diogenes of Oenoanda is covered in *The Oxford Handbook to the Second Sophistic*, pp. 541–8.

The quotation about subject disciplines breaking free from conventional philosophy (pp. 60–1) is by Jacques Brunschwig from his article on Stoicism in *Greek Thought*, p. 987. Geoffrey Lloyd's quotation in the same paragraph is from his article 'Galen and his Contemporaries', Chapter 2 in R.J. Hankinson (ed.), *The Cambridge Companion to Galen*, p. 34.

Adamson, Peter, *Classical Philosophy*, Oxford University Press, 2014.

Adamson, Peter, *Philosophy in the Hellenistic and Roman Worlds*, Oxford University Press, 2015.

Alcock, Susan, *Graecia Capta, The Landscapes of Roman Greece*, Cambridge University Press, 1993.

Alcock, Susan, 'The Eastern Mediterranean', Chapter 25 in Scheidel, Walter, Morris, Ian and Saller, Richard (eds.), *The Cambridge Economic History of the Greco-Roman World*, Cambridge University Press, 2007.

Barringer, Judith, *Olympia: A Cultural History*, Princeton University Press, 2021.

Bowman, Alan, *Egypt After the Pharaohs, 332 BC–AD 642*, British Museum Press, 1986.

Brennan, Ted, *The Stoic Life, Emotions, Duties and Fate*, Clarendon Press, 2005.

Brunschwig, Jacques and Lloyd, Geoffrey (eds.), *Greek Thought, A Guide to Classical Knowledge*, The Belknap Press of Harvard University Press, 2000.

Eidinow, Esther and Kindt, Julia (eds.), *The Oxford Handbook of Ancient Greek Religion*, Oxford University Press, 2015.

Eshleman, Kendra, *The Social World of Intellectuals in the Roman Empire*, Cambridge University Press, 2015.

Freeman, Charles, *Egypt, Greece and Rome, Civilizations of the Ancient Mediterranean*, third edition, Oxford University Press, 2014.

Goldhill, Simon, *Who Needs Greek? Contests in the Cultural History of Hellenism*, Cambridge University Press, 2002.

Goodman, Martin, *The Roman World 44 BC–AD 180*, Routledge, 1997.

Harris, William, *Ancient Literacy*, Harvard University Press, 1989.

Holiday, Ryan and Hanselman, Stephen, *Lives of the Stoics, The Art of Living from Zeno to Marcus Aurelius*, Profile Books, 2020.

Horrocks, Geoffrey, *Greek, A History of the Language and its Speakers*, second edition, Wiley-Blackwell, 2010.

Johnson, William and Richter, Daniel (eds.), *The Oxford Handbook of the Second Sophistic*, Oxford University Press, 2017.

Kennedy, George, *A New History of Classical Rhetoric*, Princeton University Press, 1994.

Kenny, Anthony, *Ancient Philosophy*, Volume One of *A New History of Western Philosophy*, Clarendon Press, 2004.

Lane Fox, Robin, *Pagans and Christians in the Mediterranean World from the Second Century AD to the Conversion of Constantine*, Viking, 1986.

Longrigg, James, *Greek Medicine, From the Heroic to the Hellenistic Age: A Source Book*, Duckworth, 1998.

MacMullen, Ramsay, *Romanization in the Time of Augustus*, Yale University Press, 2000.

Marek, Christian, *In the Land of a Thousand Gods, A History of Asia Minor in the Ancient World*, trans. Steven Rendall, Princeton University Press, 2016.

Millar, Fergus, *The Roman Near East, 31 BC–AD 337*, Harvard University Press, 1993.

Millar, Fergus, *A Greek Roman Empire, Power and Belief under Theodosius II 408–450*, University of California Press, 2006.

Miller, James (ed.), *Diogenes Laertius, Lives of the Eminent Philosophers*, trans. Pamela Mensch, Oxford University Press, 2018.

Ogden, Daniel (ed.), *A Companion to Greek Religion*, Wiley-Blackwell, 2007.

Snyder, Gregory, *Teachers and Text in the Ancient World, Philosophers, Jews and Christians*, Routledge, 2000.

Stead, Christopher, *Philosophy in Christian Antiquity*, Cambridge University Press, 1994.

Swain, Simon, *Hellenism and Empire, Language, Classicism and Power in the Greek World* AD *50–250*, Clarendon Press, 1996.

Vallejo, Irene, *Papyrus, The Invention of Books in the Ancient World*, translated from the Spanish by Charlotte Whittle, Hodder and Stoughton, 2022.

Watts, Edward, *City and School in Late Antique Athens and Alexandria*, University of California Press, 2006.

Watts, Edward, *The Final Pagan Generation*, University of California Press, 2015.

Whitmarsh, Tim, *The Second Sophistic*, Cambridge University Press, 2005.

Whitmarsh, Tim, *Beyond the Second Sophistic, Adventures in Greek Postclassicism*, University of California Press, 2013.

Woolf, Greg, *The Life and Death of Ancient Cities, A Natural History*, Oxford University Press, 2020.

Worthington, Ian, *Athens after Empire: A History from Alexander the Great to the Emperor Hadrian*, Oxford University Press, 2021.

Chapter 4. The Historian: Polybius

I have used the Penguin Classics edition of Polybius' *Universal History*, translated by Ian Scott-Kilvert as *The Rise of the Roman Empire*. F. W. Walbank is still the authority on Polybius. John Burrow places Polybius in his context as a historian.

Brunschwig, Jacques and Lloyd, Geoffrey (eds.), *Greek Thought, A Guide to Classical Knowledge*, The Belknap Press of Harvard University Press, 2000, article starting at p. 712.

Burrow, John, *A History of Histories*, Allen Lane, London, 2007, Chapter 4 on Polybius.

Green, Peter, *Alexander to Actium, The Hellenistic Age*, Thames and Hudson, London, 1990, *passim* for references to Polybius.

Walbank, F. W., *Polybius*, University of California Press, 1972.

Walbank, F. W., 'Introduction' to *Polybius: The Rise of the Roman Empire*, Penguin Classics, trans. Ian Scott-Kilvert, Penguin Books, 1979.

Chapter 5. The Polymath: Posidonius

Sadly, there are too few works on Posidonius and I have gathered together what I can find about him from the sources cited below. Ryan Holiday's biography is a good place to start. Richard Sorabji's chapters on Posidonius are not for the faint-hearted but detail the arguments that emotional feelings are not faulty judgements but, as Plato had argued, irrational emotions. The quotation on Celtic society on p. 82 is from the article by J. J. Tierney below.

Freeman, Philip, *The Philosopher and the Druids: A Journey Among the Ancient Celts*, Souvenir Press, London (now part of Profile Books), 2006.

Holiday, Ryan and Hanselman, Stephen, *Lives of the Stoics, The Art of Living from Zeno to Marcus Aurelius*, Profile Books, 2020, pp. 99–108 for Posidonius.

Sorabji, Richard, Chapters 6,7 and 8 in *Emotion and Peace of Mind: From Stoic Agitation to Christian Temptation*, Oxford University Press, 2000.

Tierney, J. J., 'The Celtic Ethnography of Posidonius', *Proceedings of the Royal Irish Academy*, 60 (1960), 189–275.

Chapter 6. The Geographer: Strabo

Duane Roller's translation of the entire *Geography* is absorbing and has a good introduction. The *Routledge Companion to Strabo* has many relevant essays which deal with his perspectives on individual parts of the Mediterranean world. Chapters 2 and 3 cover his attitudes to Rome as a city and to the Roman people. His philosophical approach is covered in Chapter One, 'Strabo's philosophy and Stoicism', by Myrto Hatzimichali.

Dueck, Daniela, *The Routledge Companion to Strabo*, Routledge, 2017.
Roller, Duane, *The Geography of Strabo, An English Translation, with Introduction and Notes*, Cambridge University Press, 2014.

Interlude One. The *Res Gestae* of Augustus and the Sebasteion of Aphrodisias

The text beginning this chapter is from the Association of 'Hellenes in Asia' from Christian Marek, *In the Land of a Thousand Gods, A History of Asia Minor in the Ancient World*, p. 316. The main theme of this chapter is to show how Augustus brought peace to the Greek east and so laid the foundations of its stability over the centuries. The standard histories I have used are listed below.

Cooley, Alison, *Res Gestae Divi Augusti, Text, Translation and Commentary*, Cambridge University Press, 2009.
MacMullen, Ramsay, *Romanization in the Time of Augustus*, Yale University Press, 2000.
Price, S. R. F., *Rituals and Power: The Roman Imperial Cult in Asia Minor*, Cambridge University Press, 1984.
Smith, Roland R. R., *The Marble Reliefs from the Julio-Claudian Sebasteion, Aphrodisias*, 6 Mainz: Verlag Philip von Zabern, 2013.
Zanker, Paul, *The Power of Images in the Age of Augustus*, University of Michigan Press, 1988.
For the latest on the excavations at the Sebasteion, visit http://aphrodisias.classics.ox.ac.uk/sebasteion.

Chapter 7. The Botanist: Dioscorides

Those interested in Dioscorides are very grateful for Tess Anne Osbaldeston's translation of *De materia medica*, which is sufficient in itself (http://www.cancerlynx.com/dioscorides.html contains a full text). John Riddle's book is a standard introduction.

Longrigg, James, *Greek Medicine, From the Heroic to the Hellenistic Age: A Source Book*, Duckworth, 1998, has some details on drugs.

Riddle, John, *Dioscorides on Pharmacy and Medicine*, University of Texas Press, 1986 (published as an ebook in 2013).

Chapter 8. The Philosopher and Biographer: Plutarch

Plutarch is perhaps the most appealing of my subjects and his works and mind are both flexible and sophisticated. For his own works I enjoy the Dryden translation of the *Parallel Lives*. The volume on *Morals* cited below contains most of Plutarch's essays, though it is quickly put together and not easy to use. The Loeb edition is in many volumes and would be expensive to use outside a library. Jeffrey Beneker's *How to be a Leader* confirms Plutarch's idea of duty in public life. Mark Beck's *Companion to Plutarch* places Plutarch in the context of his times (Part I), his philosophy as revealed in the *Moralia* (Part II) and his Lives (Part III). Many of the other essays cited below are stimulating.

Adamson, Peter, *Philosophy in the Hellenistic and Roman Worlds*, Oxford University Press, 2015, Chapter 24.

Beck, Mark, *A Companion to Plutarch*, Wiley-Blackwell, 2014. A wide range of essays.

Beneker, Jeffrey (ed. and trans.), *Plutarch, How to be a Leader*, Princeton University Press, 2019.

Brunschwig, Jacques and Lloyd, Geoffrey (eds.), *Greek Thought, A Guide to Classical Knowledge*, The Belknap Press of Harvard University Press, 2000, article on Plutarch from p. 704.

Goldhill, Simon, *Who Needs Greek?*, Cambridge University Press, 2002, especially Chapter 5, 'The Value of Greek. Why Save Plutarch?'

Johnson, William and Richter, Daniel (eds.), *The Oxford Handbook of the Second Sophistic*, Oxford University Press, 2017, Chapter 19, 'Plutarch: Philosophy, Religion and Ethics' by Frederick E. Brenk and Chapter 20, 'Plutarch's *Lives*', by Paolo Desideri.

Jones, C. P., *Plutarch and Rome*, Oxford University Press, 1971.

Plutarch, *Morals*, Lightning Source UK, Milton Keynes, not dated. Also available in many volumes in Loeb translations, Harvard University Press.

Plutarch, *Parallel Lives*, Dryden translation revised, three volumes, Everyman's Library, J. M. Dent, 1910.

Scott, Michael, *Delphi, A History of the Center of the Ancient World*, Princeton University Press, 2014.

Swain, Simon, *Hellenism and Empire, Language, Classicism and Power in the Greek World* AD 50–250. Clarendon Press, 1996, Chapter 5.

Interlude Two. Hadrian and the Patronage of Greek Culture

Hadrian is, of course, a key figure in the history of the Roman empire in the second century AD so any general history will have something to say about him. I have relied heavily on the two books cited below.

Birley, Anthony, *Hadrian: The Restless Emperor*, Routledge, 1997.

Worthington, Ian, *Athens after Empire: A History from Alexander the Great to the Emperor Hadrian*, Oxford University Press, 2021, Chapters 14 to 15.

Chapter 9. The Stoic Philosopher: Epictetus

Any general history of Stoicism will include Epictetus so readers should look at the histories cited for the first three chapters. The *Discourses* have been well translated by Robin Hard and I have used the edition in the Oxford World's Classics. A full account of

Epictetus' philosophy can be found in the 2021 article by Margaret Graver in the (online) *Stanford Encyclopedia of Philosophy*.

Adamson, Peter, *Philosophy in the Hellenistic and Roman Worlds*, Oxford University Press, 2015, Chapter 13 for Epictetus.

Graver, Margaret, 'Epitectus' in *The Stanford Encyclopedia of Philosophy*, 2021.

Hard, Robin (ed. and trans.), *Epictetus, Discourses, Fragments, Handbook*, Oxford World's Classics, Oxford University Press, 2014.

Holiday, Ryan and Hanselman, Stephen, *Lives of the Stoics, The Art of Living from Zeno to Marcus Aurelius*, Profile Books, 2020, pp. 251–68 for Epictetus.

Chapter 10. The Politician, Historian and Philosopher: Arrian of Nicomedia

I have used the Martin Hammond translation of Arrian's history of Alexander and Indica. Daniel Leon places Arrian in the context of his times and Greek historiography. Philip Stadter's is the standard biography.

Atkinson, John (ed.), *Arrian: Alexander the Great and the Indica*, trans. Martin Hammond, Oxford World's Classics, Oxford University Press, 2013.

Leon, Daniel W., *Arrian the Historian: Writing the Greek past in the Roman Empire*, University of Texas Press, 2021.

Stadter, Philip, *Arrian of Nicomedia*, University of North Carolina Press, 1980.

Chapter 11. The Geographer and Astronomer: Ptolemy

I have simplified the complex mathematical achievements of Ptolemy but the sources below will provide a more complete and accurate picture for more committed mathematicians. There is no one better than Geoffrey Lloyd to put Ptolemy within the wide context of Greek science. Michael Hoskin and David Lindberg and the essays in *Greek Thought* will provide a more general introduction to this great polymath.

Brunschwig, Jacques and Lloyd, Geoffrey (eds.), *Greek Thought, A Guide to Classical Knowledge*, The Belknap Press of Harvard University Press, 2000, article on Ptolemy from p. 731; see also 'Astronomy', p. 269 and 'Geography', p. 299.

Hoskin, Michael, *The Cambridge Concise History of Astronomy*, Cambridge University Press, 1999, Chapter 2 'Astronomy in Antiquity'.

Lindberg, David, *The Beginnings of Western Science: The European Scientific Tradition in Philosophical, Religious and Institutional Context, Prehistory to* AD *1450*, second edition, University of Chicago Press, 2007, *passim.*

Lloyd, G. E. R., *The Revolutions of Wisdom, Studies in the Claims and Practice of Ancient Greek Science*, University of California Press, 1987, *passim* for Ptolemy.

Lloyd, G. E. R., *Magic, Reason and Experience, Studies in the Origins and Development of Greek Science*, Bristol Classical Press, 1999, pp. 180–200.

Netz, Reviel, *A New History of Greek Mathematics*, Cambridge University Press, 2022.

Chapter 12. The Satirist: Lucian of Samosata

Lucian is inexhaustibly interesting and I hope I have shown the breadth of his writings in this chapter. I have taken extracts from Lucian's texts from the website The Lucian of Samosata Project. The webmaster F. Redmond has waived all copyright and related or neighbouring rights to the project, for which Lucian admirers will be forever grateful. The following chapters below fill out his personality and discuss the challenging question of his identity as it relates to his Greek contemporaries.

Goldhill, Simon, Chapter 2, 'Becoming Greek with Lucian', in *Who Needs Greek?*, Cambridge University Press, 2002.

Johnson, William and Richter, Daniel (eds.), *The Oxford Handbook of the Second Sophistic*, Oxford University Press, 2017, Chapter 21, 'Lucian of Samosata' by Daniel Richter.

Swain, Simon, *Hellenism and Empire, Language, Classicism and Power in the Greek World* AD *50–250*. Clarendon Press, 1996, Chapter 9, 'Lucian'.

The Lucian of Samosata Project. Comprehensive website on Lucian with links to his works.

http://lucianofsamosata.info/wiki/doku.php?id=home:lucian_website_home

Chapter 13. The Medical Man: Galen

Galen has received a great detail of attention in recent years. Of the two full biographies by Susan Mattern and Vivian Nutton, I have relied mainly on Mattern's. As Galen is also seen as a philosopher as much as a physician, I have included the *Stanford Encylopedia of Philosophy* entry for him. *The Cambridge Companion to Galen* contains many articles on his philosophy and method of working. The editor, R. J. Hankinson, introduces 'The Man and his Work' in Chapter 1, and in Chapter 2, 'Galen and his Contemporaries', G. E. R. Lloyd sets him in a wider context, emphasising the competitive arena in which Galen functioned. Vivian Nutton in his authoritative *Ancient Medicine* provides the fuller context of Galen's place within the medical profession – I have noted his admiration for Hippocrates. Coarelli is good on the Rome in which Galen practised.

Adamson, Peter, *Philosophy in the Hellenistic and Roman Worlds*, Oxford University Press, 2015, Chapter 20.

Brunschwig, Jacques and Lloyd, Geoffrey (eds.), *Greek Thought, A Guide to Classical Knowledge*, The Belknap Press of Harvard University Press, 2000, article on Galen from p. 618.

Coarelli, Filippo, *Rome and Environs: An Archaeological Guide*, English translation of original text by James Clauss and Daniel Harmon, University of California Press, 2007.

Hankinson, R. J. (ed.), *The Cambridge Companion to Galen*, Cambridge University Press, 2008.

Johnson, William and Richter, Daniel (eds.), *The Oxford Handbook of the Second Sophistic*, Oxford University Press, 2017, Chapter 24 on Galen by Susan Mattern.

King, Helen, *Greek and Roman Medicine*, Bristol Classical Press, 2001.

Mattern, Susan, *The Prince of Medicine, Galen in the Roman Empire*, Oxford University Press, 2013.

Nutton, Vivian, *Galen: A Thinking Doctor in Imperial Rome*, Routledge, 2020.

Swain, Simon, *Hellenism and Empire, Language, Classicism and Power in the Greek World* AD *50–250*, Clarendon Press, 1996, Chapter 11 on Galen.

Chapter 14. The Travel Guide: Pausanias

This chapter is informed by my own visits to several of the sites Pausanias mentions – Mycenae, Tiryns, Messene and Olympia among others. The study edited by Susan Alcock and others represents the increasing interest in Pausanias as a guide who is valued for the accuracy of his descriptions of locations in ancient Greece. William Hutton's essay on Pausanias in *The Oxford Handbook of the Second Sophistic* is useful, but – since he seems to have made no impact on his contemporaries – it is next to impossible to bring Pausanias alive as a personality. Judith Barringer's cultural history of Olympia is a contemporary study of the site for which Pausanias provided one of his most comprehensive descriptions. I have used Peter Levi's translation of the *Guide to Greece*.

Alcock, Susan, Cherry, John and Elsner, Jas. (eds.), *Pausanias, Travel and Memory in Roman Greece*, Oxford University Press, 2001.

Barringer, Judith, *Olympia: A Cultural History*, Princeton University Press, 2021.

Johnson, William and Richter, Daniel (eds.), *The Oxford Handbook of the Second Sophistic*, Oxford University Press, 2017, Chapter 23.

Pausanias, *Guide to Greece*, two volumes, trans. Peter Levi, Penguin Classics, 1971.

Swain, Simon, *Hellenism and Empire, Language, Classicism and Power in the Greek World* AD *50–250*, Clarendon Press, 1996, Chapter 10.

Interlude Three. City Life in Second-century Asia Minor: Sagalassos

My own visits to Sagalassos confirm it as one of the most interesting abandoned Greek cities of south-western Turkey. There is a continually updated website of the history and excavations on the site but nothing equals a visit to the city itself. A full history and details of recent excavations can be found at https://www.arts.kuleuven.be/sagalassos/history and https://interactive.archaeology.org/sagalassos/

Waelkens, M., 'The Archaeology of Sagalassos', in Smith, Claire (ed.), *Encyclopedia of Global Archaeology*, Springer, NY, 2014. https://doi.org/10.1007/978-1-4419-0465-2_1121

Chapter 15. The Politician and Orator: Dio Chrysostom

Dio of Prusa was widely regarded as one of the most flexible and effective orators of his generation. I have brought together material from the sources below. Philostratus is the best contemporary source. Unless one has access to the Loeb edition of the *Discourses* one has to search online for his orations which are not in chronological order. The easiest access is via https://penelope.uchicago.edu/Thayer/e/roman/texts/dio_chrysostom/discourses. The oration on concord with the Apameians with which I open this chapter is Oration 40. See Oration 7 for the shipwreck on Euboea, Oration 12 for the oration at Olympia and Oration 36 for Dio of Prusa's visit to Borysthenes.

The oration concerning Charidemus is Oration 30, that on the rivalry between Nicomedia and Nicaea Oration 38, and the address to Tarsus Oration 33. The 'kingship orations' are Orations 1–4. I particularly like Claire Jackson's analysis of the orations, cited below.

Bekker-Nielsen, Tennes, *Urban Life and Local Politics in Roman Bithynia. The Small World of Dio Chrysostomos*, Aarhus University Press, 2008.

Johnson, William and Richter, Daniel (eds.), *The Oxford Handbook of the Second Sophistic*, Oxford University Press, 2017, Chapter 14 on Dio by Claire Rachel Jackson.

Philostratus, *Lives of the Sophists*, reprint, publisher unknown (also available online).

Swain, Simon, *Hellenism and Empire, Language, Classicism and Power in the Greek World AD 50–250*, Clarendon Press, 1996, Chapter 6.

Chapter 16. The Rhetorician: Aelius Aristides

Aelius Aristides was a fussy man, full of complaints about his ailments but obsessed with his superiority over his contemporaries. The main part of the translation of his famous speech on the benefits of Roman rule quoted here is by S. Levin, but I have used extracts from different online translations where I considered it appropriate. One has to search online for translations of Aelius' orations (although they are available in a Loeb edition). The *Panathenaicus* is Oration 1, those to Smyrna Orations 17 to 21. The *Roman Oration* (Oration 26) is easily found online. The *Sacred Tales* are Orations 47–52. Laurent Pernot discusses Aelius' relationship with Rome in Chapter XI of Holmes' and Harris' volume. Simon Swain's chapter on Aelius is especially good: see pp. 274–84 for Rome and pp. 284–97 for the orations to Rhodes and Smyrna.

Harris, W. V. and Holmes, Brooke (eds.), *Aelius Aristides Between Greece, Rome and the Gods*, Brill, 2008.

Johnson, William and Richter, Daniel (eds.), *The Oxford Handbook of the Second Sophistic*, Oxford University Press, 2017, Chapter 17 on Aelius by Estelle Oudet.

Petsalis-Diomidis, Alexia, '*Truly Beyond Wonders*', *Aelius Aristides and the Cult of Asklepios*, Oxford University Press, 2010.

Philostratus, *Lives of the Sophists*, reprint, publisher unknown (also available online).

Swain, Simon, *Hellenism and Empire, Language, Classicism and Power in the Greek World* AD 50–250, Clarendon Press, 1996, Chapter 8.

Chapter 17. The Politician and Philanthropist: Herodes Atticus

Other than Hadrian, Herodes left more of a legacy in buildings than any other of my subjects. Jennifer Tobin's study of Herodes is comprehensive and she provides a good map of Herodes' benefactions. The life of Herodes Atticus contained within Philostratus' *Lives of the Sophists* is the fullest near-contemporary account. Berringer's cultural history of Olympia discusses the famous fountain at the shrine. The quotation from Aulus Gellius' *Attic Nights* comes at the start of the *Nights* and is easily found online (e.g. Project Gutenberg, Internet Archive).

Johnson, William and Richter, Daniel (eds.), *The Oxford Handbook of the Second Sophistic*, Oxford University Press, 2017, Chapter 15 by Leofranc Holford-Strevens.

Philostratus, *Lives of the Sophists*, reprint, publisher unknown (but also available online).

Tobin, Jennifer, *Herodes Attikos and the City of Athens, Patronage and Conflict under the Antonines*, J. C. Gieben, 1997.

Interlude Four. The Clouds Darken – The Greek World in an Age of Crisis

The opening quotation of this interlude comes from Christian Marek's *In the Land of a Thousand Gods* (p. 355). The rest of the interlude was compiled using the sources below.

Bowman, Alan, Garnsey, Peter and Cameron, Averil (eds.), *The second edition of The Cambridge Ancient History, Volume XII The Crisis of Empire*, AD *193–337*, Cambridge University Press, 2005, especially Chapter 2.

Marek, Christian, *In the Land of a Thousand Gods, A History of Asia Minor in the Ancient World*, trans. Steven Rendall, Princeton University Press, 2016, especially pp. 350–60.

Millar, Fergus, *The Roman Near East, 31* BC–AD *337*, Harvard University Press, 1993, Chapter 4.

Potter, David, *The Roman Empire at Bay*, AD *180–395*, Routledge, 2004.

Chapter 18. The Philosopher: Plotinus

The Life of Plotinus by Porphyry is incorporated as a preface in the *Enneads*. I have used Stephen MacKenna's translation, cited below, and supplemented it with material drawn from other sources as listed below.

Adamson, Peter, *Philosophy in the Hellenistic and Roman Worlds*, Oxford University Press, 2015, Chapters 29 to 33.

Brunschwig, Jacques and Lloyd, Geoffrey (eds.), *Greek Thought, A Guide to Classical Knowledge*, The Belknap Press of Harvard University Press, 2000, article on Plotinus from p. 693.

Dillon, John (ed.), *Plotinus, The Enneads*, trans. Stephen MacKenna, abridged, Penguin Classics, 1991.

Gwerson, Lloyd, 'Plotinus' in *The Stanford Encyclopedia of Philosophy* (online), article dated 2018.

Chapter 19. The Platonic Theologian: Clement of Alexandria

Clement and his mentor Philo are discussed both in Peter Adamson's volume and, more discursively, in Christopher Stead's *Philosophy in Christian Antiquity*. The original texts of Clement can be found online in the Christian Classics Ethereal Library (ccel.org), *Ante-Nicene*

Fathers Volume Two, where Clement is included among other Church Fathers.

Adamson, Peter, *Philosophy in the Hellenistic and Roman Worlds*, Oxford University Press, 2015, Chapter 23 on Philo of Alexandria discussed in this chapter; Chapter 40 for Clement.

Bowerstock, G. W., *Hellenism in Late Antiquity*, University of Michigan Press, 1990, especially Chapters 1 and 2.

Johnson, Aaron, 'Early Christianity and the Classical Tradition', Chapter 40 in Richter and Johnson (eds.), *The Oxford Handbook of the Second Sophistic*.

MacCulloch, Diarmaid, *A History of Christianity*, Allen Lane, 2009, 'Alexandrian Theologians, Clement and Origen', pp. 147–54.

Osborn, Eric, *Clement of Alexandria*, Cambridge University Press, 2005.

Osborn, Eric, *The Philosophy of Clement of Alexandria*, Hassell Street Press, 2021

Stead, Christopher, *Philosophy in Christian Antiquity*, Cambridge University Press, 1994.

Chapter 20. The Biblical Scholar: Origen

The text at the opening of this chapter comes from a letter of Origen to a student, cited in Edward Watts, *City and School in Late Antique Athens and Alexandria*, p. 165. Mark Edwards' entry on Origen in the *Stanford Encyclopedia* has a useful link to English translations of his works. Henry Chadwick provides a good introduction to his translation of *Contra Celsum*.

Barton, John, *A History of the Bible: The Book and its Faiths*, Allen Lane, 2019.

Chadwick, Henry (ed. and trans.), *Origen, Contra Celsum*, Cambridge University Press, 1953, revised 1965.

Edwards, Mark, 'Origen', *The Stanford Encyclopedia of Philosophy*, 2022.

Grafton, Anthony and Williams, Megan, *Christianity and the Transformation of the Book: Origen, Eusebius and the Library of Caesarea*, Harvard University Press, 2008.

Heine, Ronald, *Origen: An Introduction to his Life and Thought*, Cascade Books, 2019.

MacCulloch, Diarmaid, *A History of Christianity*, Allen Lane, 2009, 'Alexandrian Theologians, Clement and Origen', pp. 147–54.

Stead, Christopher, *Philosophy in Christian Antiquity*, Cambridge University Press, 1994.

Watts, Edward, *City and School in Late Antique Athens and Alexandria*, University of California Press, 2006.

Interlude Five. Constantinople and the Promulgation of Christian Orthodoxy

The sources listed below provide a standard introduction to the changing nature of religious government in the fourth century AD for those who wish to explore the subject further.

Drake, H. A., *Constantine and the Bishops, The Politics of Intolerance*, Johns Hopkins University Press, 1999.

Freeman, Charles, AD *381, Heretics, Pagans and the Christian State*, Pimlico, 2008.

Grig, Lucy and Kelly, Gavin (eds.), *Two Romes, Rome and Constantinople in Late Antiquity*, Oxford University Press, 2012.

Hughes, Bettany, *Istanbul, A Tale of Three Cities*, Weidenfeld and Nicolson, 2017.

Krautheimer, Richard, *Three Christian Capitals, Topography and Politics: Rome, Constantinople, Milan*, University of California Press, 1983.

Lenski, Noel (ed.), *The Age of Constantine*, Cambridge University Press, 2006.

Millar, Fergus, *The Roman Near East, 31 BC–AD 337*, Harvard University Press, 1993, Chapter 5.

Chapter 21. The Court Orator: Themistius

I especially recommend Heather and Moncur for their detailed examination of Themistius' oratory in support of successive emperors.

Heather, Peter and Moncur, David, *Politics, Philosophy, and Empire in the Fourth Century, Select Orations of Themistius*, Liverpool University Press, 2001.
Swain, Simon, *Themistius, Julian, and Greek Political Theory under Rome*, Cambridge University Press, 2013.

Chapter 22. The Last of the Pagan Orators: Libanius

There are many excellent articles in Lieve Van Hoof's volume on Libanius. The editor contributes Chapter 1 on Libanius' autobiography and his life. I have also relied on Raffaella Cribiore's superb study of Libanius and would recommend it strongly as an introduction. It includes translations of 200 of Libanius' extant letters.

As Van Hook says in his Epilogue: 'For a long time, Libanius has remained a dark horse, difficult to assess.' He lists what English translations there are and one has to have a copy of Van Hoof to access these. Oration 30, 'On the Temples', is, however, easy to find online, as is Libanius' Oration 18 on the death of the emperor Julian.

Cribiore, Raffaella, *The School of Libanius in Late Antique Antioch*, Princeton University Press, 2007.
Van Hoof, Lieve, *Libanius, A Critical Introduction*, Cambridge University Press, 2014.

Chapter 23. The Neoplatonist Philosopher and Mathematician: Hypatia of Alexandria

There are many contrasting accounts of Hypatia, assessing her importance as an intellectual and feminist. Edward Watts' biography, by an expert in the intellectual life of late antiquity, is very welcome and I have used it as my main source. See also the next chapter 'Afterlives'.

Rapp, Claudia, *Holy Bishops in Late Antiquity, The Nature of Christian Leadership in an Age of Transition*, University of California Press, 2005.

Watts, Edward, *City and School in late Antique Athens and Alexandria*, University of California Press, 2008.

Watts, Edward, *Hypatia, The Life and Legend of an Ancient Philosopher*, Oxford University Press, 2017.

Chapter 24. Afterlives

I used many standard histories of European thought to compose this chapter. I have selected below those books that provided specific material not found elsewhere.

Beck, Mark, *A Companion to Plutarch*, Wiley-Blackwell, 2014. Part IV of this *Companion* deals with the reception of Plutarch in later centuries, including chapters on the Italian Renaissance, Montaigne and Shakespeare and the early American Republic.

Bolgar, R. R., *The Classical Heritage and its Beneficiaries*, Cambridge University Press, 1954.

Dalché, Patrick Gautier, 'Strabo's Reception in the West (fifteenth to sixteenth centuries), Chapter 28 in Daniela Dueck (ed.), *The Routledge Companion to Strabo*, Routledge, 2017.

Fitzgerald, Allan (ed.), *Augustine Through the Ages*, William Eerdmans Publishing Company, 1999, the article 'Plotinus, The Enneads' for Augustine's attitude to Plotinus.

Freeman, Charles, *The Awakening, A History of the Western Mind* AD *500–1700*, Head of Zeus, 2020. US edition, *The Reopening of the Western Mind, AD 500–1700*, Knopf/Doubleday, 2023.

Grafton, Anthony, Most, Glenn and Settis, Salvatore (eds.), *The Classical Tradition*, The Belknap Press of Harvard University Press, 2010. The entry on Plutarch is by Robert Lamberton.

King, Ross, *The Bookseller of Florence, Vespasiano da Bisticci and the Manuscripts that Illuminated the Renaissance*, Chatto and Windus, 2021.

Nesselrath, Heinz-Gunther and Van Hoof, Lieve, 'The Reception of Libanius from pagan friend of Julian to (almost) Christian saint and back', Chapter 8 in Lieve Van Hoof (ed.), *Libanius, A Critical Introduction*, Cambridge University Press, 2014.

Nutton, Vivian, 'The Fortunes of Galen', Chapter 14 in R. J. Hankinson (ed.), *The Cambridge Companion to Galen*, Cambridge University Press, 2008.

Picture Credits

1. Historic Images / Alamy Stock Photo
2. Prisma by Dukas Presseagentur GmbH / Alamy Stock Photo
3. Margarete Lovison / Alamy Stock Photo
4. Granger - Historical Picture Archive / Alamy Stock Photo
5. Odoxo / Wikimedia Commons
6. iStock / Getty Images Plus / Getty Images
7. Zde, WIkimedia Commons
8. CPA Media Pte Ltd / Alamy Stock Photo
9. ART Collection / Alamy Stock Photo
10. elgreko/ Getty Images
11. Guven Ozdemir, iStock / Getty Images Plus
12. Daderot / Wikimedia Commons
13. Jorge Tutor / Alamy Stock Photo
14. Constantinos Iliopoulos / Alamy Stock Photo
15. incamerastock / Alamy Stock Photo
16. Cambridge University Library
17. Edward Grant, Celestial Orbs in the Latin Middle Ages, Isis, Vol. 78, No. 2 / Wikimedia Commons
18. Interfoto / Alamy Stock Photo
19. British Library
20. © British Library Board. All Rights Reserved / Bridgeman Images

Index

Charles Freeman is a specialist on the ancient world and its legacy. He has worked on archaeological digs on the continents surrounding the Mediterranean and develops study tour programmes in Italy, Greece and Turkey. Freeman is Historical Consultant to the Blue Guides series and the author of numerous books, including the bestseller *The Closing of the Western Mind*, *Holy Bones, Holy Dust: How Relics Shaped the History of Medieval Europe* and, most recently, *The Awakening: A History of the Western Mind AD 500–1700*. He lives in Suffolk.